Consultative Selling™

Other AMACOM books by Mack Hanan that support the strategies of Key Account Selling (Consultative Selling™) are:

Successful Market Penetration: How to Shorten the Sales Cycle by Making the First Sale the First Time

Customer Satisfaction: How to Maximize, Measure, and Market Your Company's "Ultimate Product"

CONSULTATIVE SELLING™

*The Hanan
Formula for
High-Margin Sales
at High Levels*

Fourth Edition

Mack Hanan

American Management Association

Library of Congress Cataloging-in-Publication Data

Hanan, Mack.
    Consultative selling : the Hanan formula for high-margin sales at
high levels / Mack Hanan. — 4th ed.
        p.   cm.
    ISBN 0-8144-5013-X
    1.Selling.   2. Selling—Key accounts.   I. Title.
HF5438.25.H35   1990   90-34874
658.81—dc20   CIP

Printing number

10 9 8

To my partners,
Jim Cribbin,
Jack Donis,
and
Herman Heiser,
who set out with me to improve the profits of our clients and who, along the way, enriched me with their knowledge, their skills in implementing it, and their discipline in refusing to settle for anything less than customer satisfaction as our standard of performance.

Contents

Appendixes

Foreword

The Customer Manager's Mindset

For the past few years, it has been my pleasure to work with Mack Hanan as he traveled around the country training sales managers and their representatives in selling. My role as the crusty old Mr. Box One, the top-level customer decision maker who critiques each Profit Improvement Proposal™, has been a relatively minor one. Nonetheless, I have had an excellent opportunity to observe the reactions of hundreds of sellers as Mack opened their eyes to a new way of selling and laid on the challenge. Almost without exception, sales representatives who have spent a career vending to purchasing agents and technically oriented engineers are excited but cautious about putting to work the Box One mindset the way that top business managers, and therefore middle managers, think about investing money in order to improve their profits through Consultative Selling™.

I spent more than thirty-eight years in the automotive industry—all at Ford and the last nineteen of them as an officer of the company. Looking back, I have difficulty remembering all of the Box Ones that I knew on a first-name basis. (Of course, I never did call Henry Ford II "Henry.") The list includes most of the head people over the years of General Motors, Ford, Chrysler, American Motors, and major tire companies and automotive suppliers, several advertising agencies,

and the people who ran dozens of other corporations in De-
troit, such as K Mart and the banks. I should also include the
heads at Nissan, Mazda, a couple of British companies, VW of
America, and the presidents of the United Automobile Workers
union over the years.

I knew many of these industry leaders before they became
Box Ones. In fact, a few of them worked for me at one time or
another. I recite all of this simply as a way of qualifying myself
to make some comments about the Box One mindset that I
hope you will find useful.

Box One managers are richer than you are. They belong to
the most exclusive clubs all over the world. They probably
spend five times as much for a suit as you do. Box Ones move
around in corporate jets and enjoy other perks, all of which
tend to feed what was already a pretty good ego. They exude
self-confidence. After all, they never would have made it to the
top if they had second-guessed their own decisions. But life
isn't all a bowl of cherries. Box One probably buys Rolaids by
the box, he may not sleep too well, and he could have more
problems with his wife and children than you do. Beyond that,
the odds are that he is somewhat overweight, may be running
a little high on cholesterol, and could even be getting a little
hard of hearing.

But he *is* Box One.

The point I want to make is that you don't have to be like
him to understand how he thinks and how his Box Two
managers—the men and women you will partner with as a
consultative seller—are required to think in order to do business with him.

The first thing to realize is that he is a lot like a banker.
The big difference is that while bankers lend money to others
to make money, Mr. Box One invests money in his own
business to make money.

To Mr. Box One, money is a business tool. A smart CEO is
always willing to spend to capitalize on a profit opportunity.
In fact, he is quite willing to borrow other people's money to
capitalize on his profit opportunity. In the final analysis, a
good manager is simply one whose revenues exceed his total

expenditures. The great ones are those who successfully take risks that expand the revenues.

Box One looks at money differently than you might. In the first place, cash isn't really cash. Don't let that first line on the balance sheet fool you. The green stuff is all invested in short-term instruments with hardly enough cash actually around to buy the coffee and croissants for the staff tomorrow morning. For example, funds are deposited in banks all around the country by wire Thursday nights to cover the payroll checks that are passed out Friday mornings. So learn Lesson 1 from Mr. Box One: Money should never be idle. Money is to be used to make more money—twenty-four hours a day, seven days a week—even while you're asleep or on vacation.

Every CEO learned this a long time ago in his personal life. It wasn't hard for him to see that the really rich never got that way by saving $10 or $100 or even $1,000 from each week's pay. Of course, he knows the value of saving—that's how almost all Box Ones got their start. But he also knows that it is the capitalization of an income stream that creates real riches.

That's the way business managers think. How much is $1,000? Enough for a week of fun at a mountain resort? Just what you need to send the kids to camp? That might be the way you look at it. But Box One's reaction is that $1,000 is a year's interest on $15,000—money at work earning money. A CEO who retires on a pension of $20,000 per month looks at it as if it were an 8 percent return on a $3 million trust fund. In fact, he would consider the $3 million as part of his own net worth. Without question, the very existence of his imaginary trust fund would influence how he invests his other assets.

Box Ones lead two financial lives—personal and corporate. While the scope of the numbers is vastly different, the same ground rules apply: Money should make money. They rarely invest in gold bullion because it doesn't earn money and is costly to safeguard. Many Box Ones carry very little money in their wallets. They are big spenders, of course, but all the bills get paid by check, more often than not written by their secretaries. The truth is that they just hate to actually open their wallets and hand somebody a couple of real $20 bills. To their credit, however, the super-rich often "return" much of their wealth to the community through the establishment of charitable foundations that will perpetuate their names.

Now all of this doesn't mean that Box Ones think of nothing but the bottom line. They simply look at money in a different way than most people do—as a way of making more money. And that makes them an easy mark for Consultative Selling. They are ready, willing, and able to spend money to make money. They find time to listen to proposals that will increase productivity, increase efficiency, reduce costs, increase quality, and strengthen their competitive position, all of which should lead to increased sales and higher profits. They are willing to invest money to make these gains if the risk/reward ratio is attractive enough. This is the mindset they instill in the Box Two managers who report to them.

So what's so frightening about dealing with the Box One mindset? Now that you better understand what motivates it, it should be clear that they and middle-level customer managers would rather listen to a good Profit Improvement Proposal (PIP) from you than meet with someone else who is pushing something that will increase their costs rather than their profits.

What makes a good proposal? All you have to do is raise one question, "Are you operating as cost-effectively as you can?" and answer others:

- How much money do we have to put up to make money? The answer tells the *incremental investment.*
- How much profit will it produce? The answer tells the *incremental profit.*
- What is our return? The answer tells the *incremental rate of return.*

To put it in numbers, your proposal might say, "In summary, Mr. Box One, an incremental investment of $4 million will generate incremental profits of $3 million annually. That is an incremental return of 75 percent per year before taxes [*$3 million divided by $4 million = 75%*]."

Now let's get down to your business.

Go back and look at some of the sales you have closed recently. Reconstruct one of them to reflect the PIP approach in Consultative Selling. If you made a sale of $200,000, what you recorded as the total sale should now be viewed as the customer's incremental investment. Did you calculate that the equipment or process you sold the customer would give him a cost reduction of $50,000 per year? If so, that should now be viewed as the incremental profit. In retrospect, then, you provided your customer an incremental return on investment of 25 percent per year. Run through a couple more of your past sales and restructure them as consultative sales. Then put a PIP together for a new transaction that you haven't closed yet.

Try it. It works. You'll like it!

Will Scott
Vice-President (Retired)
Ford Motor Co.

Preface
to the Fourth Edition

The power of Consultative Selling as a multiplier of profits from sales is proved by its track record since 1970. In the same way that McDonald's keeps a record of its hamburgers—"X billion sold"—I have quantified to the best of my ability the incremental values that have been contributed by Consultative Selling to the sales forces that have implemented its strategies.

In total, these values range from a low of $100,000 to a high of $3.5 million in profits per sales representative during the first twelve months of implementation. This is true across all products and services sold to all markets. By far the greater share of these profits has come from sales that were being made by first-time consultative sellers to customers who were buying from them consultatively for the first time and who have testified that they would not have placed these orders had they not been sold to them in a consultative manner.

About 20 percent of these customers had never bought from their sellers before. In one case, a consultative sale was made to a customer who had refused to buy from the seller's company for fifty years.

Saluting the Vendor's High Noon

The 1980s represented the decade of truth for vendors. They saw that sales were, as they had always been, either a push or pull process. Vendors realized that they were being pulled into their sales by having to react to customer demand. They began to identify themselves with hamburger stands; they gave a customer what he ordered when he ordered it. If there were no customers at the stand, there were no orders. On the other hand, many vendors saw how consultants push sales. Consultants anticipate demand by taking the initiative, pushing proposals toward their customers because they know the leads are there and they know what they can do about them.

While Consultative Selling has been ascendant, vending has reached high noon when it comes to selling to major customers on the basis of the features and benefits of technology. A combination of six factors have come together in most marketplaces to invalidate price-performance selling as a way of creating value:

1. Major suppliers have largely achieved competitive parity.
2. Further pressure to accelerate development cycles has become too costly for too little incremental gain with too little certainty of payback, let alone payoff.
3. Higher performance is not essential, nor is it easily affordable, especially if it entails the added costs and disruptions of new training for customers.
4. With significant investments already sunk in technology, breakthroughs—even if they prove feasible— threaten to invalidate existing customer asset bases.
5. Customers have discovered the inherent cost-ineffectiveness of the traditional open bidding process and are coming to prefer the consolidation of their purchases with one or two strategic suppliers.
6. In order to maximize their installed bases of equipment from several suppliers and to minimize training costs, customers are mandating "open standards" among all suppliers. In this way, they are effectively nullifying proprietary technologies.

By saying "enough" to vendor selling, customers in major markets are setting the new ground rules for selling. "Tell us," they are urging, "what the application of your technology will do for us—not what you have done for your technology. Will we be competitively advantaged by it? If so, by how much? How soon? How sure?" Suppliers without answers, or without the most compelling answers, are watching the values generated by vending become exceeded by their costs.

Vendor selling and Consultative Selling are worlds apart. In vendor mythology, identifying decision makers is a major problem. Consultative sellers go right for a customer's business managers and managers of business functions that are critical to customer success. Vendors worry about how to generate inquiries. Consultants are the inquirers. Vendors operate in an adversarial environment. They practice anticipating objections because they get a lot of them and spend a lot of time trying to overcome them. Consultants anticipate cooperation. They use objections as their negotiating platform, not to overcome them—which is arrogant and presumptuous, suggesting that a customer does not know his business—but to incorporate them into their solutions.

Vendors are preoccupied with listening. Consultants are preoccupied with asking the kind of questions whose answers are worth listening to. Vendors spend most of their time handling price as a problem. Consultants dispose of price, transforming it into an investment and selling its return.

Vendors have to sell against their competition. Consultants sell competitive advantages over their customers' competition. Vendors make cold calls. Consultants always have a customer's hot button to press. Vendors make trial closes. Consultants let the customer close. Vendors ask for an order, which represents a cost to their customers. Consultants offer improved profits that represent a gain.

The case of Symbolics, Inc., is symbolic.

Symbolics was once a shooting star in artificial intelligence. It started up in 1980 and grew like a house afire with its proprietary computer workstations and applications software. Six years after its founding, Symbolics had achieved annual sales of $114 million and was said to be on its way to becoming a $700 million company three years later. Then everything fell apart.

The ten computer scientists who founded Symbolics focused all their attention on putting the value of their technology into their products, adding to their cost. Customer value was ignored. Symbolics managers never agreed on what their value to a customer really was. They sold on price and performance, adding more and more performance but selling it for less and less price. The managers fought among themselves over what their value could be. They were never able to reach a conclusion. Their customers knew, but they were never asked. Eventually, the directors brought in a new president whose first act was to fire the entire marketing department. He reasoned that its function was to sell value, and it could not sell value if it did not know what the value was. The directors liked the fact that costs were reduced but still thought that a company should have a marketing function. As customers watched from the sidelines and waited to learn about the value of Symbolics to them, they lost confidence and stopped buying. Investors stopped funding. The directors stopped deliberating and fired the new president who had gotten them into all this trouble in the first place.

Forced to sell their products on less and less price and more and more performance, traditional vendors like Symbolics are at the high end of the cost chain in their own businesses and at the low end of the value-added chain in their customers' businesses. Positioned as costs by their customers, they often only added more to their own costs than to their profits by their fifteen-step sales cycles even when they were successful in making sales.

Positioning on the Value Chain

As an agent of corporate acculturation, Consultative Selling has been a creatively destabilizing influence. It has forced companies to ask whether they have been selling the right thing, by which they mean their products, instead of the profit impact that their products can make on customer operations. It has shocked companies into realizing that while their products and people have always made a financial impact on customer operations, they have never known its value, and therefore, they have not been able to sell it. Without selling it, they have never had cause or opportunity to know it. This is the vendor's vortex, and companies that are endlessly caught in it have no recourse as their margins go down the drain.

The shock of discovery that you do not know your value is one thing. The shock of discovering your value is another. Almost without exception, companies are astonished at the ratio between the value they add to their customers and the price they have been able to get for it. In many industries, the customer's incremental rate of return is routinely in three figures and is quite often so far into four figures that it must be called infinity. Any semblance of fair pricing goes out the window when it is realized how many of these sales have been bought, not sold, by discounting.

If a customer knows your value—if he has calculated your costs and your benefits on a return-on-investment basis—and you do not, he is your consultant and you can never be his. He will know your worth to him and, even though you add significant value to his business, he will not pay you for your value because you cannot be paid for what you do not sell. He will pay you only for your products, whose value is set by the competitive prices in your market and not by the competitive advantage you contribute to the customer. You will be paid in proportion to how much you allow yourself to become less competitive instead of how much you make your customer more competitive.

Vendors as a group tend to go on manufacturing and selling today what their customers wanted yesterday. Their motto is "Don't mess with success," a corollary of "Don't fix it if it ain't broke." They follow their competitors more than they follow their customers. This is why they go on selling the last big-winner product they have made long after its rate of growth has begun to decline and margin maturity has already set in.

In the same way, they go on selling with the same strategy, figuring that they must have been doing something right.

The opportunity to sell something new—not necessarily a new product or service but a new "it," *new profits*—and to sell it in a new, consultative manner is often perceived by inveterate vendors as more of a threat than a promise. The risk of being first is seen as the risk of being wrong. It is part of the vendor mystique to bemoan a lack of meaningful differentiation from competitors yet simultaneously to do nothing innovative. Vendors ask themselves, What if our competitors *don't* do it? Vendors who can be saved ask, What if our competitors *do*—even worse, What if they *do it first?*

Selling based on value, which is the core of the consultative approach, is the basis of sole sourcing, the ability to be a single dedicated source of supply to your customers. In packaged goods, it is the basis for retail category management. Similarly, it is the basis for systems integration in computers and telecommunications networking. Without Consultative Selling, none of these positions will be available to you. The longer you vend and the less you know of your value, the longer you will have to go on vending and the less of your value you will ever have the need or the chance to know.

Hard-core vendors cling to selling products because they appear to be tangible. Value, especially since they do not know it, seems conceptual. In reality, the customer from the Box Two middle-management level on up sees things the other way around. A product's performance is conceptual: the alleged reactions of chemicals, the mythical flow of electrons that no one has ever seen, the concept of improving the productivity of a customer's people by enabling them to make better decisions faster. The only tangible that a customer comes away with is the dollar value these things can add to his profits. That is how he knows that your reagent works and why your bits and bytes are worth something. Because he can hold the added dollars in his hands, count them, and take them to the bank, they represent the only true tangible in his business. Consultative Selling allows you to sell them to him and be paid for them in full.

Figure P-1 shows how the consultant's value chain is 180 degrees away from the vendor's chain. The vendor leads with his hardware—his product—and his software—supplies and other consumables—supplemented by their related services. At the very end of the chain, a vendor may offer applications and training services that can be supplemented by consultation. The consultation will generally be taped on and often furnished by a third party. The consultant leads with his consulting services, counseling his customers on where he can add value to them, how much he can add, and how soon he can add it.

According to the vendor chain of values, value—and therefore price—is concentrated in the hardware and software. Consultants know where their value is concentrated. They put it first. Their hardware and software come along, pulled by the leads that consultation generates. None of the links in the consultant's chain bears a price. Instead, price is the result of the total value that the consultant adds.

The consultant's value chain says, in effect, "I will show you my value (your improved profits) before I show you my hardware and software (my costs)." Vendors show their costs first. This makes the "it" of what they sell incomparably different. The vendor's "it" is product. The consultant's "it" is value, new profits for his customer.

Fulfilling Primal Needs

All customers have two primal needs in common. One is to maximize the satisfaction that their customers have with the values they add to increase their customers' competitive advantage. The second is to maximize their own competitive advantage.

Everything a customer does should result from or support one or both of these needs. This includes doing business with you.

How do you help your customers maximize the satisfaction of their own customers? The only way that counts is to

Figure P-1. Value chains.

Vendor Chain

5	4	3	2	1
Consultation	Applications and Training	Technical Services	Software	Hardware

VENDOR → CUSTOMER

Consultant Chain

5	4	3	2	1
Hardware	Software	Technical Services	Applications and Training	Consultation

CONSULTANT → CUSTOMER

help your customers make, market, or apply their products in ways that improve their customers' profits. How do you help your customers maximize their competitive advantage? The only way that counts is to help your customers improve their own profits.

Only new, improved profits from doing business with your customers will satisfy your customers' customers. Only new, improved profits from doing business with you will competitively advantage your own customers. In fulfilling both primal needs, profits are the key. Whatever you sell, it must add to profits at two points along the value chain—with your customers and then with their customers—or you will be competitively disadvantaged in your own industry.

In business, profits are the only advantage. Everything else is a cost, a disadvantage. Technology is not an advantage; it is a cost. How does it contribute to a customer's profits? Service is not an advantage; it is also a cost. How does it contribute to a customer's profits? Just-in-time inventory, customer support, cooperative advertising, and technical information and advice are all additional costs. How do they contribute to a customer's profits? Unless you can answer, they will remain costs. They will make no contribution at all to your own profits because you will be unable to sell them at their value. You will, in fact, be lucky to sell them at their cost.

There are only two ways that you can improve a customer's profits when you sell to him: You can help him decrease his costs or you can help him increase his revenues and earnings. Your customer has the same two options when it comes to improving the profits of his own customers. There is no third option. If you reject the two options for improving profits, your only recourse is to vend based on price and performance. If you do, your customers will still try to improve their profits, but they will do it at your expense. They will take it out of your margins.

When you sell in a way that improves your customers' profits, you have the chance to have your own profits improved as well. When you sell products based on price, you have no chance to improve your profits. At best, you will be able to limit your discounts.

Consultative Selling is selling in a way that improves customer profits and your own as well. It meets the primal needs of your customers for *customer satisfaction* in their own markets and for *competitive advantage* in their own industries. At the same time, it meets the same primal needs of your own business as well.

Taking Perverse and Unquantifiable Pleasures

As I have conceived Consultative Selling, taught it, and counseled on its application and institutionalization, I have presided over its spontaneous combustion. It has come about over a period of time that began when there was a strong consensus in the business community that a certain way of selling—vending, in this case, where products are sold on their price and performance—was the only way to go and that the only need was to do it better. But vending became decreasingly productive. As products achieved broad-scale parity in their features and benefits, vending left them vulnerable on price. Margins began to be traded away for sales. It took ever longer and costlier sales cycles to make the trade. Caught in the classic squeeze between shrinking margins and rising costs, one company in one major industry after another departed from the consensus and came with me. The first ones, I thought, were brave because they were unsure. All the rest that have followed have been very sure. They had been on the receiving end of Consultative Selling and they had found out what it could do to improve profits. Now the ones that do not sell this way, I think, are brave.

Beyond profits, there have been other pleasures from Consultative Selling, some perverse and others unquantifiable. In one of the few reverse transactions in the balance of trade between our two countries, the Japanese have adopted Consultative Selling. They call it *Kaizen,* which they translate as the improvement that comes from a constant reevaluation of a customer's business operations in order to find ways to increase his profits.

Consultative Selling has achieved its remarkable record by enabling suppliers to sell higher volumes of sales at higher margins to higher levels of customer decision makers. Consultative Selling also condenses the sales cycle. It encourages urgent purchase because it offsets the most coveted product of all to every customer—new profits that cannot be achieved as cost-effectively in any other way. This is the stuff, the only stuff, of which true and long-lived business partnerships are made.

Once a sales force has been trained to sell consultatively, it can conceive of no other way. It becomes hooked on the results. So do its customers. They do not want to be sold to in any other way. This makes a mockery of competitors who try to "sell high" based on the typical vendor's price and performance arguments that put forth product features and benefits. Fortunately for them, they are not likely to be invited by the customer to do it again. When they leave, vendors take away with them a startling realization: Once partnered, a consultative seller cannot be depositioned by price or performance appeals. No other practitioner of any other sales strategy can make that statement.

Ever since I invented Consultative Selling in 1970, I have been asked one question over and over again: "Of the three-legged stool you have created—positioning, proposing, and partnering—which one is the most important?" For a long time, I answered that they all were; how could one leg of a stool be more important than the other two? But one of them is. It is partnering.

A seller cannot consult except to a partner. To everyone else, he can only vend. Nor can a seller have access to his customer's managerial-level decision makers and to their data on their businesses unless he can partner. Partnership is what positioning is all about. A seller who fails to position himself as a partner has nothing else to do but vend on price. Finally, proposing—the third leg of the stool—is a fully partnered act. A preliminary partnership is the objective of each Profit Improvement Proposal. The presentation of proposals, their implementation, the progressive measurement of their results, and their migrations are all further acts of partnership, impossible any other way.

Consultative Selling is, to be sure, economic selling to a sufficient degree to be called *profit improvement selling,* which is how I often describe it. But it is essentially "partnered selling" because it takes two to make each consultative sale: a Box Two customer manager who plays the internal role of your economic seller and you, the external seller. You must sell him. Then he, as your partner, will be able to sell for both of you.

Consultative Selling is more than a sales strategy. It is the profit-making fulcrum for a business because it determines how the business relates to its source of funds, its major markets. Nothing is more crucial. It makes total customer drive mandatory, not a discussion item. It brings customer needs into a supplier's business where they cannot be ignored or denied, fixing them as the business drive force that will affect its products and services, its values, and the strategies by which these values are transferred to customers. It will build the bridge for strategic alliances and provide the platform for the category management and systems integration of customer operations. And it is the keystone to creating and evaluating the ultimate objective of all sales strategy, customer satisfaction.

No joy is greater than that of the first-time consultative seller who sees the power of Consultative Selling begin to work for him or her—except perhaps, the joy of his or her manager, who has made the investment to train the seller. From time to time, sellers I have trained and their training directors share their experience with me. They are not all as exuberant as the one that I have chosen to reproduce here, but the success that it evidences is the rule:

> On June 13, Will Skinner presented his first Profit Improvement Proposal. It was accepted. You trained Will May 9 and 10. Will's sale has already earned enough incremental

profits to pay back our entire investment to train him and the rest of his class in Consultative Selling. Thanks, Mack.

P.S. Will says your ninety-day norm for the first sale is two months too long. Either that or you've just never trained anybody like Will Skinner before.

Consultative Selling™

Introduction

The Consultative
Selling Mission

Consultative Selling is profit improvement selling. It is selling to high-level customer decision makers who are concerned with profit—indeed, who are responsible for it, measured by it, evaluated by it, and accountable for it. Consultative Selling is selling at high margins so that the profits you improve can be shared with you. High margins to high-level decision makers: This is the essence of Consultative Selling.

Since 1970, Consultative Selling has revolutionized key account sales. It has helped customer businesses grow, and supplier businesses achieve new earnings along with them. Everywhere it is practiced, Consultative Selling replaces the traditional adversary buyer-seller relationship with a win-win partnership in profit improvement. This is no mean feat. To accomplish it, Consultative Selling requires strategies that are totally divorced from vendor selling. It means that you stop selling products and services and start selling the impact they can make on customer businesses. Since this impact is primarily financial, selling consultatively means selling new profit dollars—not enhanced performance benefits or interactive systems, but the new profits they can add to each customer's bottom line.

Consultative Selling is selling a dollar advantage, not a

product or process advantage. There is no way to compromise this mission. Anything less is vending.

Vending is discount selling, giving away value to make a sale. Consultative Selling, on the other hand, is high-margin selling. Full margins are the proof of value. When they are discounted, that is proof that their value was not sold. The most frequent reasons are that it was not known or that it could not be proved.

Performance values put into a product or service are validated by the financial values a customer gets out of them. Performance values are important only insofar as they contribute to the value of a customer's operations—either they add the value of new or more profitable revenues or they help preserve that value by reducing or avoiding costs that would otherwise subtract from it.

Discounting denies that superior value has been put in. Or it denies that superior value can be taken out—or, if it can, that it can be documented. With each discounted sale, value is either denied or downgraded. It is obvious how this deprives the seller of a proper reward. Less apparent, perhaps, is how his customer is also deprived. Unless he can know in advance what value to expect, which means how much new profit he will earn and how soon he will earn it, he cannot plan to put it to work at once. He incurs opportunity loss even though he adds value, because he cannot maximize it. His own growth is impaired along with the growth of his supplier.

As long ago as the early 1970s, Bill Coors of the Adolph Coors Company said that "making the best beer we can make is no longer enough" of a value on which to base a premium price. Making the customer best in some way or other would be necessary to maintain the margins that were once easily justified by product quality alone. In 1977 a company named Vydec was finding it increasingly difficult to cost-justify its high-quality, high-priced information systems when competing against the decreasing costs of competitive systems. Its managers realized too late that the justification of a premium price could no longer be attributed to hardware performance.

"Future hardware will all look alike," they realized after the fact. "The greatest values will be in training, software, and system support. You will be able to almost give away the hardware."

A decade later, Lew Platt made Vydec's discovery all over again. When he tried to build credibility for Hewlett-Packard's technology by talking about how H-P was dealing internally with "the challenges that face us," he noticed that customers fell asleep. What woke them up was information on how H-P could help them reduce their own inventories, shorten their own product design cycles, and lower their own manufacturing costs. Improving the productivity of Hewlett-Packard's assets was meaningless to H-P's customers. Making its customers more productive was news.

A decade from now, managers will probably still continue to position themselves as "quality vendors" and will be focusing on selling "technical solutions" instead of solutions to their customers' business problems that they can translate into a return on their customers' investment. They may acknowledge that there is a better way but, under the relentless pressure to achieve quota, they will have no time for it. By doing things their standard way, they will content themselves with being as strong as any other vendor and finishing among the top two or three suppliers.

By then, however, few customers will need a third supplier—in many areas of their business, customers may not need more than a single dedicated partner—and the standard ways of vendor selling will be obsolete. Their sales forces will be following an out-of-print book that says, "A salesman needs to relax his prospect by talking about something in which the prospect is interested, such as his favorite sports, his hobbies, the recent weather, or a current event."

Meanwhile, other sales representatives will be getting the business by talking about something in which prospects are always interested—improving their profits. These sales representatives will be practicing Consultative Selling.

Consultative Selling vs. Vending

Vendors sell price-performance benefits to purchasing agents. Consultative sales representatives sell up. They form partnerships with business function managers whose processes they improve. They also partner with line-of-business managers whose sales they improve. These are their first levels of partnership. They also partner at the purchasing level, forming a relationship that permits both partners to work with function managers and line managers in a triad of mutual interests. This is the consultative uniqueness. No vendor using allegedly "professional selling skills" can replicate it.

Vendors have many adversaries, both customers and competitors. Consultative sellers have partners. This relationship is bedrock. As a consultative sales representative said:

> Your unique Consultative Selling has helped me earn the President's Award twice. This is an unprecedented achievement in the history of my company. To quantify that, it represents thousands of bonus dollars plus a European vacation for two. I know I will take my wife. But my customer partner deserves it more.

Vendors bid in a crowd, reacting to requests for proposal. Consultative sellers takes the initiative and seek out profit opportunities for their customers. When they propose, there are no crowds.

Vendors use their product catalogs as their sales database. Consultative sellers use databases of facts and figures about their customers' operations as their source of knowledge about what to sell, how, and to whom.

Vendors are only as good as their last price. Consultative sellers are as good as their last improvement in customer profit and the continuity they have built into it so that the next opportunity, and the next, are implicit to the customer.

Vendors spend their sales life trying to be accepted as an alternative supplier of products. Consultative sellers gain acceptance as exclusive partners in creating new profits. Vendors can be terminated by a small difference in price. To dislodge a consultant requires proof of a significant difference in profits and a deteriorated partnership.

For these reasons, no vendor can compete with a properly trained consultative sales representative. Even retrofitted vendors cannot stay in the game if they have been given only the cosmetics of consultative positioning without a solid foundation in the economics of customer operations and the financial savvy to make a positive change in them.

When they try to pass as consultants, cosmetized vendors have their powdered wigs blown off not by their competitors but by their customers. It may take the customer a while after a sale to find out whether a vendor's product works. But the customer knows even before the sale whether a consultant's proposed profit it really going to be forthcoming and whether his proposal is based on accurate knowledge or guesswork.

The differences between vending and Consultative Selling are significant. They are, in many respects, differences of 180 degrees. Their languages are different. Their mindsets are different. Their definitions of product, price, performance, customer—yes, even of selling—are different, as Figure I-1 shows. The main difference is in their ability to produce profits on sales.

Consultative Selling takes a position about the sales process. It says that there are two ways to sell. One is the way of the outsider, which is the way that most suppliers approach their customers. The outsider's gateway into a customer's business is through his purchasing function. Sometimes it is called just that. In many industries, it has different names: MIS (management information services), telecommunications director, and so on. In every case, though, the manager of the function has a single major concern: How much performance can he buy for how small a price?

The other way to sell is the way of the insider. This is how middle-level managers in customer companies already sell their plans, proposals, and projects to senior management. They create what are essentially investment proposals and ask upper-level managers to fund them in return for growing the

Figure I-1.   Consultative Selling vs. vending.

Consultative Selling	Vending
The seller supplies profit as his product.	The seller supplies product.
The seller offers a return on the customer's investment.	The seller charges a price.
The seller uses a Profit Improvement Proposal.	The seller uses an order form.
The seller quantifies the benefits from his customer's investment.	The seller attempts to justify his cost.
The seller attaches his investment to the customer's return.	The seller attaches his price to his product.
The seller helps his customer compete against the customer's competitors.	The seller competes against his own competitors.
The customer closes.	The seller tries to close.
The seller sells to a business manager.	The seller sells to a purchasing manager.
The seller features his customer's improved performance.	The seller features his product's performance.
The seller's product is improved customer profits.	The seller's product is equipment, a service, a process, or a system.
The seller sells to a dedicated industry and to dedicated customers within it.	The seller sells to a dedicated territory.

funds at a rate that equals or exceeds the managers' hurdle rates: the minimum returns on investment that they will accept. Consultative Selling lets you sell to insiders and through insiders. By enabling you to partner with them, it lets you sell like an insider too, which will benefit your margins because insiders sell value, not price; they sell financial performance, not operating performance. It will also benefit your sales cycle. Insiders want to close deals, often and quickly. They need the growth that deals afford them. They also must avoid the opportunity losses that come from delay. They are the corporate hustlers and they are always on the lookout for a competitive edge.

Making the Right Choices

Selling offers its managers three choices. If they make the right ones, they can maximize the earning power of their products and services. Before that can happen, they must first realize that the choices are available to them and, second, that the answers that lead to nontraditional profits and revenues are, themselves, nontraditional answers.

1. *What do you want to be compared with?* All selling provokes comparison. The traditional comparison positions one supplier's product as better than another's. If you choose to make your customers compare your product features and benefits with those of a competitor, the customer will cancel out the similarities and devalue the differences by asking you to discount their worth. If the only difference is price, you will suffer fierce margin pressure.

On the other hand, you can choose another comparison. Instead of competing against the value of a rival supplier, you can compete against the current value that a customer is receiving from one of his businesses or business functions that you can affect. If it is a cost center, what is its current contribution to cost? If it is a profit center, what is its current contribution to profits? In either case, the customer's current performance is your competition. Can you give him a competitive advantage by helping him differentiate himself from his own competitors? This is what he tries to do in his own business. If you can help him, you can sell him.

When you choose to make a customer more competitive, you compete against his own rivals: his own costs that are unnecessarily high or his own revenues that are unnecessarily low.

2. *Where do you want to attach price?* Price is always "of something." The traditional object of price is a product or service. If you choose to attach your price to your product, the customer will compare it to the prices of competitve products. If your product is more similar than superior to them, or not sufficiently superior to make a difference, or is equal or inferior to its competitors, your price will be downgraded.

On the other hand, you can choose another attachment for price. Instead of inviting comparison with competitive prices, you can position your price as an investment and attach it to the customer's return. When the customer compares the return against the investment required to achieve it, the rate of return will enable him to compare the productivity of investing with you against the rate of return from other incremental investments he is making all the time. The customer's investment performance is your competition. As long as you equal his hurdle rate for incremental investments, you represent an acceptable deal.

When you choose to make a customer more money, you become a supplier of funds instead of a disbursement. Your price, now no longer a cost but a returnable investment, can be directly compared against the return, and is therefore freed from comparison with competitive product prices. Instead of having your price reduced, the customer may increase his investment if it will disproportionately increase the return.

3. *Who do you want to make the decision?* There are two kinds of customer decision makers. One is a purchasing manager who buys a product's price-performance. The other is a business manager who operates a cost center or profit center and who does not buy at all. Instead, he sells proposals to add value to the function he manages, requesting funds from top managers to improve his function's contribution to profits.

The traditional buyer is a cost-controller. If you choose to confront him as your decision maker, he will faithfully negotiate away your margins in order to lower "the cost of goods bought." That is his job. Your relationship will be win-lose and you will lose more than you win.

On the other hand, you can choose to partner with managers who will act as your "economic sellers" inside their businesses, promoting your proposals to improve their contributions to profits. They compete for access to funds against all other managers; if they do not get funds, their operations cannot grow nor can they grow along with them. They will sell for you—actually, they will be selling for themselves, with your help—if you can add to the value of their proposals by allowing them to promise a greater return or a faster return or a surer return.

If you make the three right choices, you will be in position to compare your value against a customer's current value, attach your price in the form of an investment to your value, and partner with a business manager who will sell your value. You will be selling like a consultant.

No vendor sales force can stand up to a competitor who sells consultatively. The computer industry discovered that when it tried to vend against IBM. A decade later, IBM made the same discovery when some of its business units, exhilarated by their technology, lapsed into vending. They had to discount by up to 50 percent until they could reaffirm their mission to sell improved profits instead of improved boxes. AT&T discovered the power of Consultative Selling when it was forced to become competitive against MCI and U.S. Sprint. R. J. Reynolds made the same discovery when Philip Morris trained its entire cigarette sales force in Consultative Selling and reversed Reynolds' historic role of category leader within a single year. At the other end of the size spectrum, the fledgling home health care industry discovered the power of Consultative Selling when Jim Sweeney used it to make his Home Health Care of America the fastest growing business of the 1980s.

Each of the tens of thousands of sales representatives and their managers who practice Consultative Selling has a bird's-eye view of the same predictable phenomenon: Even when no customer wants to buy more product, even when a customer industry is deeply recessed or a customer business has become mature, these same customers still need more profits—in fact, at such times, they need new profits even more. These are when consultative sellers come into possession of their markets.

It is for reasons like these that Consultative Selling has become the standard solution in major industries—not just the preferred solution but the basic strategy for doing business. In high-technology businesses, for example, Consultative Selling is the "open standard" that all competitive suppliers use, and must use, to gain competitive parity, let alone advantage. It would be unthinkable to try to be in the computer or telecommunications businesses, or in health care, without it. The same holds true for consumer packaged goods and financial services. The alternative in industry after industry is always the same: Vend on price and performance and leave your value on the table because you do not know it, cannot sell it, have no one to sell it to, and cannot base your price on it.

Applying the Consultative Selling Process

Consultative Selling is a four-part process. Once the fourth part of the process has been reached, the process recycles itself endlessly, learning from each successful selling experience and plowing back its earned knowledge so that each successive cycle starts smarter than the one before. Figure I-2 shows this smart process.

The process of selling so that customer profits are improved is data-intensive. Consultative Selling originates in two kinds of data, one of which concerns a customer's industry and the other his business operations that you can affect. The crucial categories of data are the values that his critical success factors contribute to his businesses or their functions and how they, in turn, contribute to his competitive advantage in his industry. Are they costing him too much? Are they earning him too little? By comparing their values against your norms— which represent the values you are experienced in achieving

Figure I-2.   Consultative Selling process.

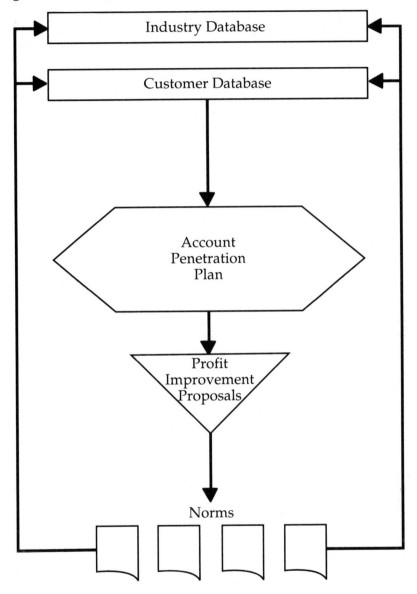

for his success factors—you will know if there is a position open for you as his consultant.

If there is, which means that your cost norms are lower or your revenue and earnings norms are higher than his current values, the second part of the process is a plan to penetrate the customer's business. His product lines or operating functions are your penetration gateways, your entry points over and above the purchasing manager level. Their managers will be your natural partners. They will be the clients for your consultation on how they can more closely approach your norms in their operations. Your account penetration plan is the basic partnering tool that sells them your strategies for making them more cost-effective and therefore more competitive in the contributions they can make to the profits of their business.

The third part of the process is the creation of the Profit Improvement Proposals (PIPs) that will achieve your plan's objectives. Each PIP is a strategy of the plan. It prescribes how much value it will add to the customer's operation, how soon it will add this value, and how the value will be added. The value contained in each PIP becomes your product. It is what you sell, what your customer buys, and what you get paid for.

When it has been successfully delivered, the value of each PIP becomes a part of your track record and should be entered on your "permanent record card" symbolized by your norm for each specific cost or revenue factor you affect. This is the fourth part of the process. Your norms are your best reference for consultative expertise. They are your most important possessions; consultants are known by the norms they keep. They should therefore be brought into your customer database so that they can help you detect your next set of opportunities to improve customer profits.

Marketing Financial Values

The decision to concentrate on key account selling as the bull's-eye of sales management is, first of all, a decision to manage from a base of customer data, not products. It puts you in the information business. It acknowledges your recognition of the central fact about top-tier selling: For both seller and buyer, information makes up 90 percent of every transaction. Nothing moves until the information moves.

Knowledge of how to improve their businesses is the principal element in any sale to key account customers. It possesses reality because it is their business. Nothing, including your physical hardware, is as real for them as that. When you talk about your products, you may think you are discussing tangibles if they have weight, size, shape, texture, color, or aroma. But these are simple bits and pieces of information. They become significant only when you can connect them to the reality of a customer's business by showing the financial values they will deliver. In Consultative Selling, *only financial values*, not products, are tangible.

When you decide to concentrate on the penetration of your top-tier business opportunity, you must give up the traditional positioning of your business. If you currently define the nature of your business in product terms, or in terms of its raw materials or its processes, you will remain a vendor. So it will be with any definition that has to do with your own business instead of your relationship to the businesses of your key accounts. From the customer's perspective, which must now become your own, your business is a financial service business whose "product" is improved customer profit.

Financial service businesses are information businesses; they deal with information about monetary values. They act as stewards of their customers' financial well-being and consult on the most cost-effective strategies for appreciating each customer's current worth. They are evaluated by results that appear in black and white on the customer's bottom line. Were customer profits improved? Were they improved as much as promised? Could they have been improved even more? Could they have been improved even faster? Will they continue to be improved? Can someone else improve them more?

How consultative are your key account representatives? Their report cards are contained in their customers' answers to these questions. But what about the age-old question, Can they sell? Unless the other questions can be answered positively by their customers, selling—in the vendor mode of price-perform-ance comparisons—may be the worst thing that top-tier sales representatives can do.

Key account representatives must position themselves as financial service representatives. This does not mean they *sell* a financial service; it means they *provide* a service that delivers improved profitability for their customers. They sell the profit. If your business has a strong product heritage, it may be initially difficult for you to reposition your mindset—to stop thinking about your product as something that goes into a customer's business and begin thinking about it as the profits that come out of it.

If you are in the electronic data processing business, you will have to learn how to sell the improved profits that result from solving a customer's problems through data processing rather than selling an EDP system itself.

If your company manufactures materials cleaning machin-ery, you will have to learn how to sell the improved profits that result from solving a customer's cleaning problems rather than selling cleaning equipment itself.

If your company processes food, you will have to learn how to sell the improved profits that result from stocking your products rather than selling the products themselves.

A financial service business lives or dies on its ability to create measurable and attributable gains on a customer's bot-tom line. The gains must be presented in dollar terms, the customer must be able to attribute them to you, and you must be able to do it again. The customer's added profit is your "product."

The "V word"—*value*—is the key word in Consultative Selling. The consultative seller knows his value, sells his value, positions his value as his product, and prices its value. He takes pride in his value and is sure about his ability to deliver it to his customers. His value is not in providing a service. Instead, his service is providing his value.

Condensing the Sales Cycle

When you sell as a vendor, you invite the two-pronged costs of a drawn-out sales cycle. You incur the direct costs of selling over and over again until a sale is made or lost. Either way, you also incur opportunity cost. While you are waiting to close with one customer, you are delayed in starting up a new sales cycle with another. You pay this part of the price in lost opportunities or inflated costs for staff that could be smaller if it could be freed sooner to make the next sale.

Vendor sales cycles are unnecessarily prolonged because it is in the customer's interest to trade off time for the price cuts that inevitably accompany it. Consultative Selling makes time the customer's enemy. Delay works against him because it increases his opportunity cost of not improving his profits day by day, week by week, and month by month. The longer he waits the more he loses. Once a revenue improvement or cost reduction is available to him, he must begin to flow it into his operations or he loses it, either in whole or in part.

This internal pressure to improve profits provides customers with a strong incentive to close proposals. Each day's delay postpones payback of their investment and moves the eventual return on the investment at least one more day into the future. Because of the time value of money, each dollar they can obtain from working with you is worth more to them today than it will be worth tomorrow. If they have it today, they can invest it. By not having it until tomorrow, they sacrifice the value of both the principal and its interest.

By prolonging your sales cycle through vending, you sacrifice the contribution your own sales force can make to your profits. Assume that you currently have a twelve-month sales cycle, which is a common cycle in telecommunications and data processing system sales. Make the further assumption that each sales representative has an annual quota of $1.5 million and costs you $300,000 a year. If you can shorten the sales cycle by only one month through Consultative Selling, you can save $25,000 on the cost of each representative each year. The extra month of selling will give you an incremental yearly gain of $125,000 in sales by each seller.

This adds up to a total improved contribution per each representative of $150,000 a year. If ten representatives deliver the same incremental contribution, you will have achieved the equivalent contribution of one additional representative each year: $1.5 million that you will not have to spend a single dollar to obtain. This "equivalent sales representative" will be your most productive seller because he will generate only revenues, no costs. He will never be sick, have to leave the field early, take vacations, ask for a raise, or suddenly decide to quit and go to work for a competitor.

Figure I-3 shows the interminable sales cycle of a typical vendor. The close takes place, if at all, at the end of eleven successive steps, assuming the sales representative is able to move through them progressively without backing and filling. In Figure I-4, a foreshortened sales cycle shows how consultative sellers get to close far more quickly.

The consultant's selling cycle starts by uncovering customer needs for the added value of improved profits. When the needs are qualified and quantified, a consultative proposal begins the partnership process with the customer's business managers. As soon as agreement is reached on the single best solution, a close is achieved. At this point, the sale is effectively made because an "economic seller," a manager inside the customer organization who will sell for you, has been partnered. A presentation of a Profit Improvement Proposal will have to be made to formalize the sale. But the selling cycle is effectively closed.

Bringing the Customer In

The traditional vendor concept of "penetration" suggests a unilateral objective, getting into customer businesses. In consulting, penetrating works both ways. While you are broadening and deepening your presence inside customer businesses,

Figure I-3.   Vendor sales cycle.

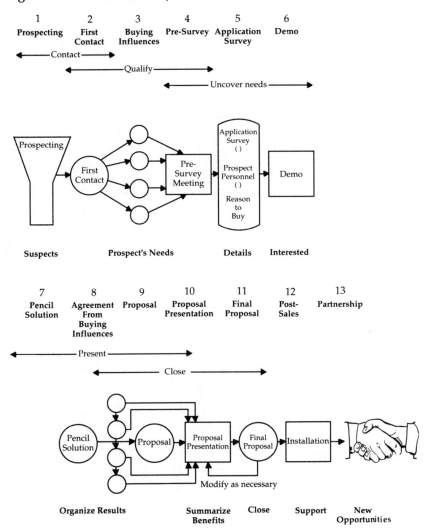

Figure 1-4. Consultative Selling cycle.

1	2	3	4	5	6
Uncover Needs	**Qualify**	**Contact**	**CLOSE**	**Present**	**Grow**

PROSPECTING

DEMO

INVEST-MENT

| Create database through market research in which customer needs can be stored on a business-unit/business-function basis. | Search database to identify best prospective opportunities for improving profit contribution of managers of business units/business functions. | Develop demonstration proposal to indicate potential added value. Also show references and arrange technical validation to rule out performance objections. | Reach agreement on single best solution with business-unit/business-function managers. Finalize demonstration proposal in partnership with them. | Present partnered proposal to decision makers who control allocation of investment funds. Sell on basis of return on investment. | Measure customer satisfaction and develop repeat business from references. |

the customer knowledge that is being gained is flowing back to you. The customer is being brought in.

Nothing more salubrious can happen to the sales function. The customer has always been its missing link. Historically, it has contained product knowledge, process knowledge, pricing knowledge, and promotional knowledge in profusion. These are all internal areas of information that have dramatized the "me-ness" of most sales functions. Rarely have they been sufficiently customer oriented to the "they" out there. The closest to knowing about what goes on "out there" has been competitive knowledge. But even this has been focused on competitive products, processes, pricing, and promotion.

A key account penetration database internalizes customers. It brings them inside your business in the form of data about their most significant problems and opportunities that you can affect.

Bringing customers into your business means knowing their cost problems, the values they assign to their opportunities, and their objectives. Their objectives are their targets, and they will try to reach them by two types of strategies: solving their cost problems and expanding their sales opportunities. Consultative Selling allows you to help them do both. But you will be unable to help them until you know what they know.

To bring in your customers means never having to say you don't know.

When customers are inside your decision-making system, you will be unable to ignore them at the all-important initial stages of proposal, where all sales are really made. The presence of customer knowledge will affect not only your proposals but how you go about making them. "Get the customer in here"—in the form of customer data—will become your most insistent demand. Without it, you will be embarrassed at your nakedness.

Customers, no longer strangers, outsiders, or adversaries, will become familiar. You will get the feel of their businesses. Their problems and opportunities will be your starting points for selling, not your products. All the usual vendor sales points—how the products are made, how they perform, and what their price may be—will become subservient to what you know about your customers. If sales features have value, it will be in relation to adding operating and financial value to your customers. If they can add no value, they can claim no value.

When customers have been brought into your business as residents in your sales database and when you have penetrated their businesses in depth, breadth, and height, the traditional distinctions between buyer and seller will become diffused. Their basis, which lies in the absence of mutual objectives, will have disappeared. Win-lose sales strategies will have no place. Because your customers must win if you are going to have a growing market, and because you must win if your customers are going to have a growing improvement in their profits, your combined need for win-win relations will foster a new union in your roles.

The line between selling and buying will gray out. The zone where customer interests conflict with your interests will thin down. Your need to overcome them will be converted to a need to come over to their way of assigning priorities to their problems, defining the kinds of solutions they can most readily accept, and together with them, implementing the solutions inside their businesses.

You will still have to compete to serve them. But once accepted, you will become their partners in profit. Your common objectives will be identified in your penetration plans; both of you will have signed off on them. Their strategies will be known to both of you and approved by your customers so that they can work together with you to achieve shared objectives.

In such a scenario, which is commonplace in Consultative Selling relationships, who is buyer and who is seller—and what difference does it make? Your role will be that of a customer extender, acting as an extension of your customer's own people and their capabilities to solve their problems. Thus you can become positioned as a true adder of value. Your contribution is perceptible; it is also quantifiable.

The essence of role blending is your combined ability to achieve the dollar objectives of your account penetration plan.

This is your pivot point in moving away from vending toward consultation. If you fail, you fall back to being a vendor. You separate out of the partnership and become a supplier once again, perceived as having your own self-serving objectives that are bound to be inconsistent with—indeed, adversarial to—the needs of your customers.

It is not unusual for a key account representative to say the following:

> For the first time, I feel that my customers are really listening to me. And why not? It's their businesses I'm talking about, not mine. They really want me to sell, because they want the improved profits they know I can bring. As a result, it's no longer clear to me whose job I'm doing, theirs or mine. It's no longer clear to them, either. Maybe that's why we're working so well together.

Improving Not-for-Profit Customers

The objective of applying Consultative Selling strategies to profit-making customers is to help them improve their profits. But profits are not the objective of nonprofit or not-for-profit customers such as educational organizations, public institutions and government agencies, bureaus and departments on the local, state, and federal levels. In their hierarchy of objectives, profits do not exist.

Many customers in the government and education markets have revenue-generating functions akin to sales. These involve licenses, permits, fees, and taxes. In these areas, Consultative Selling can increase revenues by expanding sales volume.

All nonprofit and not-for-profit customers have costs that are susceptible to Consultative Selling. Their costs are of two types. One is the cost of acquisition, the one-time cost of purchase. The other is life-cycle costs of ownership. They are the total costs of operation, maintenance and repair, personnel and training over the useful market life of the purchase. Of the two, life-cycle costs are more important because they are always larger. In computer systems, for example, every dollar of cost to acquire computer hardware is overwhelmed by $10 to provide it with software and $100 to train operators to use and maintain it. This does not include repair and replacement costs not excluded in the warranty, or costs of upgrading.

Decreasing operating costs can also help improve productivity by allowing a current work force to get more work done per dollar of wages and benefits or by allowing a smaller work force to produce as much work as a larger one. In order for productivity gains to be measurable, and therefore quantifiable, they must be related to increases in the value of usable or marketable output or the cost-effectiveness of a work force in generating it. Either the value must go up or the cost must go down to certify a productivity gain. Reducing the contribution of labor content, or reducing the level of labor skill required and thereby reducing its expense, is one way. Stepping up output per worker is the other.

No intermediate benefits, however, count toward productivity gains unless their contribution to added value or reduced costs can be measured. Better or faster access to data that can lead to better and faster decisions may or may not have an improved impact on productivity. Faster or earlier decisions may not be better decisions. Better decisions may still not be good enough. Working harder is not necessarily working more productively. But whenever true gains in productivity can be quantified, nonprofit and not-for-profit organizations are continually in the market for them.

All cost savings and provable productivity gains count for the same advantages in nonprofit or not-for-profit organizations. For one, dollars that are saved are the equivalent of more dollars appropriated or allocated, netting out the same as an increased budget: A dollar saved is a dollar earned. This means that managers have more money to spend without having to request it. Another advantage to public administrators is that reduced appropriations requests signify good management practice that earns brownie points with directors, legislators, and constituents.

Reconciling the Two Faces of Consultative Selling

One way to look at Consultative Selling is to see it as a system that empowers a sales force to act as surrogates for its customers. Equipped with an acute working knowledge of the customer operations they can affect, consultative sellers can be true customer representatives, standing in for customers within their own companies. "My customer has these needs for cost reduction in this critical success function," they can say to their product developers. Or, "My customer has these needs for market penetration in this critical success business," they can lobby with their engineers or manufacturing people or support services. "Here is what it can be worth to us to supply them."

By knowledgeably representing customer satisfaction, consultative sellers can motivate their organizations to respond based on the same strategy of profit improvement they use with customers. "Here," they can say to their own people," is what is in it for our customers. And here is what is in it for us: Here is our return on investment, the net present value of our profits at this and that volume, and our payback and cash flows over the next three years. Can we do a deal?"

This is the only businesslike way in which a customer can be represented, not in terms of his raw needs, which can appear amorphous and provoke a "so what?" response, but in terms of the improved profits that the needs represent. It no longer becomes a question of "Wouldn't it be interesting to do this or that?" or "Do we have anything better to do?" but "How attractive are the financial rewards for our customers and for us? If they are attractive enough to a customer, we can improve our satisfaction rating with him. If they are attractive enough to us, we can improve our profits."

By selling consultatively inside the seller's own company, customer needs can be presented from the strength of their call on business judgment, not as an appeal to fancy or in conflict with the comparative clamor of other competing proposals.

There is a second way of looking at Consultative Selling

that sees it from inside the customer's business rather than a supplier's. In this view, the consultative seller is not only a customer surrogate. He or she is also the supplier's expert in adding incremental value to a customer's critical operating function or critical line of business. The consultative seller represents his company's expertise and experience as an applier of its capabilities that can reduce or eliminate costs or expand revenues and earnings. This is a true consultant's posture as the resident expert who applies his norms to customer operations, measures their deviations, and sets about to bring them closer to being more competitively advantaged.

In this role, the consultative seller is a reverse lobbier, representing his company's solutions to a customer's problems and opportunities as more valuable than alternative approaches, or valuable within a shorter time frame, or more certain of delivering their proposed value. Once again, the seller will appeal to the quantifiable values of his solution, proposing their return on investment, net present value of profit contribution, payback, and cash flows. He or she will use the same profit-improvement type of proposal and will provoke action by similar appeals to competitive advantage.

These are the two faces of the consultative seller, the one internal and the other that customers see. They come together as one, however, combining the seller's twin roles as customer surrogate and supplier expert in the unified role as "honest broker" between the two companies he or she serves. The seller is a deal maker, bargaining for the short-term use of invested funds in order to convert them into an incremental return that benefits both of his clients as well as himself. It is not only win-win. It is win-win-*win*.

Deciding Which Customers to Counsel

The easiest customers whose profits you can improve are customers whose profits you are already improving. These customers are your "growings," the companies you are growing today. They are your growth base: tomorrow's "installed base for growth." A second group of customers whose profits you can improve are companies whose needs for competitive advantage are similar to those of your "growings." These customers are your "growables," companies you are not growing today or are not growing at your maximum level of capability. Taken together, the growings and growables will constitute the 20 percent of all customers who can contribute up to 80 percent of your profits because they are the 20 percent of all companies in their industry to whom you can contribute in the 80 percent range of their own profits.

This commonality of contribution, where each of you is vitally important to the other's growth, is the basis for your natural partnership.

As a partner in improved profits with your growing and growable customers, you will be contributing a high rate of return on the assets they invest to do business with you. Similarly, they will be equally high contributors to your own return on the assets you invest to grow them. They will cost you more to serve. But they will yield much more in return for each dollar you invest with them.

For the dollars of direct SG&A (Sales, General & Administrative) costs and other assets you allocate against your major growth customers, your return in sales volume and gross margin will exceed severalfold the return you make on vendor sales. If you rank your customer partners according to their contributions to your profits instead of revenues—the same way you will want them to rank you in your role as their profit improver—you will be able to customize the optimal mix of services you must provide each of them in order to return maximum profits.

Consultative sellers and their support staffs are every company's prime sales assets. They are true "knowledge workers," irreplaceable over the short term in their roles as partnered value-adders to major customers. Where should you allocate them? How much time should you allocate them for? On what projects? All of your answers must be factored by two considerations:

1. What is the most likely impact of each budgeted dollar on customer profit improvement?
2. What is the most likely impact of each budgeted dollar on our own profitability—on our return on asset allocation per consultative seller per project per customer?

In order to understand the optional deployment of the consultative sellers who are your most precious and most constrained resource, you must know at all times your sales cost for each seller as well as all the attributable added costs of goods sold, service costs, product and product development costs, just-in-time inventory costs and other allocated costs. When you compare these denominator-type costs with their commensurate revenues and earnings, you will know who your most and least profitable customers are. You will also know who your most and least profitable consultative sellers are, and why.

Once you have measured your consultative sales force's performance, you can set standards for it. You can also create a reward program based on profit-making performance. Instead of paying off on the revenues each seller generates regardless of their costs, you can pay for performance based on return on sales investment. If you really want to encourage partnering, you can adjust your compensation schedule to match that of your sellers' customer managers. You can pay them on the basis of the profits they create for their customers: the return on customer investment with them. This is the ultimate bonding strategy with a customer: not just adding to his value creation but being rewarded or penalized by how much you add.

Answering Questions Sales Representatives Ask

"How do we know we can become consultative sellers?" Sales representatives often ask this question as they try to match their own perceived abilities with the strategies of the consultative approach. "How can we tell that we have what it takes?" The only way to know for certain, of course, is to apply consultative strategies to a key account. But even beforehand, sales representatives can preview themselves in a relatively straightforward manner by evaluating three aspects of their talent mix.

Motivation comes first. Do you have the desire to develop professional knowledge about a customer's business, especially its manufacturing and marketing processes? *Dedication* is a second consideration. Do you have the dedication necessary to explore a wide range of optional strategies to improve a customer's profits, knowing in advance that you will have to reject or rework most of them before you can hope to install them, and that even then you will have to monitor and measure their progress long after the excitement of their novelty has worn off? The third essential talent is the ability to achieve your own *self-actualization* largely through contributing to the enrichment of your customers.

Sales representatives also want to know how their key accounts are likely to react to them when they make their opening consultative approach. "Will we have to motivate a customer to accept us in our new role? How do we get started: Do we suddenly announce that from now on we are going to be consultative?" When you try for the first time to position yourself consultatively with a key account, you may encounter reactions ranging from polite curiosity to skepticism. You will have to change your image with care and credibility. A good way to face the problem is to introduce the change something like this:

> Up to this point, my contribution to our relationship has been based on assuring you of a supply of products and product-related services that have been helpful to you in earning a greater profit from your operations or on the sales you make to your customers. Now I want to begin to emphasize my ability to improve your profit in a more systematic manner.

The response you seek is in the question "What is your plan?" You can then reply, "My plan is to help reduce the cost of one of your major operations by $x or y percent." Or "I propose to help you improve the profit from sales of one of your major products by $x or y percent."

When the customer asks the magic question "How?" you can begin the consultative sell.

Because Consultative Selling obviously requires a serious time commitment to a customer's business, sales representatives want to know how to reconcile it with results. "Suppose we get ourselves deeply involved? What happens if we lose the account? How do we justify our investment?" By getting involved in a customer's business through adding profit to it, a seller is taking the single most effective step toward consolidating a long-term and lasting relationship. Profit improvement is the best insurance policy against all but capricious account losses or those that occur for reasons removed from the seller's interaction with the customer. By definition, key accounts are too valuable to lose. For this reason they are worth serving with the strategy that can help them most and bind them the closest to their most helpful source of supply.

In selling, sauce for the goose soon becomes sauce for the gander. However unusual it may be, no product or sales strategy remains exempt from competitive imitation for very long. "Is this not also true of Consultative Selling?" sales representatives often ask. "What happens when everybody is selling consultatively? Haven't we just escalated competition to a higher level of cost and complexity?" Since Consultative Selling is the standard for all key account relationships, there is no doubt that each supplier will have to match competition by adopting it. The greatest rewards will go to the company that adopts it first.

But even if all suppliers copy each other's Consultative Selling strategy and even if each offers to improve profit for customers, Consultative Selling does not permit exact replication. This is because *it is a service and not a product.* Only products can be standardized. Services can always remain "branded"—that is, made unique, because of the personal nature of their application.

All suppliers in an industry may practice Consultative

Selling. Each customer will prefer to deal with only one of them, however, because of the specific relationship between one seller's values: the way that "how much" value relates to "how soon" it will flow to "how sure" the customer can be of receiving it. In case of a tie, duplicate prizes will not be awarded. The business will go to the supplier with whom a customer feels the most sure. This is as much a function of the seller as of his deal.

In making the transition from vending to Consultative Selling, the best strategy is to start with "a thin edge of a long wedge." This makes use of the "power of one," beginning with *one* proposal to improve the profit contribution of *one* business function or line of business in *one* operation of *one* customer in *one* industry. This gives you a toehold on the "thin edge." Once you have been successful, you can commence building a learning curve by taking the next step up the "long wedge" to use the power of one with the same business function or line of business in another customer's operation. Then, when you have achieved proficiency in one operation, you can move farther up the same industry's wedge by penetrating another operation or another function or line of business in the same operation.

Making Yourself the Number-One Asset

A useful definition of *management* is "getting the most out of the least amount of assets." An asset is a cost, something that has been invested in with the expectation that it will produce a return that exceeds the investment. This is what every customer decision maker tries to decide every day: Which assets should I invest in to maximize my return? Consultative Selling is your best strategy to get on his list.

Customer managers are employers of assets. Their supervisors measure them on how profitably they employ their assets to produce sales. Some assets are in the form of cash. Other assets are in the form of cash yet to come, which is called receivables, and cash sunk, which is called inventory and plant

and equipment. Inventory and equipment come from suppliers. Through Consultative Selling, you can find out how
much of a return the customer is getting on the assets he has
acquired from you in the past and you can project how much
he will be able to yield on new assets you are proposing.

The way the customer determines his return on the investments he makes when he buys from you is to divide the profits
they contribute by the amount of the investment. This tells him
whether he is going to come out with a net gain by doing
business with you and, if he is, how much it is likely to be and
how soon he can expect to get it. It is up to you to tell him how
you will make money for him. Will you help him increase his
volume or his margins? Or will you help him reduce his
operating costs? Or will you do both? If you can answer yes to
any of these questions, you will be able to sell to him on the
basis of your return instead of your cost.

Once you free yourself from being positioned as an added
cost, the customer will be able to regard you as an adder of
value—an asset whose investment pays back a profit. The price
that you ask him to pay to invest in the assets you want to sell
to him can now be freed from being attached to the asset itself
and can become related to the customer's return. By relating
your price to your value as a profit contributor instead of to the
performance features of your asset or to the price of your
competitors' assets, your price will appear small and insignificant. Even more important, it will be seen as an investment in
a profit-making asset.

In these ways, Consultative Selling changes the unit of
sale, converting it from an added cost to an added value. It
also changes the way the customer perceives the source of
value from the sale. No longer is value expected to flow from
the combination of high performance and low price. Value will
henceforth be looked for from a positive return on investment.

Part I
Consultative Positioning Strategies

1

How to Become Consultative

In just three sentences you will reveal whether you are a consultative sales representative.

In the first sentence, a consultant identifies a customer problem in financial terms—what the problem is costing the customer, or what the customer could be earning without the problem. If you mention your product or service at this point, you are vending and not consulting.

In the second sentence, a consultant quantifies a profit-improvement solution to the problem. If you mention your product or service at this stage, you are vending and not consulting.

In the third sentence, a consultant takes a position as manager of a problem-solving system and accepts single-source responsibility for its performance. In the course of defining the system in terms of contribution to customer profit, you will be able to mention products and services for the first time.

If you are selling as a consultant, it is easy to predict what the fourth sentence must be. It will be a proposal of partnership with your customer's top-tier managers in applying your system to solve the customer's problem.

A consultant's problem-solving approach to selling requires helping customers improve their profits, not persuading them to purchase products and services. To solve a customer's problem, a consultant must first know the needs that underlie it. Only when a customer's needs are known can the expertise, hardware, and services that compose a system become useful components of their solutions. This is the difference between servicing a product and servicing a customer. It allows your relationships with customers to be consultative rather than the simple sell-and-bill relationship that characterizes traditional customer-supplier transactions at the vendor level.

The ideal positioning for a consultative seller is *customer profit improver*. You can achieve this position by affecting one of a customer's operating processes in two ways: reducing its contribution to cost or increasing its contribution to sales revenues. A consultative seller's primary identification with profit improvement rather than with products, equipment, services, or even systems themselves gives the sales approach a decided economic cast. It focuses attention on the ultimate end benefit of a sale, not its components or cost. This gives you the same profit-improvement objective as the top tier of your customer has. It also professionalizes your mission by expressing it in business management terms, not sales talk.

Consultative Selling positions the seller as the vital ingredient in the selling process. It has become necessary to do this in one industry after another—and to convert product sales representatives into consultative sellers—because products and equipment have lost uniqueness in value. They have become commodities, parity products without differentiation from each other. As a result, they have lost premium value as the basis for their price.

To remain profitable, many suppliers have come to the realization that they must sell something more than commodity products. Product-related services provide part of the answer. But the major contribution to conferring premium value on a customer, and hence the major justification for charging a premium price, is *added value*—the value that can be added to a commodity product by a consultative seller who can apply it to improve customer profit.

Selling Return on Investment

From a top-tier customer's point of view, a consultative sales representative is an integral part of every sale. Unlike product vendors, who are identified as a part of their own company and therefore do not go along with the sale of their product or service, consultative sellers are embedded in their systems and are "packaged" along with it. While a piece of equipment may endure longer than the equipment vendor does, the consultative seller generally goes on making an important contribution to customer profit long after the original system has been installed. The seller's durability with a customer aptly defines the vital role a seller plays over and above the other elements of a consultative system.

A system sale is not the sale of products or equipment. Nor is it the sale of product-related services. It is not even the sale of the system itself. A system sale is the sale of a positive rate of return on the customer's investment; in short, *the economic effect of the system.*

Implicit in every system sale must be the assumption, held by seller and customer alike, that the system's return on investment (ROI) is undeliverable without the consultative seller. The consultant's personal intervention is central. It begins with prescribing the system and flows through its delivery, installation, coming on stream, continuing maintenance, periodic upgrading, and eventual replacement. As long as the consultant is perceived as the critical element, the system can hold together; it will not be "desystemized" into separate selective purchases made on the basis of competitive price. The consultant is the guardian of a system's premium price. If the consultant is unable to deliver a return on investment that justifies a premium price, the system will fall apart into its components.

Desensitizing Your Product Drive

The most difficult challenge to consultative sellers is to stop selling products and start selling the added financial values that they can contribute to a customer's business. This requires more than merely substituting one vocabulary for another; it means substituting one mindset for another. Before this can be done, however, you must first undergo a desensitization to traditional product affiliations.

Most sales representatives metamorphose into consultants through a two-stage process. The first stage is to forsake performance benefit orientation for financial benefit orientation. This is akin to the classic features-versus-benefits conversion that all vendors undergo. It is the next order of magnitude. But in Consultative Selling, performance benefits are insufficient reasons for a customer to buy. Performance benefits describe what a product *is;* they are its operating specifications. Consultative Selling requires a seller to describe what a system *does;* these are its financial specifications. It is the end accomplishment of a system's performance benefits that must be sold.

The second stage in translating performance benefits to financial benefits is the calculation of their dollar values. These values, referred to as incremental profits, are the consultative seller's stock in trade.

Product desensitization starts with awareness that systems selling is a translated dialogue. All systems components, including the systems seller, must be translated into a customer value. Hanging out a laundry list of systems components is meaningless unless their individual contribution to the customer's incremental profit is quantified. Mentioning product, elaborating on the technological superiority of equipment, extolling its construction characteristics or other qualities—all are meaningless unless their incremental contribution to the system's capability for profit improvement is quantified.

Translating product performance benefits into incremental profit benefits is the way consultants must think. "What is the contribution to customer profit?" is their key question. They sensitize themselves to bottom-line thinking because they have learned that intermediate-line thinking fails to accomplish two key objectives. It fails to position their customers as clients, since a client is a bottom-line beneficiary. And it fails to position themselves as consultants, since a consultant is a supplier of bottom-line benefits.

Nothing will deposition a seller from a consultative stance faster or more certainly than lapsing back to preoccupation with product. It is the consultative seller's deadliest sin and an ever-present pitfall. At a customer's top tier, it can be fatal. The word *product* rather than *profit* lies poised from long habit on the tips of most vendors' tongues, ready to undo them. The best way to avoid slips of the tongue is to learn to use the new frame of reference in parallel with the old one and translate as you go. Whenever a product is mentioned, define it immediately in terms of its contribution to customer profit. This is what customers do; they listen for the numbers. Consultative sellers must become sensitive to this need and deliver the benefit that customers seek: quantification of the dollar values they will receive, not enumeration of the products or their performance specifications.

Applying the 80-20 Rule

Preparation for Consultative Selling begins with identification of the customer accounts that are the best prospects for profit improvement. These accounts will be your principal source of profitable sales revenues. By concentrating on them, you will have your priority market segments pinpointed as major targets.

In every market, the familiar 80-20 rule will prevail: 80 percent of sales come from 20 percent of accounts. For consultative sellers, this means that only about 20 percent of all customers will contribute to profit heavily enough for them to become clients. Yet these relatively few customers will contribute as much as 80 percent of your profitable sales.

The 80-20 proportion is a generality. In some markets, it will require somewhat more than 20 percent of all customers to supply 80 percent of your profitable volume; in others, far less than 20 percent may do it. In this way, the 80-20 rule averages out.

Since client accounts will be those in the 20 percent category, the core of every consultative business is obviously quite small. This is a sobering fact. Every key account is precious; to lose one is to lose lifeblood. You must become as important to every key customer as the customer is to you. Only when you become a customer's preferred profit improver can this happen. You must know more about the customer's processes than anyone else does. And you must be able to supply profit-improving strategies to those processes better than any other seller can.

Not all of your profitable sales volume will come from key accounts. If up to 80 percent of profit comes from 20 percent of accounts, then 20 percent of profit must come from the remaining 80 percent of accounts. This is good money; it need not be left on the table. But it will almost always be more expensive to earn, because its sources are far less concentrated, their needs 6or individualized treatment may be considerably greater, and they may not offer the same opportunity for repeat, high-volume follow-on sales.

For these reasons, you must create a different strategy in serving non-key accounts. In order to maximize profit, you should use a mix of two strategies. For the 20-percenters, sell as a consultant. For the 80-percenters, create standardized, ready-to-install, off-the-shelf systems; these can be cost-effectively sold or leased as commodities.

Converting Customers Into Clients

In order to consult with a customer on how he can improve his contribution to profits from an investment he makes with you—in something you may call your "solution"—you must counsel with him in his own terms. These are not the vendor's terms of product features and benefits or price and performance. They are, instead, the basic language of business management in its most elementary form: Business Management 101.

At the Box Two level, "business-ese" is the only language

spoken. It is transaction talk, the language of money being transacted. It is charged with action verbs: funds being *invested*, investments being *returned*, cash *flowing*, payback *occurring*, profits *improving*, costs being *reduced*, revenues being *increased*, and market share being *gained*. But these are simply ways of expressing what is happening to the subjects of these verbs, the dollars themselves. Box Two talk is money talk.

What do you have to know in order to "talk money" well enough to be conversant in "business-ese?" There are two requirements. One is to know how money is classified. The other is to know a customer's current money base of costs and revenues and how much you can affect them.

Classifications of Money

Money is classified into six major categories:

1. *Investment*—what a customer pays out.
2. *Return*—what he gets back on what he pays out. The rate of return is the ratio of return to the investment.
3. *Payback*—when he gets his investment back.
4. *Net profit*—what he makes on his investment, or his increment over and above payback.
5. *Cost*—an investment on which there is no return.
6. *Opportunity cost*—the profit he could have made on a different investment.

Customer Money Base

Consultants ask for incremental investments, money that is over and above the basic fixed-cost investments in the business as a whole. In return, they propose incremental profits. Incremental investments are discretionary. Customers choose among them on the basis of the best combination of muchness, soonness, and sureness that meets their needs.

Most consultative sellers propose incremental profit improvement. The rate of return is calculated only on the incremental investment in the proposal, which tends to make it

exceedingly high. The customer's total investment in his business as a whole, or his total corporate return, are irrelevant.
Consultative Selling takes place in the arena of a customer's
microeconomics.

For that reason, the customer's balance sheet and income
statement are neither causes nor effects of Consultative Selling.
They will rarely if ever suggest leads. Equally rarely will they
be impacted by a consultative seller's incremental improvement
of any one business manager's contribution to profits. Yet, for
the individual business manager whose profits are improved,
the consultant's contribution can be a matter of life or death. If
enough business managers have their profits improved by
consultative sellers, their combined contributions may then
make a significant impact on total corporate competitiveness.

The consultant's micro impact makes a customer's annual
report and 10-K interesting background reading but generally
unproductive in suggesting leads for Profit Improvement Proposals. These reports can convey value, however, in three areas
of lead generation:

1. Where funds are flowing inside the company, you can
learn which of a customer's business functions and business
lines are considered critical enough to his success to be funded.
This will clue you in to a customer's "Critical Success Functions" and "Critical Success Businesses."

2. Within Critical Functions and Businesses, you may also
be able to learn their "Critical Success Factors," the key operations and processes that are being funded for renovation or
replacement to make them more cost-effective to their functions.

3. The life cycle position of a customer's business functions and business lines can clue you in to his specific needs
for cost avoidance or reduction and revenue increase.

The rest of what you need to know in order to qualify
consultative needs cannot be found in reports. It is business

function–specific and business-line–specific and consists of two categories of data:

    1. In a cost-centered Critical Success Function, what are the current contributions to the function's costs being made by its critical factors that you can affect? What is the gap between the current contribution of a factor and the function manager's objective to reduce it? Can you help him close the gap enough to make you a compelling partner?

    2. In a profit-centered Critical Success Business, what contributions to its revenues and earnings being made by its critical products and services can you affect? What is the gap between the current contribution of a product or service and the line manager's objective to increase it? Can you help him close the gap enough to make you a compelling partner?

When you know the answers to these questions, you will be ready for your first conversation in "business-ese" with a Box Two customer manager. Your objective will be to reposition both of you: your customer into a client and yourself into a consultant.

Zeroing In on Your Targets

In order to be able to improve the profit contribution of a customer's business or business function, you must know three things:

    1. The current values in the customer business or function that you can affect—the dollar values of a customer's current costs, current productivity levels, and current sales
    2. The prospective dollar values that you can add
    3. The worth of your added dollar values

Knowing Current Customer Values

All customer operations are cost centers. Only one, the sales function, can also be a profit center if profits from sales exceed the cost of sales. Customers have a choice of three strategies for managing their operations. One is to avoid or reduce costs while maintaining productivity. Another is to increase productivity while maintaining, reducing, or even increasing costs. The third is to eliminate an operation altogether, either spinning it out as an independent profit center to remove it from the corporate books or outsourcing it instead of manufacturing in house.

In order to consult with a customer function manager, you must be expert in his operation. This means that you must have three kinds of smarts. You must be *process smart,* knowledgeable in the flow of the customer's process and where the critical costs cluster. You must be *applications smart,* knowledgeable in how to apply your product to the customer's process so that his costs can be reduced or his productivity can be increased. And you must be *validation smart,* knowledgeable in how to quantify your contribution.

"Knowing your customer's business" means all three types of smarts. In the areas of your expertise, you must know how a customer's process flows. You must be able to chart it from start to finish. You must know the 20 percent of its critical success factors that contribute up to 80 percent of its costs. You must know the value of these costs. You must know your norms for these operations and by how much the customer's costs deviate from them. You must know how to bring the customer's costs closer to your norm if they exceed it or keep them below it if the customer is doing better than the norm. You must know by how much you can do this and how soon. When you know all these things, then you can say that you know the customer's business as far as the operations you affect are concerned. Anything less is vendor selling.

In order to consult with a customer business manager, you must be expert in his markets and his marketing to them. This means that you must have three kinds of smarts. You must be *process smart,* knowledgeable in the flow of the customer's products through their distribution processes and where their critical values are added. You must be *applications smart,* knowledgeable in how to apply your products and services to the customer's sales and distribution process so that his revenues or margins can be increased. And you must be *validation smart,* knowledgeable in how to quantify your contribution.

"Knowing your customer's business" means all three types of smarts. In the areas of your expertise, you must know how a customer's distribution process flows. You must be able to chart it from start to finish. You must know the 20 percent of its critical success factors that contribute up to 80 percent of its income and earnings. You must know the value of these revenues and profits. You must know your norms for the products and markets that account for his profits and by how much the customer's earnings deviate from them. You must know how to bring the customer's profits closer to your norm if they are below it or keep them above it if the customer is doing better than the norm. You must know by how much you can do this and how soon. When you know all these things, then you can say that you know the customer's business as far as the products and markets you affect are concerned. Anything less is vendor selling.

Knowing Prospective Customer Values

Vendors like to say that they are value adders. Yet all they can usually quantify is the value of the cost they add when a customer buys from them. Rarely, if ever, do they know the value of the customer costs they reduce or the productivity they increase or the new revenues and profits they contribute to. Yet these are every supplier's most crucial values. Unless you know them, you are selling blind. You will only be as valuable as your most recent discount.

Even worse, you are selling costs, not improved profits, when you vend. If you do not know the value you add to a customer, you must sell what you know: your product's cost and its justification. As soon as you sell cost, you will come under the control of the customer's purchasing function, whose primary purpose is cost control. You will be imprisoned in vending.

In Consultative Selling terms, a *sale* is a transfer of values: a customer's resources—time, talent, and money—are transferred for the contribution to customer profits made by a supplier's products and services. In the same terms, a *sales call* must be an exchange of values as well. The customer must come away with new knowledge: He must be aware of the supplier's norms for profit contribution and how the current contributions of his operations compare with them. The supplier must come away with new knowledge as well, consisting of data on customer businesses or business functions whose profit contribution can be brought closer to the supplier's norms—in other words, he must come away with *leads*. Unless the supplier comes home with data on which to base a Profit Improvement Proposal, or with an approved proposal itself, he has not made a sales call. He has been socializing on company time.

All value is customer value. Adding value does not take place at the factory. It takes place in a customer's business. If you are going to add to a customer's value, you must first know what it is without your addition. This is the customer's "before." The new value will be the customer's "after." The difference between before and after is the *value added by your business*. In truth, it *is* your business. It is what you do and the reason why you are in business to do it.

For the purposes of Consultative Selling, the value you add must become the product you sell. You must become a value-added seller. This means that you must know your "product," the value that you represent.

In common with all products, value has its own specifications. These give it its performance capability, that is, what it is able to do inside a customer's business. Your performance capability is customer-dependent and will vary for each customer application. Each of your "products" will be unique to its customer. Except by chance, no two values will be the same. As a result, you will no longer be able to print a price list. As value differs customer by customer, moving up and down within the range that establishes your norms, the price you require in the form of a customer's investment to achieve the value will also differ.

Value has three specifications:

1. *It has "muchness" or "littleness."* You will be able to add a lot of value or only a little.
2. *It has "soonness" or "delayedness."* You will be able to add value quickly or not for a while.
3. *It has "sureness" or "vagueness."* You will be able to add value with a high degree of certainty or you will hedge.

A mix of "muchness," "soonness," and "sureness" forms the value features that you will be able to offer to each customer. You must be able to quantify each one. Otherwise, if all you can say is something like "We are pretty sure that we can provide a lot of value to your operation very soon," you will be saying nothing. Once you have quantified your value, then you will be able to know your most important sales tool: what your added value is worth to your customers.

Knowing the Worth of Your Added Values

If you are able to offer your customer the added value of one dollar as the result of doing business with you, what are you really offering him? The dollar has three values. One is its money value. A dollar is a dollar. Another value is its time value. A dollar today is worth more than the same dollar will be worth tomorrow. Finally, the dollar has investment value. It can be invested at a rate of return that will multiply its original value several times.

Your value is worth what a customer can do with it—a function of how much he gets from you, when he gets it, and what he does with it. This is the ultimate worth of your dollar. Like value, dollars appreciate only inside a customer's business. In order to create new worth for a customer, you must therefore get into the customer's business—into his critical lines of business and critical business functions—and help him manage them. You cannot create worth without him. Nor can he achieve the added worth you offer without you. To magnify the worth of a business, you and your customers need each other. This congruence of need makes you natural partners.

As a consultant, the most important knowledge you can have about your business is *your value* to your customers; that is, how much you typically contribute to their profits and how long it typically requires to make your contribution.

If you do not know your value, you should discover it at once. Without it, you are doomed to vend. Through a process of *reverse engineering,* you can reenter a customer installation you have sold that has been up and running for twelve months or more and retrieve its "before" costs and contribution to revenues. You can then compare them against the changes made in them after your installation. The differences will reflect your added value. If you follow this process in several similar installations, as shown in Figure 1-1, you will be able to average out your findings into norms.

When you know what your value is worth to a customer, you and your customer can tell what kind of consultant material you represent. If your value is the same as the customer can obtain working alone without you, you are not consultant material. If your value is worth more than the customer can obtain working alone or with any other supplier, you may be prime consultant material.

If you want to be a customer's consultant, you must offer him the prime value. Nobody must be able to offer him better value specifications—as much value or as soon or as sure. If you can achieve this position, your value will become the industry standard. Not only will you deliver the greatest value but it will be worth the most to your customers.

When that happens, you will have a new basis for your price. No longer will your price need to reflect cost or competitive market value. You will be able to relate your price to the worth of your value on a return-on-investment basis. The customer's added worth becomes his return. Your price be-

Figure 1-1. Reverse engineering model.

Original
Customer Norms
As of (Date) _____

Total costs = $__ __ __   Total revenues = $__ __ __

Cost centers*		Revenue centers*	
1. _____ = $_____		1. _____ = $_____	
2. _____ = _____		2. _____ = _____	
3. _____ = _____		3. _____ = _____	
4. _____ = _____		4. _____ = _____	

*20% that
yield 80% costs

*20% that
yield 80% revenues

**INVESTMENT
TO IMPROVE NORMS**
($000)

$ __ __ __

*INVESTMENT PAYBACK
(START POSITIVE
CASH FLOW)*

(Date) + _____ **Mos.**

Improved
Customer Norms
As of (Date) _____
ROI Rate = _____ %

Total costs = $__ __ __   Total revenues = $__ __ __

Cost centers*		Revenue centers*	
1. _____ = $_____		1. _____ = $_____	
2. _____ = _____		2. _____ = _____	
3. _____ = _____		3. _____ = _____	
4. _____ = _____		4. _____ = _____	

*20% that
yield 80% costs

*20% that
yield 80% revenues

comes his investment. A premium return to the customer is all the justification you need to require a premium investment.

Positioning Your Value With Norms

A norm is the distillation of your consultative expertise in improving customer profits. Consultative sellers who sell from their norms are routinely able to say provocative things to their customers:

"According to our norms for the optimal layout for a print shop of your volume and type of production," 3M can say, "your current layout is depriving you of up to $1 million in profits every twelve months of operation."

"According to our norms for an optimal receivables collection system for food processors," AT&T can say, "you can improve the profit contribution of your current system by an average of $500,000 a year."

Norms are the ideal consultative penetration tool. All consulting professionals work from norms, which represent their track record—their single most important possession and the foundation of their repute. When their norms are the industry standard, they can use them to issue a "norm challenge" against a customer's current norms as well as competitive norms. The challenge develops leads. Here is the standard of performance for this Critical Success Factor in this business function or business line, it says. *How do you compare?* If my norms are better than yours, ask me *how* I can bring you closer.

IBM sales representatives walk along the manufacturing lines of pharmaceuticals makers and can say,

> Our model design for automating a process like yours can help you reduce up to $200,000 in labor. According to our norms, your manning is excessive by five workers. Your control process is also slower than our standard in spotting and alerting you to deviations from specification. This will be reflected in added costs for quality assurance, scrap, and downtime. You can avoid these costs by computerizing

your product testing and quality assurance. The difference
between our models in these areas and your operations
can yield you up to three quarters of a million dollars in
the first year.

Your norms announce what is special about you: You know
how to improve the profits of certain types of business operations. You know the standard specifications of what their profit
values can be for these business functions; indeed, you are
probably the discoverer and maker of many of them. If a
customer already exceeds your norms, you can help him maintain competitive superiority. If your norms are better than a
customer's current performance is, you can help bring the
customer up to your standard values.

Your norms—not your products—must become your consultative stock in trade. You sell consultatively by superimpos-
ing them over the current norms of customer businesses. A
customer's new product norm may be only a plan. It does not
matter. The plan contains a pro forma financial projection of
the business-to-be. This is its *as-if* norm: as if it were up and
running. Your norm is an *if-then* model: If the customer adopts
your solution, then the customer norm will more nearly approach your own. The customer will become, or remain, improved.

A norm highlights customer profits. It says that there is a
better way than the one the customer is currently practicing.
The profit difference between the customer's way and your
norm represents your added value. If you can enable a customer's new product, for example, to enter its market one
month earlier than its plan, the dollar value of that month's
earnings and the advance of one month in achieving payback
of the product's funding represent your added value.

The first thing that you should propose to a customer is
your norm for the customer's business or business function.
"If your operation can more closely approach my model," you
can say, "then the added values representing the differences
between them will be yours. Do you want the added values?"

What you do not ask is as important as what you do ask.

You do not ask, "Do you want my product, service, or system?" Nor do you ask, "Do you want my solution?" or "Do you want to buy from me?"

You need only ask whether the customer wants his business to more closely resemble your norm.

When you ask that question, you are proposing to sell in a consultative manner. When the customer asks *how* he can make his business resemble your norm, he has begun to buy from you.

Rising Above Industry Norms

There are two levels of profit improvement that consultative sellers can propose. One level is improvement that is "better than nothing"—a greater contribution to profits than a customer business or business function is currently able to make. The second level is improvement that is "better than anything." This is the promise you can make when your ability to improve customer profits is the standard of your industry, which means that nobody does it better.

If you can only operate consultatively at the first level, you will have to base your proposals on a matrix that compares two values:

1. The current value of a customer operation's contribution to profits
2. The customer's industry norm that represents the level to which you propose to bring the operation

Selling based on customer industry norms is commodity selling. Industry norms are commodities. They are available to you and your competitors alike. They give you no meaningful differentiation. Nor do they give your customers the competitive advantage to take leadership even if you succeed in improving their current norms to the industry level. Industry norms are competitive floors, not ceilings. To perform at or near the industry norm is merely a customer's entry pass into competition, not a badge of superiority. Competitive parity is signaled by the industry norm. Competitive advantage takes place above it.

A typical collection of industry norms is shown in Figure 1-2. They represent a standard percentage reduction in a customer's costs which can be achieved by automating several key investment categories of information technology. The normative reductions are a compost of many customer experiences with many suppliers' solutions. Presumably, any supplier can achieve the same standard cost savings. After achieving it, a customer could still be far from competitive advantage. He would be better, but better is not best.

If you are going to be the industry standard of performance for your customers, you must be the norm leader. If you want to run with the leader, you must be a close number two. Few if any industries require a third major supplier.

Figure 1-2. Industry norms.

Category	Factor	Percentage Savings Norm
Outside services	• Express mail costs	50%
	• Messenger/courier costs	50
	• Printing costs	40
Facsimile	• Facsimile costs	25
Copiers	• Purchase price	10
	• Annual lease cost	20
	• Annual maintenance costs	20
Telephone	• Long-distance service	5
Travel	• Interoffice travel expenses	25
Office space	• Copier space	10
	• Mail room space	10
	• Records storage space	15
	• Centralized word processing space	25
Salaries and benefits	• Permanent employees	5
	• Temporaries	75
	• Overtime (nonexempt)	75

As a norm leader, you can offer customers a demonstrable advantage over their competitors by bringing them closer to your norms, which should be significantly superior to the industry average. This ability—to help your customers compete more cost-effectively—is your own competitive advantage as a consultant. It transcends your product price and performance, your deals and discounts, features and benefits, or any other aspect of your business and its sales propositions. It is the added value that your customers buy when they buy from you.

The superior level of your norm value—superior to both the industry average and your customer's current performance in an operation's dollar contribution to profits—should brand you as the partner of choice. By contrast, your competitors who sell from industry norms will be selling commodities. Even though they can propose customer improvement, they cannot propose *leadership*.

Maintaining a superior norm margin is crucial to your branding. Every time you perform below it, you lower it; every time you lower it, you come back to the pack of competitive commodity suppliers. This is your main incentive to work at your best. It also warns you to work only with customers who want as badly as you do the growth that your norms promise, who have the managers and support staffs who can partner additively with you, and who will be impressive references for your track record as norm leader.

Proposing Through the Life Cycle

Selling from norms based on your experience enables you to sell to any customer whose operations or product lines are at any one of the four major stages of the life cycle, as shown in Figure 1-3. At each stage on the figure, the key opportunities for consultative leads are highlighted.

Proposing With a New Product Norm

A new product norm must be based primarily on cost avoidance for a customer as he prepares for market entry.

Figure 1-3. Life cycle leads.

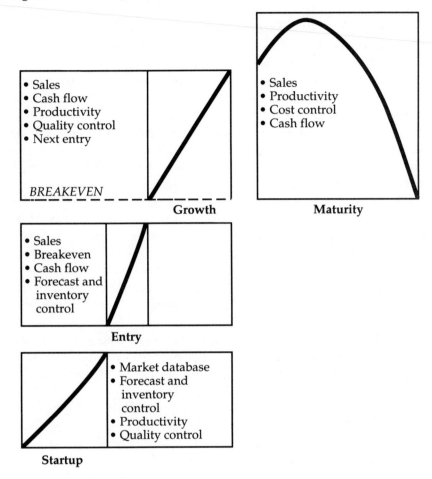

Secondarily, it can be based on preventing opportunity loss of sales.

Before it makes market entry, a new product is a collection of sunk costs. While its asset base is being planned and laid down, nothing is available for sale. Hence, its cash flow is negative. The capital funds that have been appropriated for it are being invested at a high rate of expenditure. Everything is going out. Nothing is coming in.

How many of these costs can be avoided? Every dollar saved at this point is a dollar-plus earned later. A dollar that can be saved can be invested elsewhere. Or it can be returned to the customer, lowering his total investment and, by reducing his eventual breakeven point, speeding payback.

New product norms are heavily into cost displacement or cost replacement. They wipe out a cost category or consolidate several costs into a single lower cost. They substitute a less costly solution like automation for a more costly investment like human labor. The sum total of what they save can be regarded as the equivalent of profits from sales that cannot yet be made.

The second area of new product norm concentration involves reducing the threat of incurring opportunity costs that can delay market entry or can come back to haunt a business after it has been commercialized. These opportunity areas typically involve four business functions: market analysis to make sure the market is rightly assessed from the start; product and process design to make sure that the product is right for its market and is cost-effective to manufacture; quality assurance to make sure that the product will not incur excessive warranty costs for repair or costs for replacement or recall; and forecasting and inventory control to make sure that the product is neither back-ordered, causing lost sales, nor overstocked, causing excessive handling, storage, and insurance costs.

Proposing With a Growth Product Norm

A growth product norm must be based primarily on acceleration of the sales that begin with a product's market entry. It must also be concerned with preventing the opportunity cost of lost sales.

A product's growth phase has two objectives. The first is to maximize market entry by selling up to the full manufacturing capacity of the business. This puts the emphasis on gaining market share as quickly as possible and driving the product's growth curve as high as it can go. A growth product has an insatiable appetite. It devours cash. Therefore, cash flow must be insured. It is a sin to lose sales because lack of cash or capacity prevents sales fulfillment. This means that productivity must be maintained, with its quality tightly controlled. Nothing suffocates growth like the inability to get product out the door except the inability to keep it from coming back.

How much faster can the business be grown? How much faster can inventory be turned and receivables collected? How can downtime be minimized and quality maintained?

The second objective of a product's growth phase is to prepare the business for the next product entry. A successful product not only justifies proliferation; it demands it. Market acceptance offers opportunity for market expansion.

How cost-effectively can a second new product follow on the growth of its pathfinder? What economies can be gained by sharing asset bases? How can the initial product's reputation for quality be bred into the next product? How can tie-in sales create a system for selling the first and second products together?

The objective of a growth product norm is to show how to perpetuate growth. How long can growth at a high rate of sales and profit-making be maintained? Since growth is a rate and not a state, this is the key question for growth product modeling. Every additional day that the rate of growth can be sustained is an added day of premium profits—one more day during which the onset of the declining margins of maturity can be postponed.

Proposing With a Mature Product Norm

A mature product norm must be based primarily on delaying the decline of profit per sale that is the inevitable result of reaching the endpoint of growth. Even though volume at maturity may be huge, decaying margins and increasing costs absorb revenues at an increasing rate as maturity progresses. The mature phase of a product therefore requires a delicate balance between costs, including the cost of sales, and the maintenance of a constant high rate of cash flow to pay for them. Expanding sales is more difficult in mature markets where the markets themselves are not growing. Increased penetration then requires the conquest of a portion of a competitor's share. How can sales be increased cost-effectively? How can sales be maintained more economically? How can the product be renovated marginally to provide a sales incentive yet keep costs down? How can costs—any costs, all costs—be better controlled?

Mature product norms focus heavily on productivity improvement as a means of increasing output at lower cost or the same cost. By the time a product becomes mature, its asset base has become a mixed blessing. It provides the product's capability base but is also the product's cost base. Can it be reduced? Can it be modernized? Can it be made more productive? Buying instead of making, leasing instead of buying, operating jointly instead of going it alone can provide alternatives to cost.

Just as growth product norms are dedicated to maintaining the growth phase, mature product norms must show how to maintain maturity as long as possible. How long can a mature product yield an acceptable rate of return on its assets before the assets become more valuable than their return? This is the key question for mature product managers. Every additional day that the return from a mature business can be sustained at an acceptable rate is an added day of cash flow and market presence—one more day during which divestiture has been postponed.

Leaving Your Product in the Car

What is it like to propose to a customer using only your norms and a Profit Improvement Proposal—actually leaving the product in the trunk of your car?

Figure 1-4.   Norms on a card.

Savings Categories	Total Savings ($/Ton)
Salaries, wages, benefits	$ 4.0
Chemicals	4.6
Wood	2.3
Energy	2.1
TOTAL	$13.0
For a typical 250,000 tons-per-year mill	$ 3.75 M

A sample set of norms, in this case "norms on a card," is shown in Figure 1-4. The information on this three- by five-inch card represents the cost savings that the supplier can make by installing his automated process controls in a pulp mill. Two other norm cards are shown in Figures 1-5 and 1-6. These norms are based on improvements that a supplier can make in a customer's inventory and marketing functions.

Selling from norm cards like these may make you feel naked at first. What will you say? Without your product to extol, you will have no choice. You will have to talk about the customer's business in the ways you can affect it in the following areas:

Figure 1-5.   Norms for enhanced profit contribution by inventory functions.

Function	($000)	Percentage of Sales
Goods on hand	$280	.02%
Out of stock	27	.07
Pipeline	644	.04
Shipments	172	.01

Figure 1-6.   Norms for enhanced profit contribution by marketing
              functions.

Function	($000)	Percentage of Sales
Direct sales	$107	27.0%
Sales forecasting	9	23.0
Distributed sales	3	7.9

1. Where the major costs are and how much they normally
   contribute
2. Where the major opportunities are and how much they
   normally can contribute to improved profits
3. Where you can help and, when you do, how much of a
   cost reduction typically results and how much of an
   increase in sales typically results
4. What your best conservative estimate suggests about
   the cost reductions and sales increases that you can
   generate for the customer

By the time you get to item 4, you will no longer be talking
alone. The customer will begin to talk, opening the dialogue
with you by asking the magic question "How?"—*How* can we
find out *how much* the true value of the contribution that you
can make to us can be and, if it is significant to us once we find
out, *how soon* can we get it?

By asking *how,* the customer will open your sale. By
calculating *how much* and *how soon,* he will also close it.

If you drive your sales with your product, you will have to
open by asking the customer, in one form or another, to take
the product off your hands. You will also have to close your
sales. When the customer drives your sales, he does both jobs
for you. Your job comes in between when you answer the
question "How?"

How is the acid test. It tests your expertise and your ability
to apply it. Without applications capability, expertise is academic. Letting the customer drive your sales will force you to

spend your selling time talking about your most priceless possession, which is not your product but your ability to apply it to improve the profit contribution of the customer's business or business function.

Becoming the Industry Standard

To achieve the position of specialist, to connect the mission of your business to one of the missions of its core customers, is to achieve the supreme differentiation—that of the *industry standard*. The standard supplier's impact on his customers becomes the standard impact. No one who falls below it, or who cannot prove that he does not, can compete against the standard. No one who may exceed the standard but cannot prove it can compete either. The ground rules of competition are clear. Competitors who can make an equal impact come in second. Competitors who can make only a marginally improved impact also come in second. Competitors who can make a significantly greater impact will have to prove it. They may never get the chance. What customer will abandon the industry standard on a chance? If he were wrong, the opportunity cost would be unaffordable.

If you can position yourself as a bearer of your customers' industry standard, you will have two unassailable advantages. One is that you are able to do something no one else can do. The impact you make sets the standard. The other is that you know something no one else knows. The knowledge you have of customer businesses and business functions and how to bring them up to standard is exclusively your own.

Your specialist expertise will be composed of units of knowledge about customer operations. Your impact will be composed of units of profits added to customer bottom lines. In this way, becoming the industry standard can be self-perpetuating. Specifications may say "IBM or equal," but they specify IBM as the yardstick. Performance must be "IBM-compatible" but it is with IBM performance that compatibility must be achieved. IBM is the industry standard. Everyone else is "all others."

When General Motors sets its quality standard as "Honda or equal," Nissan and Toyota are "all others." Honda is the standard brand. All others are equal to each other but not to the standard. Things equal to each other are commodities.

As the specialist, you can be the standard of knowledge about the customer businesses and functions you affect. Customers will turn first to you for information. You can tell them the one thing they need most to know: How do they compare with your standard norms? The norms tell a customer how cost-free, how productive, and how revenue-producing the customer's functions *can be*. They tell him how far he departs from the standard. If a customer is below the standard, you can work with him to come closer to your norm. If a customer is already above the standard, you can work with him to keep him there or, better yet, to improve his superiority over the norm even more.

Your mission as the specialist is clear. No one will have to ask you twice, What do you do? You possess your customer industry's norms. You keep your customers on or below them in the areas of costs. You keep your customers on or above them in the areas of productivity and sales revenues. You are, in effect, a business health maintenance organization. Below par? Maintain or regain your health. Do business according to our norms.

Your mission as a specialist is to improve the profit contribution of the customer operations that you affect. This gives your customers three opportunities to disadvantage their competitors. They can become a lower-cost supplier. They can become a more productive supplier. Or they can become the most profitable seller because of higher quality, lower cost, or better ability to lower the cost or increase the productivity or sales of their own customers.

The ultimate advantage that you can confer on your customers is *to help them become the industry standards in their own markets.*

Ruling Out Debate

Competition debilitates margins. Competition can delay the entry of new businesses and foreshorten their growth phase. Among mature businesses, competition clones all attempts at differentiation and thereby stifles prices at permanently low levels of profit. It also adds to sales cost, further weakening already-depleted commodity margins.

Only the industry standard-bearer is immune to debate on the comparative merits of his product, system, or service. The question he is asked by customers is a *how* question: "*How* can I achieve or exceed your industry standard?" The question he avoids from customers is the *how-much* question: "*How much* is your product?"

The answer to the how question is a Profit Improvement Proposal. The answer to the how-much question is a discounted price. To the customer who asks how much, almost any price will be too much.

There are only two ways that a price suspected of being too much can be justified. One is to sweeten it with some free goods or services. The other is to plead on the basis of superior performance merits. If a pleader cannot be the best, he must try to be better. Today, and forever more, hardly anyone can be best for long. Even being better—better enough to make price commensurate with value—is increasingly difficult to achieve and less likely to be sustained.

Debates on the merits of competitive products inevitably become debates on comparative price. The specialist who establishes the industry standard rules out debate on the merits of his products or the relationship between their value and his price. He sells a different product than his competitors do: the added value of improved profit.

By shielding his products from debate on their merits, the industry standard-bearer protects them from margin erosion. He also defends them against the need for ever-enlarging investments to realize the elusive and transient objective of performance superiority. Competitors find it difficult to get at him. They try to encourage debate on the merits. Meanwhile, he is busily resolving a very difficult kind of debate that he has stimulated, and will referee, with his customer managers. How can we improve the profit contribution of your operations? No wonder, as competitors complain, the customer is not listening.

Positioning as the Mixmaster

Each customer business function is a mix of costs and opportunities. Can you optimize the customer's mix—that is, can you help it more nearly deliver its optimal contribution to profits? If you can learn how to master the mix of customer costs in an industry's manufacturing process, for example, you can ensure your role as the industry's standard-bearer.

Every customer allocates certain resources to each of his businesses and their functions. This is his asset base—actually, his cost base. Some of these resources are supplied internally. They consist of his own people and the capital they use. The rest of his resources come from outside—the products, services, and systems that are purchased from a variety of suppliers. Taken together, these internal and external resources form the customer's current operating "mix." In order to partner, you will have to help create a mix that will contribute higher profits.

All customer businesses operate with a mix. Some mixes are simply conglomerations of products. Others add services such as training or maintenance. Still others are composed of systems that, in turn, are composed of subsystems or, when amalgamated, contribute to networks. You must determine where you fit in every mix, what value you can add to it, and what the worth of that value can be to you and a customer.

The mix becomes your "market." It is where you fit, where you operate, where you belong. It will become the arena of your expertise. You must know how to make it produce profits in the most cost-effective manner and you must know this better than anyone else does. You must master the mix so well that you can position yourself with customers as their industry's "mixmaster."

Customer mixes usually lag behind the optimal mix. They frequently represent a sizable investment. They are also hidebound to a customer's learning curve. His people have learned how to operate the current mix, have become familiar with its capabilities and its quirks. Training programs have been built around it. Cost and production schedules are established for it. Psychologically, it has become "the way we do things around here," a part of the gruel of "corporate culture." It must be approached remedially but respectfully. You must not want to run your customers' businesses. You must want to partner with them so that *they can run them better*.

There are three main strategies for optimizing a customer's operating mix:

1. You can supplant one or more elements in his current mix. If the mix is labor-intensive, for example, you may be able to reduce labor content by substituting an automated process or eliminating an operation altogether. Or you may be able to combine multiple processes such as forecasting and inventory control, thereby eliminating overlapping and duplicated costs.

2. You can substitute your product or process for a competitive product or process that is part of the customer's current mix. The basis for your recommendation must be that improved financial benefits will accrue to the customer if the mix is altered—not simply that more advantageous performance benefits will be realized.

3. You can manage the mix as its systems integrator or facilities manager, working under a profit-improvement contract with a customer.

The specific strategies for partnering by means of optimizing a customer's mix will depend on the industry you serve. If you sell personal care products to supermarket and drug chains, you can penetrate by optimizing the mix of the number of facings that stores allocate to your products compared to competitors', the locations of your facings, and the type of displays. The proof of your optimization will have to be quantified in financial benefits, such as profit improvement per square foot, overall improvement from personal care department contribution per store, or improved profit contribution from related item sales. Or you may propose to optimize a customer's mix by becoming the manager of his personal care product category.

If you sell financial services like stocks and bonds, insurance, real estate investments, or money market funds to affluent individuals, you can optimize the mix of their portfolios in terms of growth potential, risk, and current payout. The proof of your optimization will have to be quantified in dollar benefits, such as higher earnings, lowered taxes, or increased net worth.

Overcoming the Temptation to Protect

It is comfortable for a sales representative to want to take a position of protecting a major account from competition, assuming an essentially defensive posture by "being there" a lot and providing a high degree of personal service. Yet the only protection is in continued growth. Unless a customer is constantly provoked to grow and stimulated to compare his current values against the seller's values, someone else will challenge the customer. This will force the seller to react defensively, aggressively marketing his values as he should have been doing all along. The customer will always wonder afterward, "What other values is he sitting on?"

The temptation to look around will be born.

Consultative sellers must understand that their customers are preoccupied with growth. In business, you grow or die. Without growth, costs overtake you, new technologies outmode you, and competitors outmarket or outflank you. Customer managers take partners precisely to hedge against these risks.

All consultants discover that it is easier to reduce a customer's costs than to expand his sales, and it is a good deal easier to quantify the resulting improvement to his profits from cost reductions. But consultants also come to learn that no customer business exists to control costs. Customers are in business to make money, and the only way to make money is through sales. A consultant who is positioned as a cost reducer can be important to a customer. But a consultant who is positioned as a sales developer is vital.

New profits from increasing a customer's volume at the same margin or increasing margins at the same volume are the stuff of which growth is made. As a result, a customer can control more of a market or he can be the profit leader if not the leader in market share. There is nothing wrong with being the low-cost producer. But if a consultant is expert in cost reduction, he should learn how to translate his impact into its effect on revenues so that he can be positioned as a growth contributor.

All cost reductions can be translated into their sales equivalent. A reduction in the cost contributed by unnecessary inventory expense can be interpreted as the equivalent of a corresponding increase in sales revenues. This is equally true for a decrease in the cost contributed by scrap from off-specification production, from rejects or rework, from failures to make same-day delivery, from late billing, and from late collection of accounts receivable. If these costs are reduced, their earnings equivalent is the dollars saved or avoided: How much profit on how many dollars' worth of how many units sold over how much time stated as "the equivalent of profits from the sale of 500,000 cartons each week—or 1,000 carloads every 72 hours—or 10 additional aircraft operating each day at an 80 percent load factor."

2

How to Penetrate High Levels

Top-tier customer management rarely deals with vendors, and then only under duress. They speak different languages. Vendors speak price and performance: management speaks value and profit. Vendors speak of their competitors; management is concerned about its own competition. Vendors wonder when management will ever buy; management wonders when vendors will ever leave.

Vendors who stand before their customer's top tier will not do so for long, or soon again. For consultative sellers to make a stand, and make it again and again, they must be prepared to speak the language of management, address customer concerns instead of their own, and put to work their knowledge of the customer's business so that a demonstrable improvement—not just a shipment of goods—takes place.

Key account sales representatives who want to penetrate the top customer tier must position themselves to discuss, document, and deliver their answers to the question "How much profit will you add?"

In order to be accepted as profit improvers, sales representatives must pledge allegiance to the Consultant's Credo, reproduced in Figure 2-1. Only by understanding the consultant mindset—which is the mirror image of the customer manager mindset—will you be able to partner at the Box Two level

Figure 2-1.   Consultant's credo.

Consultants sell money, not products. They transact returns from investments, not sales. Their price is an investment, not a cost. Their performance is measured by the amount and rate of the customer's return, not product performance benefits. They work inside their customer businesses as partners, not from the outside as vendors. They relate directly to customer business function managers and profit center managers, not purchasing agents. They work at these middle management levels on a long-term, continuing basis, not from bid to bid. Their focus is not on competitive suppliers but on competitive profit making for their customer partners and for themselves.

---

shown in Figure 2-2. It is at this level that the customer business line managers and business function managers are concentrated, reporting directly to Box One where the funds are.

By partnering at Box Two, you can capture customer managers to act as your "economic sellers," who will help you do your job so that you can help them do their jobs more successfully.

If you are a Box Two manager, what constitutes success? It means always improving your contribution to profits. For a business line manager, it means expanding revenues or increasing margins. For a business function manager, it means reducing costs. And where does the money come from to do these things? It comes from Box One. What is your role in this process? You must help your customer partners get more funds, get them more quickly and more surely so that they can increase more revenues or margins and decrease more costs.

As Figure 2-2 shows, Box One is the keeper of the keys to the corporate treasury. He is Box Two's only funder. He is open to suggestion twenty-four hours a day seven days a week from his Box Two managers on how the corporate funds can be invested more cost-effectively—in other words, how to get "the biggest bang for the buck." Box Two managers are always in a proposal mode with their Box One funders, claiming a stake in

Figure 2-2.   Customer manager hierarchy.

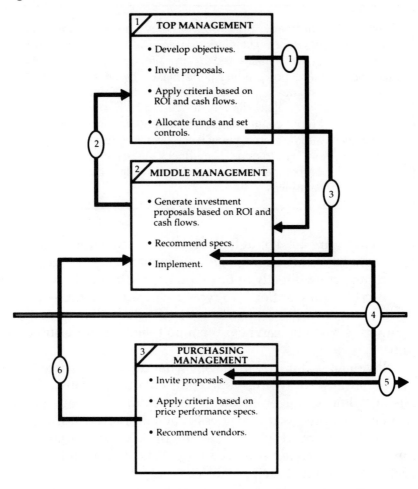

the funding process for their own businesses or functions. When Box One favors them, he does so on the basis of the strategic fit of their proposals with his corporate growth policy and their adherence to his financial objectives for each dollar he invests with them. What rate of return will he achieve? When will his investment be paid back? How will the cash flow? What is the degree of risk?

With every release of funds to a Box Two manager, a control procedure goes along with it to make sure that the invested funds are, first of all, paid back on time, and then maximized for the greatest return. The Box Two managers who get the most funds the most often are the best internal sellers. If you can help them get even more, or more often, they will "go partners" with you to do it again and again.

Allying With Box Two

Consultative sellers succeed or fail on their ability to ally themselves with their Box Two counterparts. They cannot sell without them because Box Two *sells for them* in ways that they cannot. Their alliances are founded on creating an ongoing stream of Profit Improvement Proposals for the customer managers to sell internally, thereby obtaining the funds to support the consultative seller's strategies. In order to act consultatively, the seller must conform to the requirements outlined in Figure 2-1.

Box One thinks, feels, and acts in ways that are standard operating performance for all Box One managers, emulated by all Box Two managers who interface with them, and virtually unknown to everybody else. Box One's position self-description is that of a money manager. Box One's personal business mission statement—the commitment that is really operative in making the business go and not the gassy "emission statement" that is publicly proclaimed—defines a company for what Box One knows it to be. At Borden, Inc., Box One's personal mission is stated this way:

I want Borden to be the lowest-cost producer of all its products and to have an optimal mix of national and regional brands—and most important, I want Borden to be a perpetual cash machine.

It is very much the same at other companies:

We calculate everything we can put a number on. You can think liberally but you must move conservatively when the money is on the line.

*   *   *

I put the highest value on survival. My job is to conserve the critical mass of the corporation.

As a money manager, Box One is preoccupied with financial stewardship, the management of other people's money. This involves making prudent, duly diligent investments, the control and fractionalizing of risk into small, survivable bites, and a conservative management style that emphasizes certainty over the chance for a windfall, incremental gains over breakthroughs, and consistency over flashes in the pan. The following Box One quotations set forth these universal positions:

How would I feel about investing $100 million with a fifty-fifty chance of losing it or making $500 million? Most likely, I'd end up making less than the maximum, maybe $200 or $300 million. But if it were a case of $500 million or broke, I would seldom elect to take it even at fifty-fifty.

*   *   *

When I have a high-risk decision, I make it divisible. If the total risk were $150 million, with a 10 percent chance of losing it and a 90 percent chance of making $500 million, I would risk $15 million to the point of first withdrawal—if it is our kind of technology and we know what to do so we can take a higher risk. If it is not our own technology, I will risk $5 million on step one with a 15 percent or so expectation of success. After spending a second $5 million, we may have a 90 percent expectation. Now we can put in $25 million. If a competitor gets in first while we're pussy-footing around, we may have only a $100 million business instead of $500 million. But we still get some of it. The important thing is that we are not betting the business.

* * *

In the end, how much of a gamble I would take depends on how much money is involved—$25 million is one thing but $250 million is something else. I would risk the smaller number but not the larger one. If I lost $250 million, it would mar earnings.

Your alliances at the Box Two level depend on the same standards of performance as your Box Two counterpart's internal alliance with his own Box One: the contributions that you make to competitive profit making. When you work in partnership with a Box Two function manager, the added contribution you make to him becomes incremental to the contribution he is committed to make to his Box One. That is why he will partner with you. The incremental value of your contribution becomes his test of how much you are worth as a partner.

The definition of *business partner* is therefore the customer manager's definition: someone who can add incremental value to the manager's contribution to profits. If you are going to qualify as a consultant partner, you must make yourself incrementally valuable to a business function manager. This means you must deliver one or both of three types of added value:

1. You must enable your partner to *add more profits* than he would be able to contribute without you.
2. You must enable your partner to *add profits sooner* than he would be able to contribute without you.
3. You must enable your partner to *add profits with greater certainty* than he would be able to contribute without you.

These "deliverables" set the standards of performance for consultative sellers. You will be judged for your partnerability by the manager's answers to three questions: *How much* value do you propose to add: *How soon* do you propose to add it? *How sure* can I be that you will add as much value as you propose as soon as you propose to add it?

These are very different questions than the traditional ones raised at the Box Three purchasing interface. When vendors make their sales calls there, they are asked how much performance they can propose and how little price they can charge for it. But Box Two does not buy product; he invests in value. Box Two does not buy at all; he sells proposals to obtain funds for his own operations. The Box One managers he sells to are your customer's ultimate buyers. They buy investment opportunities that can put their money to work at the highest rates of the surest return within the shortest periods of time.

They judge their Box Two operating managers by how good they are as money managers. If I give you one dollar, they ask in effect, "How much more will you give me back? How long before I get it? How sure can I be?" A manager who partners with you as his consultative seller is betting that you can help him enhance his performance by enabling him to return more money than he could alone, or return it faster, and return it more surely.

When you reduce one of a Box Two manager's critical cost factors, you can help him improve the contribution he returns from his operation. When you increase one of his critical revenue factors, you do the same. These are the mutual objectives of your cooperative partnerships because they are the achievements that improve your mutual profits.

Empowering Box Two With Your Value

Box Two managers have a simple set of needs:

1. They want money.
2. They want it now—yesterday would be even better.
3. They want money so they can make more money with it.

In order to position yourself for Consultative Selling, you must be able to prove to a customer manager that you can help him get his hands on money, that you can help him to get it soon, and that you can supply him with a steady stream of investment opportunities that will enable him to make more money. These are the empowering features and benefits that will make you compellingly partnerable.

As your products and services become more closely replicated by competition, their features and benefits can no longer be differentiated enough to command a premium price. This places the burden of differentiation on you. Can you help a customer manager make or save more money than your competitors can? Can you help him make or save it faster? Can you make him more certain by working with you? *Yes* answers are your sole competitive advantage because they provide the sole competitive advantage of your customer managers.

Most vendors sell by asking purchasing managers at the Box Three level to let the seller do his job: "Buy from me." Consultants sell by helping their Box Two partners do their own jobs better: "Win with me." If you put your money to work with me, the consultant's position says, you will have more money back sooner and surer. At the same time, you will have a greater market share of a current market or you will have gained entry into a new market or you will have a reduced cost burden in an important operation or greater productivity. You will be competitively advantaged as either a market share leader or the industry standard of value as the low-cost producer.

The true value of the competitive advantages you bring to a customer is not in his new profits themselves but in their investment value when he puts them to work. How much more can he make on what he has just made with you? Funds always seek work. Idleness incurs opportunity cost. For this reason, you must have your next investment proposal in your hip pocket—actually, in your Account Penetration Plan—ready to present as soon as your current project has reached payback. This maintains your position squarely in the flow of funds while simultaneously repositioning your customer for the next round of being competitively advantaged by his partnership with you.

As your customer partner positions you, you are an optional investment opportunity. This is how you must come across to him. It tells you how you must define the nature of your business with him:

- If you are in the telecommunications business, you must not simply be in the telecommunications business. You must not sell switches, networks, or rates.
- You must not, simply be one more "problem solver." You must not just sell "solutions."
- You must not be simply a "consultant."

You must be a *profit improver*, a partner whose expertise and experience in the customer's business can help the customer increase the amount, speed, and certainty of the profits he contributes to his top-tier managers in Box One. You must understand the world that your partner lives in. If he is "in manufacturing" and considering robotics, he lives in a world of cost contributors such as Figure 2-3 shows. Which of them can you help him control? Your contributions are your tickets of entry into his world. How much you can contribute, how soon, and how reliably will determine whether you will be invited to live in your customer's world as his partner or be just passing through.

Selling the Way Box Two Sells

Box Two managers approach their top tier as the principals in a four-act play. Key account sales representatives would do well to follow this scenario, both in sequence and in content.

Act I: "Why Do You Want to See Me?"

Everyone who approaches top-tier management must offer justification. Management's brainpower is every company's most precious resource, and it must be profitably engaged every minute. Downtime is time lost forever. Management

Figure 2-3.   Robotics cost checklist.

Initial Costs

- The robot and its tooling
- Facilities, equipment revisions, and rearrangements
- Application engineering
- Process and product changes
- Training and transfers
- Installation
- Direct labor costs

Continuing Costs

- Cost of capital
- Taxes and insurance
- Maintenance labor, supplies, and spare parts
- Energy
- Training
- Scrap and rework
- Safety and potential cost of disability

knows what is profitable and asks, Do you? Management knows what needs improvement to become more profitable and asks, Do you?

In your role as a consultative seller, you must be prepared to declare what you want to see customer decision makers about. It must be either a problem of significant cost or a major revenue opportunity, and it must be solvable within a reasonable period of time. Issues that meet these criteria are the proper business of top-tier management. Any other issues—especially those within your own business—will bring the response that management is too busy with its own business to deal with them. Act I can be the final act unless the customer's business is spotlighted on center stage.

Act II: "What Do You Want Me to Do About It?"

Management-level decision makers make decisions; they do not conceptualize or contemplate idly. You cannot raise an issue with management merely to provoke intellectual curiosity; you must offer a remedy. Once management knows why you want its attention, it next must know what you want it to do. In the end it is you, of course, who will end up doing something about the issues you have raised. But customer management must do something first: It must appropriate assets in the form of dollars and people.

Assets are allocated for solutions, to prevent or relieve problems. Management must be told what solutions are available. Some may already have been tried and failed. Should any of them be considered anew? Some attempts may already be in implementation. Can they be reinforced? Should they be superseded before they fail or prove cost-ineffective? Is there a best solution; if so, how can we tell it is best? What can its contribution be expected to amount to?

When customer management evaluates solutions, it is not evaluating products, services, or systems. It may know little about them and care less. Top management assesses only the financial results of a solution, not its components or their performance. Operating managers will be interested in systems, but at the top the dialogue of Act II will be principally in dollar terms: how much profit you are prepared to offer management and how much, in return, you want as your reward.

Act III: "How Do I Know It Will Work?"

If management likes what you want it to do—in other words, if it likes the amount of added profit you want it to be able to make—it will want to know how it can realize your proposal. "How do I know the profits you promise will actually accrue?" That is what top management means by "Will it work?" It is not a question of whether the gears will mesh or the system will integrate; these performance benefits will have to be demonstrated to operating management. Throughout the top tier, a proposal works when it produces the profit that you claim for it. If it operates mechanically, chemically, or electronically but the profits are not forthcoming, it does not work.

In Act III you must attest to the workability of your

solution. You must document the profits, showing their source, their flow over time, and their cumulative total. You must also document your system: What major components will it contain? What is their contribution to improved profit? How do they conform to state-of-the-art technology, and what are their track records?

Act III can therefore be divided into two sequential scenes. First, you must strike a partnership with managers of customer business functions on the profit contributions of your proposals. Then, when a consensus agreement has been reached at this operating level, the financial contributions should be proposed to top management. This bottom-up phasing of approval permits top management to obtain the immediate concurrence of its operating decision makers: "Is this what you want? Will it work the way they say it will?" It also prevents resentment at the operating levels; instead of having a decision handed down, they will participate in handing it up.

Act IV: "When Do We Get the Show on the Road?"

When key account sales representatives sell consultatively, the call to action will most likely come from the customer in Act IV. As soon as your solution is perceived to work financially and operationally, top management will want to implement it. Time is money. Every minute's delay decreases promised profits.

Implementation consists of four elements. The first three concern what will be installed, when it will become operational, and who from each side will be involved. The fourth element is the sum total of the first three: What resources will have to be provided from the customer's business to match the resources contributed by you and your support services? Only when money and people—their time and talent—are allocated does something get done in business. You must be prepared to specify what both parties will have to put up in order to get the show on the road.

Key account representatives must be trained to produce their four-act plays at a fast clip, requiring a minimum of props and moving smoothly from one act to the next. Like all good plays, consultative proposals should be presented orally, with a copy of the libretto left behind for each member of the audience. An hour, allowing time for interruptions, is the maximum length any performance should take. The audience has other plays to go to.

Where are the trap doors under top management's carpet? Everywhere. Act I can close out your performance if you focus on a problem that customer management does not perceive as significant or if you fail to describe a truly significant problem correctly in management terms. You will be dismissed as not understanding the customer's business.

If the solution you propose in Act II pays out too little profit or is too late in coming, it may be rejected. If the profit is too great in amount, your credibility may be suspect—can you really do what you say you can do? If you are deemed not to be credible, you will not be trusted with management's approval. Even worse, if your solution appears to be unlikely and you provide supportive testimony from another company in another industry, you may be summarily dismissed as not understanding the differences between your customer's business and all others.

If fault is found with your financial documentation of profit contribution in Act III, especially if the errors are in your favor, your image or your credibility will be downgraded. You may nonetheless survive if the corrected contribution remains significant. If your profit analysis fails utterly, you will be dismissed as not understanding the first thing about the business of consultation in profit improvement: how to measure profits.

Act IV is the proof of the pudding. If you cannot implement, you will be dismissed as not understanding the second thing about your business: how to bring new profits in.

Looking Differently at Competition

Vendors compete against each other. Their customers pay their Box Three managers to manage this competition, playing one vendor against another to get the best—that is, the lowest—price. Competition, whether among vendors or others, is based on comparison. When vendors compete for Box Three, they compare themselves against their competition product by product, feature and benefit by feature and benefit. When all the distinctions without a difference cancel out, vendors compare their performance to their price. In this way, they force debate on the relative merits—or, to say the same thing in other words, they force competition on themselves. The winner makes the sale but, in the process, trades away his margins.

It is not uncommon for the margin loss to exceed 50 percent. In one typical case, a sales representative "sold" a $3 million order for computers to a retailer at a 54.75 percent discount that, the customer was told, would "elevate your awareness of the benefit of doing business with us by increasing your overall profitability." The discount was composed of a 46 percent price break plus free cooperative advertising funds, prepaid freight, the services of a team of marketing and sales representatives together with a product trainer and a rebate program. As the representative said who made the sale, "The customer practically sold himself."

The transcendent objective of Consultative Selling is to maintain premium margins. To do this, consultants must create a new concept of competition; that is, they must sponsor a different set of comparisons, none of which is with "other vendors." In addressing Box Two, consultants can position two types of comparison for their customers to evaluate:

1. For cost center managers who run customer business functions, consultants can create a comparison between a manager's current operating performance and the consultant's norms. Where the consultant's norms are superior, he can propose to add his value to the customer by helping to reduce or avoid costs.
2. For profit center managers who run customer business lines, consultants can create a comparison between a manager's current sales and share of market and the consultant's norms. Where the consultant's norms are

superior, he can propose to add his value to the customer by helping to increase volume or margins.

In both cases, the consultative seller is challenging his customer to compare his current competitive advantage with a proposed superior advantage. Is a competitor taking greater advantage of a market opportunity than you are? If so, I can help you come closer to equality or leadership. Are unnecessarily costly operations taking needless advantage of your profits and preventing you from being a lower-cost producer? If so, I can help you come closer to equality or leadership.

When a customer focuses on comparing what it is costing him now, in both direct costs and opportunity costs, to be competitive with what it could cost him if he were partnered with the consultant, his concentration is on his own competitive position and not the consultant's. Other vendors are driven from his field of vision. They are out of sight and out of mind because the questions the customer asks himself have nothing to do with "the best price." He is, instead, preoccupied with questioning the deal at hand. Is it credible—can I believe the numbers? Is it sufficient—will it make enough of a difference? Is it doable—can the proposed people and systems and strategies do the job? Is it realistic—can I reasonably expect to get the predicted rate of return on my investment within the promised time frame?

What if he asks, "Are there other suppliers who could do the same thing or do it more cheaply or better or faster?" He already knows the answer: "Perhaps." He also knows that because time is money, he will risk opportunity loss if he wants to find out. He will be far more concerned with evaluating today's opportunity today—the bird in the hand—and not speculating about tomorrow. All he can ever be sure about is today. Today's opportunity taken tomorrow is already operating at a competitive disadvantage.

Making Peace With Box Three

Consultative Selling permits you to move up from a vendor relationship with a customer's Box Three purchasing manager to a partner relationship with a Box Two business manager. In the process, you must be careful to avoid alienating the Box Three manager. The best way to ensure his participation and support—or at least his passive permission—is to offer to take him with you.

You must make your offer in Box Three terms: What is in it for him? These are four potential advantages:

1. Increased visibility at the Box Two and Box One levels
2. Increased access to knowledge about the business issues that drive purchase requirements
3. Increased mobility on the corporate career path as a result of increased visibility and knowledge
4. Decreased demand on his budget when Box Two managers make investments from their own budgets to fund consultative projects

It is a business paradox that it may be easier for a Box Three manager to move up with you rather than alone in his own company's hierarchy. This is true because the Consultative Selling process provides him, just as it offers you, the opportunity to add value at the Box Two level. Instead of relating primarily outward with vendors, Box Three can relate upward with his own managers who have been his users and customers but who can hereafter be his partners.

By offering to include Box Three in your Box Two consultancies, you risk nothing. Box Three may say *yes,* which is the best case, or he may say *yes but;* he will remain a passive participant who wants to be kept informed as a member of the loop but prefers to take no active role. This is the next-best case. A certain number of Box Three managers will say *no.* This gives you the option of trying to convert them or working with a company whose Box Three will say *yes* or *yes but* and trying to convert them later.

Because of its continuing nature, your relationship with Box Three managers is important to you. What do you say to them when you create a two-tier sales strategy by which you sell at both Box Two and Box Three? You have nothing to lose and much to gain by proposing to partner with them in the following way:

> It is our intent to continue to sell to you as we have in the past, responding to your requests for proposal with quality products at fair prices. It is also our intent to seek out additional opportunities to serve you. We anticipate finding these opportunities in your cost centers and lines of business where they may be unknown even to their managers or where the cost-effectiveness of doing something about them may not be realized. We would like to share our discovery of these opportunities with you and invite you to partner with us and your business managers in diagnosing the opportunities and proposing profit-improvement solutions for them. What do you say?

What if only two out of every ten Box Three managers want to go up—upstairs to Box Two with you or take you there? What if only one other Box Three manager does not want to go himself but is willing to let you go? You will have enough of a quorum to get started.

The Box Three types who are easy to partner have a broad-banded business orientation and a desire to expand their role as business managers. By contrast, Box Three types who are more difficult to partner have a technical orientation, often quite provincial and parochial, are cost-conscious more than value-driven or profit-sensitive, and are defensively protective about sharing customer knowledge. They may also have an acute vendor orientation, keeping all suppliers at arm's length as "outsiders" and being afraid of criticism if it appears that a supplier is doing Box Three's job. New young purchasers can be unusually aware of their prerogatives and jealous of a supplier's superior knowledge or expertise. This can make them just as stubbornly resistant as older managers, close to retirement, who are reluctant to change because they perceive no benefits to the remainder of their career lifetimes.

Box Three will partner you if his own purposes are served. Is there value to him in gaining visibility upstairs, or in learning more about the business objectives of the products and materials he purchases, or in playing a role as a profit improver instead of merely another cost center? If so, you can sell these values consultatively to him in terms of both personal profit improvement and the opportunity to make an enhanced contribution to business profits.

Many Box One managers encourage the participation of their purchasing managers in the operations aspects of their businesses. Some are even addressing the issue frontally, saying that "if all you people are going to do is buy things without knowing their contributions to the way our business uses them to make money, I will no longer be able to afford you."

The rule to follow is to try to "go with" Box Three rather than to go over or go around him. He will often be involved in giving his OK to your proposal on technical grounds or playing a role in its implementation, which makes his agreement vital. He may also be promoted to the Box Two level where you need to partner. His alienation incurs the probability of future problems whereas his partnership, or even your attempt to partner him, can be an immediate and continuing asset.

3

How to Merit High Margins

For both consultative sellers and their customers, profit is the name of the game. While the game is the same, the role you play in it is very different from that of your customer.

Setting profit objectives is the customer's business. It cannot be abdicated, nor can the customer delegate it to anyone outside the company. No one who is external to a company can ever know enough about total corporate assets and liabilities—financial, operational, or human—to set business objectives based on them. Besides, your concern with a customer's business is rarely an overall one. It is concentrated on his use of the product and service systems, and their market segments, with which you yourself are involved. As a result, your role is concerned with the additive effects that your product and service systems can have on the customer's profitability. You are his *incremental profit improver,* not his total profit maker.

A customer's primary management function is to develop strategic and tactical plans that can achieve profit maximization. Your role is limited to profit betterment. This means that you will propose your contribution from the point at which customers have finished developing their own profit plans. The end point of the customer's profit objectives becomes your point of departure.

Generating Profit Improvement Proposals

A consultative seller's day-to-day work is the generation of Profit Improvement Proposals. Each PIP adds value to your customer's profit objectives through the application of your product and service systems to the customer's business. Through such applications, you are able to merit added margins in return.

The process of generating profit proposals must be a continuing one. Once it begins, it can go on without end because the profit-improvement opportunities in a customer company are limitless.

You will find the task of selecting your profit-improvement portfolio easier if you apply five criteria. They will steer you toward Profit Improvement Proposals that have the greatest chance of succeeding.

1. *New profits should be achievable within 90 to 270 days.* Longer time frames incur unpredictable risks; they not only defy ready calculation but invite disenchantment or cancellation.
2. *New profits should be significant for both you and your customer.* Shared profit improvement should not be confused with equal profit. The first objective—profitability for both—is a vital aspect of the concept of partnership. The second—equal profit—is both impossible and unnecessary.
3. *New profits must draw on a major product or service capability* to be profitable for your company. Similarly, in order for your customer to profit, your proposals must affect a major product, service, or operation.
4. *New profits must be measurable* in terms of a net increment or a decremental investment in operating assets. If it cannot be measured, or if no provision is made to quantify it, agreement on whether it even took place may be impossible to obtain.
5. *New profits should not be an isolated entity* but a module

that leads naturally to the next infusion of profit and
then to the next one after that.

Contributing to Asset Management

Box Two business managers are managers of cost centers or
profit centers. Whatever operation their particular business
function may perform or whatever markets their line of business may sell to, they are essentially in the business of asset
management. They are funded by their Box One managers
with assets in the form of cash or credit. They are expected to
invest these assets in their operations to turn a profit on the
original investment, which they will allocate to fixed and operating assets "under management." How good they are at this
determines how much they will get the next time.

A consultative seller can take on the role of contributing to
his Box Two partner's success as an asset manager in three
ways:

1. He can help his customer manager improve his ratio of
   selling successful proposals to Box One by adding high-
   quality investment opportunities to the manager's portfolio and helping him to obtain more funds.
2. He can help his customer manager improve his turnover
   rate of accepted proposals to Box One by adding more
   investment opportunities to the manager's portfolio
   and helping him turn them over faster.
3. He can help his customer manager improve his success
   ratio of implementing projects by adding expertise that
   will help earn more profits or earn them sooner and
   with greater certainty.

In business, money has one purpose: to make more
money. To be a consultative seller, you must position yourself
as adding the values of "more money faster and surer" to your
customers. This is the supreme product. All customers need it
all the time. There is always demand—no matter what you

sell—because no matter how much money is on hand, there is always a short supply. There is never enough soon enough; "more money yesterday" is the only answer a Box Two manager ever gives to the question How much do you want and when do you want it?

Every dollar that a Box Two manager has is on loan to him. The loan, in the form of allocated funds from Box One, is callable on the date that the manager's proposal has pledged to achieve payback on Box One's investment. But that is only the beginning. Box One does not invest to achieve payback. His objective is to maximize the return on his investment and to do so as quickly as possible. In this sense, the funds he lends to the Box Two managers who report to him are trust funds: Box One trusts his Box Two managers to return them at a profit.

Proposing Profit Improvement

Proposing is a three-step process: definition of a customer problem to be solved or a customer opportunity to be capitalized on; prescription of the profit-improvement benefit from solving the problem or capitalizing on the opportunity; and description of the operational and financial workings of the system that can yield the improved profit.

Step 1: Problem/Opportunity Definition

Your initial task is to establish consultant credibility. Initial credibility comes only from displaying knowledge of a customer's business. Until a customer can say, "That salesperson knows my business," the customer will rarely be inclined to say, "That salesperson can improve my profit."

In fact, you must be knowledgeable about two areas of a customer's business. First, you must know the location of significant cost centers that are susceptible to reduction. Second, you must know how a customer's customers can be induced to buy more from the customer. In the first instance, you must prescribe a system that will reduce customer costs. This is a problem-solving system. In the second instance, you must prescribe a system that will increase customer sales. This is an opportunity system.

Defining a customer problem or opportunity has two parts: what you know, and how you know it. The second part documents the first by citing the sources of your knowledge. It also reinforces your credibility. There are three likely sources of knowledge about a customer cost problem or sales opportunity. One is that the customer revealed it. This is the "horse's mouth" source. A second source of knowledge is past experience with the customer, with other companies in the same industry, or "track record." Or knowledge can come from homework. This is the "midnight oil" source.

Step 2: Profit-Improvement Prescription

The objective of the first step in a consultative presentation is to say to a customer, in effect: "You have a situation that is detrimental to your profit. Either you are incurring unnecessary costs or you are failing to capture available sales revenues." The objective of the second step is to say, "Working together, we can reduce some of those costs or gain some of those sales at a cost-beneficial investment."

In this way, you further reinforce the perception of being knowledgeable about the customer's business by framing the system's benefit in businesslike terms of return on investment. By quantifying an added value the system can make to the customer's operations, you are creating a business-manager-to-business-manager context for customer decision making in contrast to a vendor-to-purchaser context.

The prescription for customer profit improvement must specify the positive return that can predictably result from installation of your system. The return should be specified as both a percentage rate of improvement and its equivalent in dollars. These quantifications, the end-benefit specifications in money terms, rather than specifics about the system's performance or components, are the ultimate specifications of the consultant's system. These are what a customer will or will not buy. They are therefore what you must prescribe for delivery.

IBM consultants approach top-tier management of key retail customers on behalf of IBM's computer-assisted checkout station. The consultants prescribe profit improvement benefits of reduced costs and increased sales like this: "For a store with gross weekly sales of $140,000, savings are projected at $7,651 a month by faster customer checkout and faster balancing of cash registers." The time required to check out an average order is said to be reduced by almost 30 percent. In addition, IBM sales representatives claim that the elimination of time and cost expenses of correcting checker errors can contribute annual savings of more than $91,000 per store.

If a store is growing, its total savings every year can approach one week's gross sales at the $140,000 level. The net value of these savings falls directly to the store's bottom line. The essential contribution made by IBM is providing added growth funds that supplement revenues from sales and can be invested for still further growth.

Step 3: System Definition

The third presentation step is to define the system that will deliver the promised profit-improvement mix and to justify its premium price by interpreting price in terms of investment in the new mix. Customers must not be asked to buy systems; you must invite them to improve profit. They are not quoted a system's price; you must promise them a positive return on the investment in their system.

The purpose of defining the system is not to sell it, but rather to present proof that the promised benefit is derived from known capabilities that have been prescribed precisely because they will contribute in the most cost-beneficial way to the customer's profit improvement. The system substantiates your promise. Its capabilities, plus your personal expertise in applying them, are the means of conferring new profitability on the customer.

Price is an intimate part of a system. It is the single most revealing component. Not only does it have high visibility, but it also possesses high connotative power. Premium price connotes premium value. It conveys more than the system's cost; it communicates the system's value.

Premium price can be justified by a system's ability to deliver premium value. If price contributes to value by assuring a system's profit-improving quality, and if price can be recovered by a return on investment that exceeds it, a premium price is justified.

Since system price depends on a customer's improved profit, system pricing is value pricing. The definition of value in terms of the amount by which profit is actually improved will always vary from customer to customer. As a result, there is no such fixed item as "system price," even for the same system. Price will be proportional, therefore, to the degree of value contributed by a system.

As a Profit Improvement Proposal of this type is progressively presented, it should make successive claims on a customer's propensity to buy. Defining a customer problem or opportunity should condition a customer to relate to you as a business manager. The next presentation step, prescribing a quantified benefit, should condition a customer to regard the system as a profit-making investment, not as a cost or a collection of components. Defining the system and justifying its price should condition a customer to credit the prescription as believable and achievable.

The final step in a system's presentation is to set down the standards by which you will progressively monitor the system's ability to deliver the promised benefit in partnership with the customer. At least three control standards should be set so that a working partnership can be confirmed between consultant and customer:

1. Time frames for the accomplishment of each installation and operational stage
2. Checkpoints for measuring the impacts of phasing the system into customer business functions
3. Periodic progress review and report sessions to head off

problems and anticipate new applications and opportunities for system extension, upgrading, modernization, and replacement

Comparing Costs and Benefits

The comparative analysis of a customer's costs to improve his profits by doing business with you and the benefits he can expect to receive are the heart of Consultative Selling. Cost-benefit analysis, which should really be called "investment-return analysis," tells the customer how much he must lay out for how much he can get back. A typical analysis for a project with a three-year commercial life is shown in Figure 3-1, where Year 0 is the current year and Year 3 is the end of the project's useful life.

The model analysis shown in Figure 3-2 freeze-frames the investment and its return for a single year. In this model, the total incremental investment required by purchase and installation of the system is itemized. Stage 2 sets down the annual contribution to profit improvement that the system can make, in terms of a net decrease in operating cost.

Stage 3 has two parts. Part A shows the effect of the system on operating costs. In Part B the consultant can demonstrate the effect of the system on revenues. Finally, in Stage 4 the system's profit return is figured in relation to the incremental investment required to obtain it. A projected profit improvement of approximately $25,000 means a before-tax rate of return of roughly 86 percent. This earmarks an exceptionally good opportunity for the consultant to propose.

As Figure 3-2 shows, the consultant has taken three stages to get to the point where a number can be put on the value contributed by the system. At Stage 1, the total incremental investment required by purchase and installation of the system is itemized. Stage 2 sets down the annual contribution to profit improvement that the system can make. Sometimes this contribution will take the form of a net increase in revenue. In this case it comes from a net decrease in operating costs. In Stage

(Text continues on page 95)

Figure 3-1.   Useful life cost-benefit analysis.

	Year 0	Year 1 [1]	Year 2
1. New equipment investment			
2. Noncash expense			
3. Revenue			
4. Cash savings [2]			
5. Depreciation ACRS [3]			
6. Material trade-in			
7. BIT PROFIT IMPROVEMENT			
8. CASH FLOW			
9. PAYBACK (cumulative cash flow)			
10. Present value (10 percent factor)			
11. Discounted cash flow			
12. Net present value cash flow			
13. RETURN ON INVESTMENT			

[1] Years are annualized, beginning sixty days after installation date.
[2] Cost inflation not accounted for in cash savings.
[3] Depreciation based on 1985 ACRS rates.

Figure 3-2.   Single-year cost-benefit analysis.

STAGE 1. INCREMENTAL INVESTMENT ANALYSIS

1. Cost of proposed equipment	$39,600		
Estimated installation cost	6,000		
Subtotal	45,600		
Minus initial tax benefit of	3,190		
Total		42,410	1
2. Disposal value of equipment to be replaced	8,000		
Capital additions required in absence of proposed equipment	6,000		
Minus initial tax benefit for capital additions of	420		
Total		$ 13,580	2
3. Incremental investment (1 − 2)		$ 28,830	3

STAGE 2. PROFIT-IMPROVEMENT ANALYSIS
(ANNUAL CONTRIBUTION)

4. Profit improvement—net decrease in operating costs (from line 27)	$ 24,952	4
5. Profit improvement—net increase in revenue (from line 31)		5
6. Annual profit improvement (lines 4 + 5)	$ 24,952	6

STAGE 3. NEXT-YEAR OPERATING BENEFITS
FROM PROPOSED EQUIPMENT

A. Effect of proposed equipment on operating costs

(Computed on Machine-Hour Basis)	*Present*	*Proposed*	
7. Direct labor (wages plus incentives and bonuses)	$ 10.50	$ 3.50	7
8. Indirect labor (supervision, inspectors, helpers)	3.67	1.22	8

(continues)

(Figure 3-2 *continued*)

(Computed on Machine-Hour Basis)	*Present*	*Proposed*	
9. Fringe benefits (vacations, pensions, insurance)	2.15	0.72	9
10. Maintenance (ordinary only, parts and labor)	1.18	0.90	10
11. Abrasives, media, compounds, or other consumable supplies	1.32	1.10	11
12. Power	0.56	0.48	12
13. Total (sum of 7 through 12)	$ 19.38	$ 7.92	13
14. Estimated machine hours to be operated next year	2,400	3,000	14
15. Partial operating costs next year (13 × 14)	$46,512 (A)	$ 23,760 (B)	15
16. Partial operating profit improvement (15A − 15B)		$ 22,752	16

(Computed on a Yearly Basis)	*Increase*	*Decrease*	
17. Scrap or damaged work	$	$ 700	17
18. Downtime		1,500	18
19. Floor space			19
20. Subcontracting			20
21. Inventory			21
22. Safety			22
23. Flexibility			23
24. Other			24
25. Total	$ (A)	$ 2,200 (B)	25
26. Net decrease in operating costs (partial) (25B − 25A)		$ 2,200	26
27. Total effect of proposed equipment on operating costs (16 + 26)		$ 24,952	27

B. Effect of proposed equipment on revenue

(Computed on Yearly Basis)	Increase		Decrease		
28. From change in quality of products	$		$		28
29. From change in volume of output					29
30. Total	$	(A)	$	(B)	30
31. Net increase in revenue (30A − 30B)			$		31

STAGE 4. ANALYSIS OF RETURN ON INCREMENTAL INVESTMENT

32. Incremental investment (line 3)	$ 28,830	32
33. Annual profit improvement (line 6)	$ 24,952	33
34. Before-tax return on investment (line 33 ÷ line 32)	86%	34

3, savings in operating costs can be expected to come largely from a decrease in customer downtime as well as reduced scrap or damaged work. Savings will also be derived from reduced costs of labor, fringe benefits, maintenance, and power.

When a cost-benefit analysis is used to support a proposed improvement in a customer's business or business function so that it can be a better contributor to profits, a Profit Improvement Proposal or PIP results. A model PIP is shown in Figure 3-3. Its purpose is to prove the cost-effectiveness of a solution for radioactive waste disposal.

Being Good at Project Management

A Profit Improvement Proposal is a miniature project. Its site is a customer's premises, either one of his business lines or a business function. A Profit Improvement Proposal is a money-

Figure 3-3.   Model Profit Improvement Proposal.

A Proposal to Improve the Profit of
Trickle River Canyon Power Company

CHASTE WASTECORP

(1)   Problem to Be Solved
         Cost-effective disposal of low-level radioactive waste.
(2)   Prescription to Solve the Problem
         Improve profit by reducing annual costs of handling low-level
         radioactive waste by more than $400,000 and simultaneously
         maintain complete safety together with full legislative compli-
         ance.
(3.1) Solution System
         1. AECC volume-reduction system
              1.1 Handles all plant-generated liquid wastes.
              1.2 Twenty to fifty gallons per hour; will handle a two-
                    unit plant.
              1.3 Produces dry free-flowing product.
              1.4 Automatic, remote operation including system. De-
                    contamination for maintenance.
              1.5 Nonmechanical fluid bed dryer.
         2. Licensability consultation services
         3. Technical support services
              3.1 Inspection of equipment during storage—refurbish-
                    ment if required.
              3.2 Live-in engineering consultation during installation.
              3.3 Training of operating and maintenance personnel.
              3.4 Live-in engineering consultation during startup.
              3.5 Engineering participation during demonstration test.
         4. Equipment supply contract services.
         5. Maintenance contract services.
         6. Total project management consultation service to concen-
              trate single-source responsibility provided by Chaste
              Wastecorp profit-improvement team.
         7. Access to our information bank on radiation-waste dis-
              posal.
(3.2) Solution System Rate of Return
         Accounting rate of return =   29.2%
         Cost savings/year   = +$400,000

Incremental Investment

Cost of equipment	$1,000,000
Installation	200,000
Building space penalty	200,000
Total cost	$1,400,000

Operating Costs (Dollars in $000)

Costs	Present System	Proposed System
Labor	$120	$ 25
Material	200	11
Transportation and burial	280	70
Maintenance	20	30
Power	1	20
Depreciation	40	96
Totals	$661	$252

Proposed Annual Savings = $409,000

$$\frac{409,000}{661,000} = 61.9\% \text{ Cost reduction benefit}$$

Profitability Evaluation
  Accounting Rate of Return

Total investment	$1,400,000
Annual savings before tax	409,000
Annual savings after 48% tax	212,000
Rate of return	15.1%

Cash-Flow Payback (W/O Escalations)
  1. Savings after tax = $212,000 per year
  2. Straight-line depreciation (4% per year) = $56,000
  3. Investment-tax credit (10%) = $140,000 (2nd year)
     Cash payback by end of 5th year (4 years, 9 months)

making project. It says to the customer, Here is where you are incurring unnecessary costs or missing out on realizable revenues. Here is what it is costing you. Here is how much you can save or earn. Here is what it will take to obtain the improvement and how long it will be before you can see it on your bottom line.

Profit Improvement Proposals are designed to affect a customer's economy. To do this, they require adding the value of a supplier's products or services along with information in the form of advisory services and training. Sometimes financing is involved as time payments or a lease. But the essential ingredient in every project is its manager.

The art of managing a profit-improvement project is a consultative seller's prime skill. To manage it means to make it pay off as proposed, in full and on time. This requires the seller to be a good diagnostician, making sure he or she has sized up the project correctly from the outset. The seller must then be a good prescriber in order to propose the most cost-effective solution for the problem or opportunity he has diagnosed. Then he must be a good installer, implementer, and applier to fit the solution seamlessly into a customer's operations so that it becomes a part of their natural flow. He must be a good planner, exactly meeting each milestone along the way from startup through payback to realization of the proposal's objective. And at every step of the way, he must be a good partner with his customer's people, without whose cooperation he can accomplish nothing.

A project in profit improvement begins when a customer closes the seller's proposal. The project ends not with the one-time delivery of products and services but the on-time delivery of improved customer profits. In between, the seller must manage the flow of work. Even more important, he must manage the flow of new profits.

As project manager of a profit project, the consultative seller must have the answer to questions like these on the tip of his tongue on a day-in, day-out basis:

- *"How's it going?"* This means: Are we on plan so that we will make our objective when we said we would?
- *"Is everything under control?"* This means: Are our control procedures proving that we are proceeding according to plan or are they picking up variances?
- *"Any problems?"* This means: Has our diagnosis been changed by the discovery of facts we did not know

beforehand or by new events that have arisen since we began?

There are three parameters to good project management. They all concern money. Even the parameter that refers to time concerns money because that is what time is.

1. The manager must bring the project home *within budget.* He must not overrun the customer's investment.
2. The manager must bring the project home at *full realization.* He must not deprive the customer of his expected return.
3. The manager must bring the project home *on time.* He must not prolong the length of the customer's investment cycle or delay the onset of awaited funds.

It takes a tightly controlled manager to achieve these three hallmarks of good management with consistency. He must control his project's resources in order not to overinvest them and hike up the project's costs so that its payback is postponed. He must control his project's cash flow on a milestone-by-milestone schedule in order not to come up short. And he must control the clock in order not to run out of time. Managing tight is essential from a project's start to finish. Managing tight only at the end after a careless or profligate beginning is a recipe for failure.

The ability to diagnose heretofore unsolved customer problems in such a way that they can now be solved is an enviable asset for a project manager. So is the ability to conceive a simplistic solution that, for the first time, enables a customer problem or opportunity to be dealt with cost-effectively. But the greatest ability is *dependability.* Can the project manager be depended on to control the project, to keep it from getting out of hand, pick up deviations quickly and remedy them at once, to avoid cost overruns, and to be free of surprises? If the answers are either no or, even worse, sometimes, no amount of creativity or simplistic problem solving will atone for the absence of reliability.

Guaranteeing Your Results

Once a Profit Improvement Proposal has been accepted, even before it has been realized, the consultative seller's customer is already counting on the new earnings he has just contracted for. He will find sources of investment for the project's earned funds just as soon as they are available, not wanting to waste a minute in putting them to work. He will depend on them being available on time and in the amount promised. If they are not available, the customer will suffer a shortfall. He will also suffer a lost opportunity.

Since funds still "on the come" are already invested as if they were real as soon as they are proposed, it is easy to see why failing to realize them can be a catastrophe. The funds are planned for. If they are not going to be delivered, the customer will be surprised. It is not necessary to say "unpleasantly surprised." Managers learn early in their careers there is no such thing as a pleasant surprise; all business surprises are unpleasant.

A project manager is known by the profit promises he keeps. He must follow a rule of "no surprises." Each surprise means a reduced or delayed stream of earnings that have already been planned for investment and for which no replacements are readily available. As a result of being surprised, the customer will have to reduce the scope of another project, postpone it, or cancel it entirely. He will remember his surprise and the seller who surprised him for a long time.

The seller will probably remember it too. Not only will he be deprived of repute for dependability; he will also have no claim to a share of the customer's next investment.

It is easy to see why there is no substitute for guaranteed results. When you guarantee your solution, you are acting as a coguarantor, a cosigner of your proposal. Your Box Two partner is the actual guarantor. He or she is the true receiver of corporate funds, choosing to invest them with you. This makes each Box Two manager the ultimate responsible party whose career success or failure is at stake and whose reputation as a "good manager" will be enhanced or downgraded by your proposal's effectiveness. Simply by the act of endorsing your proposal and going public as its sponsor—your internal "economic seller"—a customer manager is implicitly guaranteeing that he will return his company's funds plus a profit. When you partner with him, you inherit the same obligation.

Part II

Consultative Proposing Strategies

4

How to Qualify Customer Problems

The high margins that accrue from Consultative Selling are your reward for knowing more about the customer operations you affect—and being able to improve them—than your competitors do. Margins are merited by mastery of how a customer runs the business functions that are your sales targets. The more you know about them, and the better you are able to implement what you know into proposals for performing them more cost-effectively, the greater your value will be. Accordingly, the higher the price you will deserve.

Consultative Selling is industry-dedicated. Within each industry, it is function-specific. Business functions in customer companies are your end users, your true markets. According to the way they operate, they create the costs that you can reduce or do away with entirely. They can add new sales revenues or productivity if you can show them how. Your customer's business functions are the sources of the problems you will have to solve and the showcases where the value of your solutions will give testimony to your capabilities. Scoping their ways of operating should therefore be your constant preoccupation.

Remember, if you are going to sell in a consultative manner, customer business functions will be the subject matter of your consultation. The only alternative is to talk about your own processes and the products or services they produce. In that case, you will be talking to the purchasing tier and selling on a basis of competitive performance and price. Your opportunity for high margins will have vanished.

In order to know customer functions from an operating perspective and from the point of view of their financial structure, you will have to get inside customer businesses. Generic knowledge of a function based on industrywide generalizations is important and useful, but it is insufficient. Norms and averages can be extremely helpful, especially if they are used as jumping-off places to learn the specifics of individual customer operations, but by themselves they are inadequate.

The only business function profiles that customers will recognize are their own. These are also the profiles customers guard most zealously. There is good reason for this. Little perceived value comes from releasing functional operating or cost information. There are many people and organizations that can use it detrimentally, and few if any who might use it helpfully. If you want to qualify as a helpful source, you must first pay your dues—do your homework on customer businesses. Then, on the basis of what you have learned and how well you can apply it, you may be invited to propose improvements.

The ability to profile a customer business function is essential to selling at the top tier. In customer functions, you will find the problems you will propose to solve. Unless you know the nature of these problems, their importance, their financial values, and the language in which customer top management discusses them, you will be talking to yourself when you get to the top tier.

Developing a Business Function Profile

Business functions are processes. All processes have a flow— they have a beginning, a middle, and an end. Manufacturing begins with raw materials and ends with finished goods in inventory. Data processing begins with raw information and ends with reports. There are costs at both ends; in between, there is nothing but costs.

Consultative sales representatives should be able to chart the flow of the critical customer businesses and functions they affect. They should be able to assign appropriate costs to the most critical "success factors" in each process—the 20 percent that contribute the 80 percent—and be able to prescribe the optimal remedy to reduce their contribution to costs or expand their contribution to revenues.

Some of these remedies will be therapeutic; that is, they will lower an existing cost. Other remedies will be curative; they will alter a process, combine it with another, or eliminate it from the flow. In still other cases, the remedy will be to change the architecture of a process so that a completely new set of cost or revenue centers will result.

In most customer operations, work flow is cost-ineffective. It incurs unnecessary cost or it processes work ineffectively. If you can optimize it, you can improve its contribution to profit. Every dollar of cost you take out can drop to the customer's bottom line. Every improvement you make in productivity can also lower operating cost and raise the output from each dollar invested in labor, energy, and materials.

There are two ways to scope a customer's Critical Success Function or Critical Success Business. One is to scope its funding to determine where it ranks in its company's flow of investment funds. A second way is to scope its process flow to determine its Critical Success Factors.

1. *Scoping a function's funding.* Nothing happens in business until a function is funded by a Box One manager. Once funds are allocated, they can be drawn down at the Box Two level and put to work, that is, invested. If a consultative seller wants work, he must go where the funds are flowing, which will always be to a customer's cost center and profit center managers whose success is critical to corporate strategy.

"Go where the funds flow" prevents your coming up dry by being told that "We have no money" and having proposals turned back that are effectively stamped "insufficient funds."

2. *Scoping a function's process.* When funds flow to a customer function or business, work can flow through it. You must know how this takes place. You must be able to identify the Critical Success Factors in all customer functions and businesses that you affect, you must know their current contributions to function costs or revenues, and you must know if you can add value to them and at what rate of return for a customer's investment.

Figure 4-1 shows the critical functions that determine the success of a supermarket chain's business. Where are costs higher than necessary: Is inventory stocking or order assembly inefficient? Where are revenue opportunities remaining under-capitalized: Can backhaul trucking be made to contribute, or contribute more, to profits?

The work flow for an aerospace manufacturer is shown in Figure 4-2. This process begins with the marketing function. How can it turn over more projects faster? Is design analysis and testing a roadblock to turning over the process as a whole—is time wasted, and therefore money, in moving along the projects that marketing brings in? What if model testing could be accomplished one month faster? One week faster? What value would that add to delivery, the time when an aerospace manufacturer is paid in full? In other words, what would the added value be of collecting receivables one month or one week sooner for each project?

Databasing From the Three Key Sources

To vend, you need to know your own costs. To sell in a consultative manner, you need to know customer costs. To vend, you need to know your own sales opportunities. To sell as a consultant, you need to know customer sales opportunities. Realizing that you must come up with a cost-reducing or revenue-adding option, how can you learn a customer's current costs in the business functions that are important to you? How can you get a fix on the customer's unachieved sales potential?

Figure 4-1.   Supermarket chain business functions.

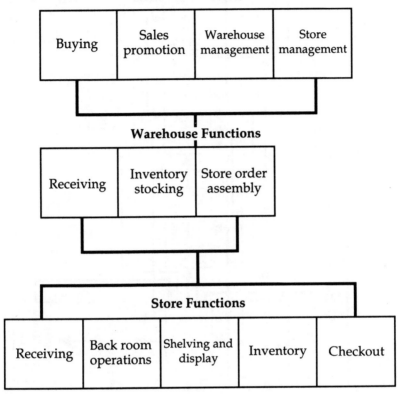

Administrative Functions

Buying	Sales promotion	Warehouse management	Store management

Warehouse Functions

Receiving	Inventory stocking	Store order assembly

Store Functions

Receiving	Back room operations	Shelving and display	Inventory	Checkout

Figure 4-2. Aerospace manufacturer business functions.

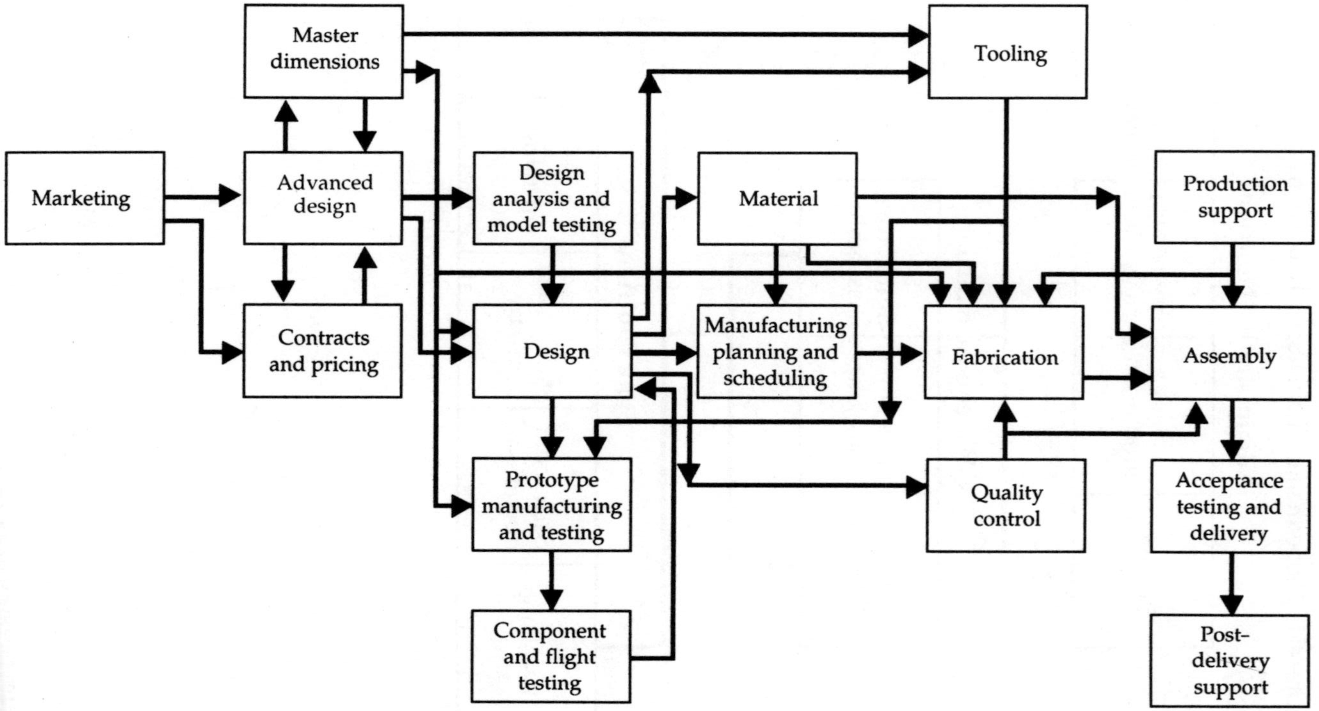

In profiling customer functions, how can you quantify with reasonable accuracy the problems and opportunities that will form the base of your penetration plans?

You will need to develop three databases, storehouses of information that will become the basic resources for top-tier selling to key accounts:

1. An *industry database* on each of the industries in which you serve key customers
2. A *customer database* on each key account customer you serve in an industry
3. A *customer's customer database* on your key accounts' key accounts

From your industry database, you will learn average costs, average profits on sales, average inventories and receivables, and other industry norms. The information in each of your key customer databases will allow you to compare customer performance against industry averages. In categories where a customer falls below the norms, you may find sales opportunity.

Your individual customer databases will teach you the concentration and distribution of customer costs. Where do they bunch up? Are these the same places for the industry as a whole? How heavy are they? What are their trends? Are they rising or are they coming under control? What variable factors affect them most significantly?

How to Qualify Customer Problems

Your customer databases will also provide you with knowledge of where potential new sales opportunities for a customer may be found. These may include existing products, new products, combined products, new or enhanced services, superproducts, or systems. How can your customers sell more? How can they sell at higher prices? How can they extend sales into closely adjacent markets? How can they invade new markets that offer superior profit opportunity? How can they anticipate or turn back a competitive thrust?

In order for you to know your customers' businesses, you must know more than the performance and cost characteristics of the internal business functions that you can affect. You must also know the markets your customers sell to. They are your customers' opportunity. Their needs cause many customer business functions to operate the way they do: to manufacture the kinds of products they make, to advertise and sell the way they do, to communicate inside and outside their businesses with the telecommunications and data processing technologies they use. Only when you know your customers' customers can you understand the complete spectrum of the consultative relationship that will be available to you, the full range of costs that can be reduced and sales opportunities that can be enlarged.

The essential elements of information you will need to know about your customers' customers are exactly the same as the data you must develop on your customers themselves. You will have to learn the major cost areas your customers affect in their own key account businesses and the main sales opportunities they help them achieve.

The joint development of information is one of the strongest bonds for partnering. Shared discovery is an alliance of adventurers, each adding new values to the other. Joint research can also be cost sharing, another partnering act. At best, your key customers will realize that they will have to expand their knowledge of their own customers if they are going to be able to help them improve profits. They will, of course, also be able to use customer knowledge to sell consultatively themselves. At worst, you may have to suggest a cooperative starter survey to demonstrate the value of market knowledge.

Learning From Industry Sources

Getting into the cost structure of an industry and its customers is a three-stage effort. Setting up your databases is a front-end-loaded undertaking. After that, it is simple and inexpensive to keep them up-to-date. The first stage is to learn as much as you can from the multiple sources that are always available without going to your customers themselves. Then, when you take on the second and third stages that deal specifically with your accounts, you will have two advantages: You will already know a great amount, so you will have less to ask of customers, and you will have a meaningful framework on which to hang the information they share with you.

In addition to the ubiquitous publications and knowledgeable career professionals of the United States government—especially the Department of Commerce—six additional sources can help you learn the costs and revenue potentials of customers in a key industry.

1. *The people and information resources inside your own company* are the first and most obvious sources. Some of your people may have been recruited from customer industries; some may even have worked for key customers. Others may have participated in market research studies that produced information relevant to your consultative needs. If your company maintains a library, its periodicals and publications can be culled for data, especially the trade magazines of your key customer industries. Your librarian can be a valuable aide in obtaining published information of all types.

2. *Trade associations* in your customer industries are staffed by people who usually devote their lifetimes to their trade. They know many generalities and often specific information about individual companies. They know the main leaders in the industry and can introduce you to them. Their associations also maintain industry libraries and computerized databases.

3. *Securities analysts* are professional researchers employed by brokerage houses to follow specific industries. They publish updated industry analyses that evaluate growth potential, highlight the major factors that determine profits and costs, and define trends that can forecast opportunities. Many analysts will provide personal counsel on a quid pro quo basis.

4. *Industry experts and consultants* can be retained on a one-

shot or periodic basis to lay down a foundation for understanding an industry's processes and their cost structure. They can also be helpful in estimating the impact of your technology on customer costs and productivity, keeping in touch with competitive technologies, and exchanging information on industry-wide business function problems and the solutions currently being implemented.

5. *Other suppliers* who sell noncompetitive products and services to the same decision makers at your key accounts may be willing to share their acquired knowledge of customer process costs and sales opportunities. They will probably approach the knowledge you seek from the bias of their own interests, making their information peripheral to your needs, but nonetheless valuable.

6. *Noncustomer companies or non-key accounts* in the same industry are sometimes easier to approach for general information than your own customers are. They operate the same business functions. Their costs tend to cluster at the same critical few crunch points. The potential sales opportunities affect their marketing strategies in the same way.

Learning From Public Sources

After you have done homework with multiple industry information sources and before you approach your key customers themselves, there is an important intermediate step. Every customer company reveals publicly many facts about its existing operations and plans for forthcoming investments or divestitures. These revelations are invaluable because they are authentic; they come from the horse's mouth. You should unfailingly investigate them, not only as you start up your learning curve in the transition to top-tier selling but on a continuing basis. There are two major sources from which you can learn what customer companies are proclaiming or complaining about themselves:

1. *Annual reports and 10-K reports* give information on your customers' current financial condition and its trends, their

objectives and the major constraints they are encountering in achieving them, how and where they are introducing new technologies and systems to alter operations that are cost-intensive, ways and areas where productivity improvement is important, and new product developments and the changes they may make in the market share configurations of existing products. This information is presented to shareholders in the annual report. The 10-K version is far more detailed and far less promotional, since it is put together for the Securities and Exchange Commission.

2. *Presidential speech transcripts* are reprinted in *The Wall Street Transcript*. Chief executive officers are often interviewed by *Forbes, Business Week, Fortune,* and other business media. CEOs are increasingly appearing for interviews on network and cable television. The interview format creates a wide-ranging agenda, sometimes eliciting off-the-cuff remarks and spontaneous declarations that can yield important insights. They will also provide useful conversational tidbits when you sit down with your customer decision makers in the third stage of your information gathering.

Learning From Customer Sources

When you have learned as much as you can from industry sources and from sources that key customers make public, then and only then are you ready to confront your customers themselves. By this time, you will have less to ask. You will be able to phrase your inquiries in customer language, the jargon of each industry. You will be able to initiate discussion by recapitulating what you already know instead of asking for help up front. You will have shown commitment to your customer businesses by your willingness to invest homework time and effort in advance of a payback. And in the course of your studies, you will get many ideas for improving customer profit that will provoke further information from customer decision makers as you introduce them into your negotiations.

No information source on a customer's business can equal

the customer's people themselves. They speak with authority, for two reasons. They have the inside track on customer operations; indeed, they originate much of the information themselves. Second, they believe the information is gospel. Right or wrong, their "facts" are the only real facts. Their numbers are the only hard numbers. Their costs are the costs you will have to work with. Their unfulfilled opportunities are the opportunities you will have to help them seize.

In an ideal world, customer facts and figures would be open for your asking. Every now and then it happens in exactly this way. A vendor supplier sits down once in a lifetime before the top-tier managers of a key account customer and presents generalized narrative benefits of working together in a two-tier manner. For the work they will do at the top tier, the supplier proposes a partnership based on Consultative Selling strategies. The supplier reveals minimal customer knowledge and asks to be provided with the rest. The customer somehow senses the value of the benefits and agrees.

This is called the Phil Smith approach, in honor of the first man known to have successfully accomplished it the first and only time he tried it.

The other approach is called Consultative Selling, because it is the strategy that almost always must be used. It is also known as the hard way. It is the cookbook strategy, because customers do not give internal operating information and its financial implications to vendors, especially to vendor sales representatives. As a result, a vicious circle is set up. A vendor needs inside customer information to switch from vending to top-tier consultation. Yet customers do not release inside information to vendors. Without the information, a vendor will forever remain a vendor. How can the circle be broken?

Quasi-Consulting Without the Numbers

There are three strategies you can use to bargain for customer numbers that you do not know. Each of them acts on the same principle: To get numbers, you must offer numbers first. Your numbers may be assumptive, perceptive, or speculative, but they will be numbers. They will save you from asking for information from scratch and, instead, make your customer's response easier by inviting him to comment on and correct what you propose.

1. *Pleading from ignorance.* The "power of one" can be used assumptively. If you cannot quantify a number, assume it in units of one, such as "Let us assume that lost revenues due to out-of-stock are only one percent of total revenues," or "Let us assume that we can only reduce scrap from work in process by one percent," or "Let us assume that we can only collect receivables one day sooner." These are all patent absurdities, apparent to your customer as well as you. If you can make your case at the one percent level, however, it can be made without question at any higher level.

2. *Planning perceptively.* An admittedly soft number, deliberately deflated if it is an added revenue and inflated if it is an added cost, can be substituted for the correct number by negotiation using a "What if?" approach. "What if we say that an hour of downtime costs this much?" "What if we say that the lack of an accurate procedure for tool tracking costs about this?" "What if we make the ratio of accepts to scrap like this and the ratio of scrap to reworks like that?" So long as the customer agrees that your perceptions of his numbers are fair approximations, you can base a preliminary proposal on them.

3. *Connecting the dots.* When you have gone as far as you can go in your homework and there are still important gaps in your numbers, you have earned the right to ask the customer to "connect the dots," if not together with you then at least by himself. "We have done our homework. This is as far as we can go. Will you fill in the gaps with us?" If the customer tells you that the real numbers are proprietary, you have two possible responses:

   a. "Can you simply tell us if our numbers are close enough to make our proposal worthwhile for you to evaluate? If not, will you just tell me where we are badly off—much too high or too low?"

b. "Will you please take what we have done and fill in the gaps privately for yourself? If the real numbers prove to be interesting to you, we can pick up from there to work further with you."

4. *You must be able to show dollar benefits* that meet the customer's threshold of what is significant. Unless you can do this, customers will have no incentive to trade information with you. Partnering must promise a clear reward. The customer must believe it to be achievable by working together and must also be able to visualize continuing to receive ongoing value after the first success.

5. *You must make it simple* for a customer to agree to trade business knowledge with you. This means that you should require as little information as possible. It also means that you should not ask for any information that a customer knows is publicly available. You should not ask for major allocations of customer resources to further your work together. Your partnering requests should involve the least possible customer staff time and expense.

6. *You must believe mightily in what you propose.* Your conviction will be contagious. It will be tested by customer decision makers who have never before worked with you—or with any supplier—in a consultative manner. Their comfort level in going ahead will be reinforced by the assurance you convey and the degree of support you are willing to commit.

Being sure of your solution means more than just being sure that it will work. Does it yield the best financial reward—in other words, do the dollar values work best? If you are wrong, millions of dollars may be sacrificed, as one customer discovered:

> We make hundreds of components that can be configured in thousands of ways to make an unlimited number of customized products. One vendor wanted to set up a just-in-time inventory of all our components. Another one gave us a system to determine the optimal configuration for each product based on customer requirements. The JIT

inventory would have saved us between $3 and $5 million. But the second vendor saved us roughly $18 to $20 million per year in manufacturing costs by reducing the number of false orders for unneeded components.

Employing the Power of One

The number one, which is the smallest whole number, can have enormous power. One more product sold every day, one more percentage point added to current revenues or profits every week, or one more day gained every month in the collection of accounts receivable can yield astonishing amounts of improved profits for a customer. Applying the power of one also appeals to customer comfort. Most managers can deal with increments of that magnitude without incurring a disruption of the business whose costs and inefficiencies can nullify the gains. Furthermore, the number one has the power of credibility. Most customers will readily concede that they can improve performance, productivity, or profits by one percent.

Some consultative sellers have codified the power of one in their businesses. For every one percent of cost reduction we can help a customer achieve, such a business can say, we can propose a 5 percent improvement in customer profits. For every one percent of added sales revenues we can bring to a customer, we can propose a 4 percent improvement in customer profits. For every one percent of added margin we can help a customer command, we can propose a 9 percent improvement in customer profits.

If you can help a manufacturing customer eliminate one part from a major product, you can free him from ten contributions to cost. He will not have to:

1. Design it.
2. Assign a part number to it.
3. Inventory it.
4. Shelve it.
5. Inspect it.

 6. Assemble it.
 7. Repair it.
 8. Package it.
 9. Handle it.
10. Deliver it.

If you partner with customers to help them expand sales, can you enlarge their market opportunity by a factor of one? If you can start new mothers using a customer's baby foods one month sooner, when their babies are five months old instead of six months, you can open your customer to millions of dollars worth of incremental annual sales.

Figures 4-3 and 4-4 are laundry lists of general opportunities to apply the "power of one" to revenue expansion and cost reduction. Somewhere in these lists may be your own best opportunities, the things you do exceptionally well that help customers improve their profits and that therefore become the definition of "what you do" as a business. These elements of "your game" target the critical success factors in customer

Figure 4-3.   Revenue expansion opportunities.

---

 1. Add operational flexibility.
 2. Add manufacturing or processing quality.
 3. Add volume.
 4. Improve effectiveness of sales department.
 5. Introduce new sizes, shapes, or materials or new and improved products.
 6. Reduce customer returns.
 7. Apply creative sales promotion strategies.
 8. Speed up production and distribution.
 9. Reduce or eliminate unprofitable products, customers, warehouses, or territories.
10. Improve market position "image."
11. Add brand name value.
12. Add customer benefits.
13. Extend product life.
14. Expand into new markets.
15. Increase distribution.

Figure 4-4.   Cost-reduction opportunities.

From Cutting Customer's Purchase Costs
1. Reduce number of types of articles in stock.
2. Standardize preferred items.
3. Shop market for optimal supplier quality, delivery, and cost.
4. Centralize negotiations for major items.
5. Plan ahead to reduce rush procurement.
6. Subject bids and contracts to periodic review.
7. Conduct make-or-buy studies.
8. Speed up invoice processing to avoid discount losses.
9. Inspect incoming shipments to minimize damage from defects.
10. Speed up disposal of slow-moving inventories.
11. Establish most economical production or ordering quantities.
12. Shift burden of carrying inventories to suppliers.

From Cutting Customer's Production Costs
1. Reduce number of operations.
2. Reduce cost of one or more operations.
3. Combine two or more operations.
4. Automate operations.
5. Reduce labor.
6. Improve production scheduling.
7. Reduce operating time to speed up production.
8. Reduce insurance costs.
9. Reduce materials consumption.
10. Recyle materials.
11. Substitute less expensive materials or otherwise reformulate product.
12. Reduce raw materials inventory.
13. Reduce parts inventory.
14. Improve controls.
15. Simplify product and package design.
16. Dedicate an entire production line to one product or customer.

From Cutting Customer's Production Downtime
1. Standardize preferred items.
2. Shop market for optimal supplier quality, delivery, and cost.
3. Plan ahead to reduce rush procurement.
4. Improve plant delivery system.
5. Inspect incoming shipments to minimize damage from defects.

(continues)

(Figure 4-4 *continued*)
    6. Install preventive maintenance program.
    7. Improve personnel training.
    8. Improve process analysis.
    9. Establish most economical production or ordering points.
    10. Correlate forecasting data between marketing and production.

From Cutting Customer's Freight Costs
    1. Centralize negotiations for freight haulage.
    2. Plan ahead to reduce rush procurement.
    3. Prescribe preferred routing.
    4. Stage incoming shipments to reduce overtime.
    5. Reduce intraplant inventory transfers.
    6. Utilize trucks more efficiently, or buy trucks instead of renting.
    7. Relocate warehouses.
    8. Reformulate product or packaging to lighten shipping weights.
    9. Reduce handling costs.
    10. Reduce insurance costs.

From Cutting Customer's Administrative Overhead
    1. Reduce number of types of articles in stock.
    2. Standardize preferred items.
    3. Plan ahead to reduce rush procurement.
    4. Combine related items on purchase orders.
    5. Establish most economical production or ordering points.
    6. Shift burden of carrying inventories to suppliers.
    7. Control additions of new articles to stock.
    8. Take inventory cycle counts when stocks are low.
    9. Combine two or more operations.
    10. Decrease labor force.

From Maximizing Customer's Working Capital
    1. Reduce number of types of articles in stock.
    2. Shop market for optimal supplier quality, delivery, and cost.
    3. Speed up disposal of slow-moving inventories.
    4. Establish most economical production or ordering points.
    5. Shift burden of carrying inventories to supplier.
    6. Control additions of new articles to stock.
    7. Correlate forecasting data between marketing and production.
    8. Make secured short-term loans of excess cash.
    9. Use large-supplier's credit department to obtain optimal bank
       interest rates.

10. Speed up production.
11. Increase process efficiency to decrease scrap and damaged or unacceptable work.
12. Combine two or more operations.

---

businesses and business functions that identify the arenas where you can make the partnership contributions that must become your industry's standards for adding value.

The world of costs is changing. Whereas labor has traditionally contributed the major share of a manufacturer's costs, now it rarely exceeds 10 to 20 percent. While the hard-core costs of capital equipment have traditionally been a principal area of customer investment, or at least have been perceived as such, this is no longer the case in businesses where information-intensive services are natural accompaniments of equipment. In buying computers, for example, a common rule of thumb is to allow $100 for training expenses for every $1 of hardware cost. In networking computers and telecommunications equipment, the support costs of making everything work together as a single coherent system normally outruns the equipment cost by five times. These customer costs for integration and application are more important to reduce, in many cases, than are the costs of the hard goods they add to.

Getting to PIP

Nothing happens in Consultative Selling until you get to PIP. At the PIP point, you make your preliminary Profit Improvement Proposal to a customer manager and begin your partnership. This begins the process of putting you in business with him. It positions you as potentially partnerable, permitting the belief that you may provide him with a compelling reason to work with you. At the same time that a preliminary PIP starts the selling phase of the sales cycle, it also forecloses to your competition the customer problem or opportunity you have projected for improvement.

The sooner you can get to PIP, the better. Until you do, you are vulnerable to opportunity loss from not being able to sell. You are also open to preemption by a competitor who can get to PIP faster or by the closing of the opportunity window if customer priorities change, managers move, or funds run out or become reallocated. Simultaneously, your customer is also suffering lost opportunity and may be preempted in industry advantage by his own competitors.

When you sell improved profits, time becomes your enemy. Time downgrades the value of money, which has a time value as well as a dollar value. The rule of thumb about money is that a dollar today is always worth more than the value of the same dollar tomorrow because today's dollar can be invested today to make more dollars. Tomorrow's dollar must wait for tomorrow. This is as true for your business as it is for your customer. The longer it takes you to get to PIP, the less money you make and the more money you spend in cost of sales to make it.

Time-to-PIP is one index of cost-effective Consultative Selling. *Time-between-PIPs* is another. Minimizing both must be prime objectives in managing your consultative practice. This means that you must condense your up-front load of data gathering time to a point that is to the right of "nothing" but well to the left of "everything." You must strip customer data to their essential *"needs to know,"* nothing less and nothing more. These stripped needs will generally be project-specific to the business function problem or business line opportunity you want to PIP. They will focus on two types of data:

1. Current contribution to profits being made by a customer's Critical Success Function or Critical Success Business that is PIPpable by you. A function or business is defined as critical to customer success if it is one of 20 percent of all customer functions or businesses that contribute up to 80 percent of customer profits.

2. Current contribution to Critical Success Function costs being made by a Critical Success Factor that is PIPpable by you

or current contribution to Critical Success Business profits being made by a PIPpable Critical Success Factor. A factor is defined as critical to function or business-line success if it is one of 20 percent of all factors that contribute up to 80 percent of function costs or business-line profits.

This miniature database will set your PIP targets. It is based on two presumptions:

1. You know your customer industry well enough to know its common Critical Success Functions and Critical Success Businesses. These are the major ways that customers in the industry invest their money and the major ways they make a return on it—for example, manufacturing in a computer company and snack items in a food company. You are good at minimizing their investments or maximizing their productivity and returns on investments. You have the norms to prove it.

2. You know the Critical Success Functions and Critical Success Businesses well enough to know their Critical Success Factors. These are the major processes and operations that cost the most money and produce the most revenues and profits— for example, inventory control in a manufacturing function and promotions in a consumer packaged foods business. You are good at reducing their contributions to function costs or expanding their contributions to business-line revenues and profits. You have the norms to prove it.

If these two sets of preconditions are true for you, two things can be said on your behalf. One, you know your customer's "business" in either a critical function that is a cost center or a critical product or service line that is a profit center. Two, you know your own business in three terms: *how much* you can affect the customer's profit contribution, *how soon* you can affect it, and *how* you can affect it. In short, you know the value of your single best solution compared to the current customer value being contributed by a critical factor in one of his functions or lines of business and you know that your value is superior to his. Your preliminary PIP's cost-benefit analysis proves it.

Therefore, the up-front data search you conduct must sweep your norms across the factors you affect in critical customer functions or businesses until you find a *value gap*— the deviation of a customer's current value from your norm value. That is the point at which you can go to PIP.

Learning to Live With Minimal Data

Any information above and beyond minimal data must pass a test: *Is it worth more than the added costs of delay in getting to PIP,* both direct costs and opportunity losses? If you get to an unapproved PIP quicker without added up-front data, you have saved nothing and may have damaged your credibility. But if you get to an approvable PIP too late, you have earned nothing on your incremental investment. Your opportunity cost is total.

Getting to PIP means getting to Box Two. Only Box Two is PIPable by you. If you partner preliminarily with him so that he will agree with your proposal as representing the single best solution, he will PIP Box One. The selling cycle objective of Consultative Selling therefore requires four steps:

1. Get to Box Two as quickly as possible with the minimal data required to make a preliminary proposal to improve his contribution to profits.
2. Get him to agree that your solution is his single best option to solve a cost problem or expand a sales opportunity.
3. In partnership with him, extend the range and depth of your data so that they are accurate enough, complete enough, and current enough for both of you to be sure that you can achieve your proposed results. Fulfilling this requirement may cause you to penetrate the office of the president.

4. Together with your Box Two partner, propose jointly to Box One for funding your proposal.

By getting to Box Two with minimal data, you force yourself to get out of the comfortable homework stage, free of commitment yet replete with costs and delays that can infinitely prolong the nonselling phases of the sales cycle, and get to the actual point of sale—Box Two. The quicker you do this, the faster you can create your preliminary partnerships, deny them to competition, and make sales. Conversely, the longer you procrastinate, the costlier each sale will be, the longer the mean time between sales, and the greater your chance of being preempted by competition.

The calculation of "minimal data" is crucial: When is enough enough? *Data are minimally sufficient when you know enough about the current values of a Box Two manager's problem or opportunity to know that your values can be superior and when you can demonstrate your superiority on a cost-benefit analysis.*

As soon as this occurs, you can get to PIP. If you put it off until you can put a little more mascara on its eyelashes or a deeper blush on its cheeks, your opportunity window may close. Customer priorities may change. Or a competitor in bathrobe and curlers may get there first.

A minimal data collection system is illustrated in Figures 4-5, 4-6, and 4-7. They compose a starter set of information on customer problems and opportunities that are currently proposable in the Critical Success Factors of an account's Critical Success Functions or Businesses. Cost factors that you can decrease will be the basis for your PIP targets for improving customer profits through cost control. Volume or margin factors in a customer's Critical Success Businesses will be your PIP targets for improving his profits through sales or earnings expansion.

Penetrating Middle-Up vs. Top-Down

Getting to Box Two means getting to your eventual partner in the most direct manner, the shortest time, and with the least

Figure 4-5.   Cost factors.

Cost factors that we can decrease	How we can decrease them	How much in $/% we can decrease them by
1. _____	1. _____	1. Avg. $ _____
	_____	Avg. % _____
	_____	
2. _____	2. _____	2. Avg. $ _____
	_____	Avg. % _____
	_____	
3. _____	3. _____	3. Avg. $ _____
	_____	Avg. % _____
	_____	

downside in terms of opportunity cost to both you and the customer.

The purpose of Consultative Selling is not to consult about selling but to sell consultatively—that is, to newly empower a customer by improving his ability to save money or make money. These monies have a time value. So do your direct costs while you are in the belly of the sales cycle and so do your opportunity costs while you are going through the sales process until you can close. Penetrating your customer businesses at the levels where saving or making money is crucial is your guarantee that your own costs will be minimized.

Selling at the middle-management levels where you will partner, and where your partners can sell for you as internal "economic sellers," points you directly to the only decision

Figure 4-6. Volume factors.

Volume factors that we can increase	How we can increase them	How much in $/% we can increase them by
1. _____	1. _____	1. Avg. $ _____
	_____	Avg. % _____
	_____	
2. _____	2. _____	2. Avg. $ _____
	_____	Avg. % _____
	_____	
3. _____	3. _____	3. Avg. $ _____
	_____	Avg. % _____
	_____	

maker who can answer the consultative question, Can this proposed solution improve my profits enough, fast enough, and sure enough to get myself involved with it? If the answer is *yes*, he will help you add to or correct your data.

This may mean that the two of you will work together middle-up in your customer organization, penetrating higher, wider, and lower wherever the remaining minimal data may be. Some of them may be in Box One. Why not start there and penetrate top-down?

There are three reasons not to. One is that it is unnecessary. Box Two is the repository of a customer's operating objectives and constraints—the home of his Critical Success Factors. Box One knows the functions and businesses that are critical to success but he relies on his Box Two managers to

Figure 4-7. Margin factors.

Margin factors that we can increase	How we can increase them	How much in $/% we can increase them by
1. _____	1. _____ _____ _____	1. Avg. $ _____ Avg. % _____
2. _____	2. _____ _____ _____	2. Avg. $ _____ Avg. % _____
3. _____	3. _____ _____ _____	3. Avg. $ _____ Avg. % _____

control their critical factors. At most, you may get a "Go see" out of Box One. Do you need it? If you know a customer's Critical Success Functions and Businesses, you should not need Box One's consultation.

A second reason is that penetrating top-down is unprofessional. Box One managers freely act as coaches and counselors to their own Box Two operators, but far less often and much less voluntarily to their suppliers. Even at the Box Two level, many managers will want to know "Why are you here?" At the Box One level, the issue is significantly more problematic. It can be image-depleting for you. Box One's methodology is based on delegation, pushing everyone and everything as far as possible down the organization. If you need Box One's imprimatur to be delegated downward, you must have a proposition for him that will move him. At his level, only two appeals act as turn-ons: very big bucks and very sure bucks. When you enter Box One, you are making a quantum leap in muchness and sureness. It is no longer one small step for incremental enhancement but a giant step in corporate finance.

The third reason not to go top-down is that it is quite likely to be unproductive. It will yield nothing at all if it violates any one of the following six rules for dealing at the Box One level:

1. *Never* ask for information about his business before you give some of your own.
2. *Never* ask for information that is obtainable anywhere else.
3. *Never* quote information from any source other than Box One or his managers or accredited industry representatives.
4. *Never* quote specific dollar figures about any work you are doing or have done with Box One's competitors.
5. *Never* position Box One's businesses negatively. Talk only in terms of improving their competitive advantage or maintaining leadership.
6. *Never* try to "wing it" or fly by the seat of your pants.

Most of what Box One knows and is willing to have you know is already in his company's current annual report and 10-K report. Some of what he may not care to talk about is in security analysts' reports on his business. If you reveal ignorance of what he has already revealed, you run the risk of being redundant, which is unproductive for both of you, or ridiculous.

An example of being redundant is to ask, "What are the top priority business goals for your organization?" An example of being ridiculous is to follow up the redundancy with these two sequential questions:

1. "Does your company have a mission statement?"
2. "Are your goals consistent with the mission statement?"

Managing Business Function Knowledge

Your expertise in customer business functions will emerge in this type of sequence:

1. You will know a little about one operation in one customer company in one industry.
2. You will know a lot about that one operation in that customer company.
3. You will know a little about another operation in the same customer company, because you will be invited to migrate your profit improvement strategy to another aspect of the same business function or to another function.
4. You will know a little about the same operation in a second customer company, as you penetrate other key accounts in the same industry.
5. You will know a lot about that same operation in several customer companies. You will be storing their facts and figures in your databases. Your reputation for expertise in bringing profit improvement to the operation will spread throughout the industry. The profits you bring will become the industry standard.
6. You will acquire similar databases and expertise for improving the profit contribution of other operations in the same business function and in other business functions in the industry.
7. You will extend your knowledge and repute to other closely related industries.

This is the capsule history of how major corporations have managed their customer knowledge, extending it from operation to operation within a business function, then to other business functions, then to other customer companies in the same industry, and then to other industries. In order to grow their key account sales at high margins, they have marketed their knowledge of customer business problems and opportunities. On the surface, they have been selling profit-improving solutions. But the underlying value has been their understanding of customer problems. They appear as solution experts. At rock bottom, however, they are process-smart, operations-smart, function-smart—that is, customer-smart. Only then can they be smart suppliers.

As you learn how to manage customer knowledge resources, you will discover two truths. No customer wants to be first with anything new. Yet as soon as something new produces superior results, every customer wants to possess it on an exclusive basis. These paradoxical attitudes will be encountered as you take the first steps from vending to Consultative Selling. Finding the first customer to work with, to let you get inside heretofore proprietary operations, will be more difficult than finding the second. Yet working with a second customer in the same industry may also be difficult because the first customer will want to monopolize your function-profiling skills and profit-improving strategies.

In spite of these initial constraints, you will know that you have achieved consultant recognition in a customer industry when a remarkable event occurs. You will be *invited* by customers to profile their business functions—not to bid on their business but to study its cost structure and its sales opportunity. At that point, your knowledge of industry norms will come importantly into play. Once you have captured the knowledge of their functions, your proposals for profit improvement will follow naturally. After all, who will be better equipped?

What you know about customer functions will not be what you sell. But what you sell will always be based on what you know.

In many sales organizations, realization is accompanied by pain as the balance of power swings from product and pricing specialists to customer operations and applications specialists. Product knowledge will always be preeminent at the vendor's purchasing tier. But a sales organization will be permanently welded into position there until it acquires the customer data that enable it to move up. The short-run agonies of change must be balanced against the long-term agonies of decreasing margins, increasing competitive parity, and rising costs that can never be retrieved by price. The difference between being able to obtain top margins at the top tier and suffering eroding margins at the purchasing tier is the value added by Consultative Selling.

5

How to Quantify
Your Solution

Customer profit improvement begins with knowledge of how customers make the profits that you are going to improve: how they make their money right now. This is the starting point for Consultative Selling. Unless Consultative Selling strategies can improve the profits a customer can make, the customer will not be a prospect for high-margin sales.

Knowledge of how customers make profits starts with their own records of performance. For public companies, these are the balance sheet and the income statement. Privately held companies must be assessed by speculation, with the best clues obtained from comparison with public companies in the same industry.

Using Customer Balance Sheets for Background

A balance sheet is a snapshot of a business that shows its financial condition at the moment in time when it is snapped. If you learn how to read it, you can picture the financial structure of a customer's business, which can be useful in helping you spot your best opportunities for profit improvement.

Balance sheets can take many forms, and the items that

appear on them may vary according to the character of each business and its particular circumstances. A conventional balance sheet appears in Figure 5-1. It contains five sections. Two appear on the left-hand, or asset, side of the statement: current assets and fixed assets. On the right-hand side are current liabilities, long-term liabilities, and capital. When the dollar values assigned to the items on each side are totaled, a balance sheet must balance. Components of the balance sheet's five elements are as follows:

1. *Current assets.* Cash as well as receivables and inventories that are expected to be liquidated into cash within one year.
2. *Fixed assets.* The land, buildings, and equipment used in the operation of the business.
3. *Current liabilities.* Accounts payable, short-term bank loans, current installments of long-term loans, bonds or

Figure 5-1.   Balance sheet expressed as a statement of assets and liabilities.

BALANCE SHEET	
ASSETS	LIABILITIES
Current Assets	Current Liabilities
	Long-Term Liabilities
Fixed Assets	Capital (Capital Stock and Retained Earnings)

mortgages payable, accrued payroll due to employees, accrued taxes, and other amounts due to third parties within one year.
   4. *Long-term liabilities.* Bonds, mortgages payable, and other loans due beyond one year.
   5. *Capital.* The value of a business to its owners; also called equity. It is created either by direct investment of funds in the business or by profits that are retained after payment of dividends to owners or stockholders. Since equity is determined by subtracting liabilities from assets, both sides of the balance sheet will balance.

To understand the character of the underlying funds, you must translate the customer balance sheet into the form shown in Figure 5-2. In effect, Figure 5-2 is an X-ray of Figure 5-1.

The left-hand side of Figure 5-2 represents the funds invested in the business operations of a customer. It shows at a particular point in time where and in what form these funds reside. Current assets are the funds invested in the circulating capital of the business. Funds invested in the facilities used to operate the business are fixed assets.

The right-hand side of Figure 5-2 shows the current sources of the funds that have been invested. From it, you can determine the specific proportion of the customer's total invested funds that has been contributed by vendors and banks on a short-term basis; by banks, insurance companies, and bondholders on a long-term basis; and by the owners and stockholders as a result of direct investment or retained operating profits.

As a rule, management of the left-hand side of the balance sheet, representing the funds invested in a customer's operations, is the responsibility of operating management. The right-hand side of the balance sheet, representing the sources of funds, is the responsibility of financial management. Since the cost of acquiring and maintaining funds differs depending on their source, money management is an important function contributing to profitability.

Consultative sales representatives who deal in products

Figure 5-2.   Balance sheet expressed as a statement of funds invested
              and sources of funds.

BALANCE SHEET	
FUNDS INVESTED	SOURCES OF FUNDS
Circulating Capital	Vendors Banks (Short-term)
	Banks Insurance Companies Bondholders (Long-term)
Facilities	Stockholders

and services related to money management—financial systems, for example—will want to pay particular attention to the
right-hand side of the balance sheet. Examining competitive
sources of funds may be useful in determining how their
products or services can reduce the customer's cost of acquisition or maintenance of funds and thereby contribute to profit.
On the other hand, consultants whose products or services
affect the operations of the customer's business—computerized
design and manufacturing systems, for example—will be more
interested in the funds invested in operating assets. Because
credit terms affect the financial management function, they
will be of interest to all consultants regardless of the products
or services they sell.

Using Customer Income Statements for Background

Increases or decreases in the value of a customer company's
capital are generally the result of one or more of three conditions:

1. Capital value will increase if additional capital is obtained.
2. Capital value will decrease if dividends are paid out.
3. Capital value will increase if the net result of operations is a profit and will decrease if the net result of operations is a loss.

By far the most significant factor in determining capital value is the net result of operations or the earning power of the business. This aspect of profit making is reported in a separate document known as the income statement or profit and loss (P&L) statement. On it, profit appears as the remainder of revenues after expenses have been subtracted. This statement of profit on the bottom line is the benchmark from which your profit improvement objectives must take off. How much better can you do than the customer is already doing? Every dollar you can add represents incremental gain for the customer and provides the basis of incremental pricing for you.

The P&L statement also shows you where a customer's money goes—where investment is most intensive and where any reduction will be welcome. A typical dealership or distributor will state its intensiveness like this:

	($000)
Materials	850
Labor	1,500
Overhead	900

You may not be able to reduce fixed assets, at least not in the short term. But labor and materials costs are prime targets for cost reduction proposals.

The Circulating Capital Principle

Profit is made by the circulation of business capital. Every business is founded on capital, or funds that start in the form of cash. The objective of business is to make that initial cash grow into more cash. The way this is accomplished is to circulate the capital, the initial cash, through three transfer points. Each transfer adds value:

1. The initial cash circulates first into *inventories*.
2. Then the inventories circulate into *receivables*.
3. The receivables finally circulate back into *cash*, completing one cycle.

This three-step process demonstrates the principle of circulating capital. Every business depends on it for its income.

Circulating capital is the current assets of a business. They go to work in profit making as soon as cash is invested in accumulating inventories. Every time raw materials are purchased or processed, inventories come into existence. Another name for production scheduling could really be inventory conversion. Manufacturing adds further to the values of inventories, and so do all the other processing functions of a business that transfer value from cash to product costs on a dollar-for-dollar basis.

Figure 5-3 shows the profit-making process that occurs as capital funds circulate through a customer's business. At A the funds are in the form of cash. As the business operates, the funds change form. The initial cash is transferred into inventories as raw materials are purchased, labor is paid, and finished goods are manufactured and sometimes transported from plant to warehouse.

When sales occur at B, funds flow from inventories—the manufactured goods—into receivables. As they flow, the magnitude of the funds increases because inventories are valued at cost and receivables are valued at selling price. This increase represents the gross profit on sales. The greater the gross profit rate, the greater the increase in funds during each rotation of the capital circulation cycle.

At C, the funds earned by the collection of receivables flow back once again into cash. Before they do, they are reduced by

Figure 5-3. Profit making through capital circulation.

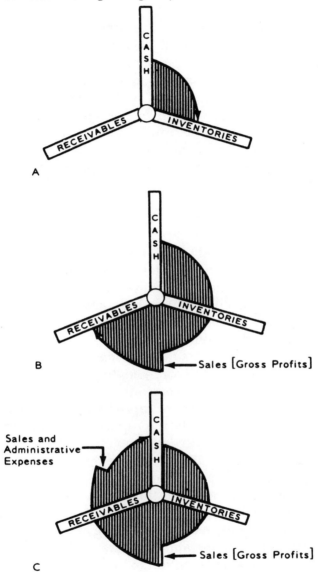

the sales and administrative expenses that have been disbursed throughout the operating cycle.

At this point, one full cycle of capital circulation has been completed. It has resulted in an increase in the number of dollars in the circulating capital fund. This increase is the difference between gross profits and selling/administrative expenses. In other words, a profit is made when the circulating capital of the business turns over one cycle. The more cycles through which you can help turn your customer's circulating capital during an operating year, the greater the profit the customer can earn. This is the principle of *turnover*.

The Turnover Principle

The circulation of capital funds in a customer's business takes on meaning only when it relates to time. Since capital funds turn over in a complete cycle from cash to inventories, then to receivables, and finally back into cash again, their rate of flow can be measured as the rate of turnover. The faster the turnover, the greater the profit.

Stepping up a customer's turnover rate through profit improvement is the consultative sales representative's most important function. Unless your profit projects are by and large directed to improving the turnover of the capital employed in your customer's business—especially the capital that is in the form of inventories—you cannot accomplish your mission.

Turnover will generally offer more opportunities than will any other strategy for profit improvement. The most common way to improve turnover rate is through increased sales volume and lowered operating fund requirements. In some situations, turnover may be improved by decreasing sales or even increasing the investment in operating assets.

You are in excellent position to help improve a customer's turn of circulating capital since, as Figure 5-4 shows, the drive wheel that rotates capital is sales. You must continually search for the optimal relationship between your customer's sales volume and the investment in operating funds required to achieve it. At the point where the optimal relationship exists, the turnover rate will yield the best profit.

In Figure 5-4, the circumference of the sales wheel represents $200,000 worth of sales during a twelve-month operating period. The sales wheel drives a smaller wheel representing circulating capital. The circumference of the circulating wheel equals the amount of dollars invested in working funds, in this case $100,000. Enclosing the circulating capital wheel is a larger wheel, also driven by sales, that represents the total capital employed. It includes the circulating capital of $100,000 plus another $100,000 invested in plant and facilities. Thus the circumference of the wheel representing total capital employed is $200,000, equal to the sales drive wheel.

When annual sales are $200,000 and total capital employed in the operation is $200,000, the annual turnover rate of total funds invested is 100 percent, or one turn per year. The portion of the total that is circulating capital, amounting to $100,000, will turn over at the rate of 200 percent, or twice a year.

Each of the three elements of circulating capital—cash, receivables, and inventories—will have its own individual turnover rate. Inventory turnover is calculated according to the number of months' supply on hand. A six months' supply would represent two turns per year, or a 200 percent annual turnover rate. Turnover of receivables is expressed as the number of days' business outstanding. If 90 days of business are outstanding, the receivables turnover is four turns per year, or 400 percent.

Since circulating capital increases every time it completes one turn, your job is to find ways to increase customer turnover through the use of your product and service systems. You can exercise two options for improving turnover. One way, option A, is by increasing sales. The other way is by decreasing the amount of money invested in circulating capital, option B. Figure 5-4 shows an opportunity to double customer sales to $400,000 per year without increasing the $200,000 of total funds employed in the business. This is option A. The turnover rate will be increased from 100 to 200 percent. At the same time,

Figure 5-4. Turnover.

Basic Relationship

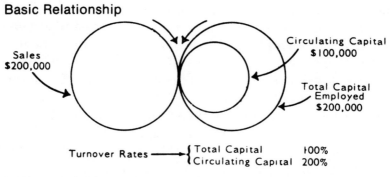

Sales $200,000

Circulating Capital $100,000

Total Capital Employed $200,000

Turnover Rates {Total Capital 100% / Circulating Capital 200%}

Option A: Increase Sales

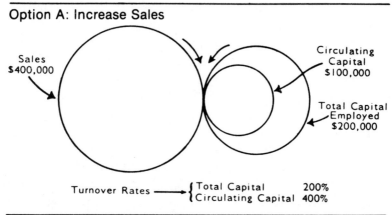

Sales $400,000

Circulating Capital $100,000

Total Capital Employed $200,000

Turnover Rates {Total Capital 200% / Circulating Capital 400%}

Option B: Decrease Capital

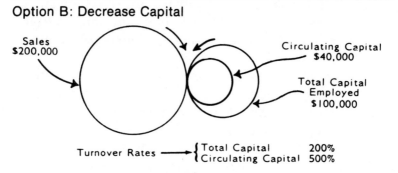

Sales $200,000

Circulating Capital $40,000

Total Capital Employed $100,000

Turnover Rates {Total Capital 200% / Circulating Capital 500%}

the turnover rate of circulating capital increases from 200 to 400 percent.

If the consultant cannot increase the customer's sales, option B offers an alternative opportunity to improve turnover. Even though sales remain at the same annual rate of $200,000, turnover can be increased if total capital employed is reduced from $200,000 to $100,000. This includes a parallel reduction in circulating capital from $100,000 to $40,000. These reductions help the consultant improve the turnover rate of total capital employed from 100 to 200 percent and that of circulating capital from 200 to 500 percent. This strategy for improving turnover means that the operating funds of the customer's business are being worked harder.

The profit improvement created by options A and B can be readily appreciated by multiplying the increase in funds generated at each turn of the operating cycle by an increasing number of turns. If the operating profit from one turn in the basic relationship shown in Figure 5-4 is $50,000, the profit realized by option A would be doubled to $100,000. In option B, profit would remain at $50,000 but $100,000 of funds would be released from operations that could be used to generate additional business or reduce indebtedness.

Opportunities abound for improving a customer's turnover. The reason is simple. The sum total of funds employed in a customer's business represents the many individual funds that make up circulating and fixed capital. An improvement in the turnover of any one of these funds will correspondingly improve the turnover of the total funds employed. Therefore, you can zero in on any component of a customer's "turnover mix" without having to consider any of the others or their sum total. For example, improvement in the turnover of any single item in a customer's inventory—including your own product— will improve total turnover and consequently contribute to profit improvement.

Contribution Margin

The key to profits is contribution margin—how much margin each product line or business unit contributes to a customer's total profits. Affecting a customer's contribution margins is a key objective of Consultative Selling. There are two ways to do this. You can help increase sales volume at the current contribution margin. Or you can help increase contribution margin at the current volume of sales.

Figure 5-5 shows how contribution margin works. It is

Figure 5-5. Analysis of profit contribution by product line (dollars in thousands).

	Total	Product Lines		
		A	B	C
1. Sales	$2,600.0	$1,742.0	$650.0	$208.0
	100.0%	67.0%	25.0%	8.0%
2. Cost of sales	$2,106.0	$1,440.0	$520.0	$146.0
	81.0%	82.7%	80.0%	70.0%
3. Gross profit (1 − 2)	$494.0	$302.0	$130.0	$62.0
	19.0%	17.3%	20.0%	30.0%
4. Wages	$221.0	$134.0	$65.0	$22.0
	8.5%	7.7%	10.0%	10.5%
5. Other	$26.0	$10.0	$13.0	$3.0
	1.0%	0.6%	1.9%	1.5%
6. Total (4 + 5)	$247.0	$144.0	$78.0	$25.0
	9.5%	8.3%	11.9%	12.0%
7. Contribution margin (3 − 6)	$247.0	$158.0	$52.0	$37.0
	9.5%	9.0%	8.1%	18.0%

calculated by subtracting variable costs from sales revenues. In the example, a customer's total contribution margin is $.095. That means that each single dollar of sales is currently contributing a margin of 9.5 cents to cover the customer's fixed operating overhead of $221,000. It takes a lot of $1 sales to contribute enough 9.5 cents' worth of margins to cover $221,000 of overhead. Even when sales do that, the customer merely breaks even. That is where you come in. If you can increase sales or decrease the variable costs that subtract from sales revenues, you can improve customer profits.

The consultant's choices are shown in Figure 5-5. If you want to work on product line A, you can improve profits best by improving sales. While it has only a 17.3 percent gross profit, it also has a 9.0 percent contribution. Any increase in sales volume will produce new profits. On the other hand, if you work on product line B, you will have to reduce its variable costs. Its 20 percent gross profit exceeds that of A. But it is making only an 8.1 percent contribution after variable expenses. If you can reduce its expenses, you can improve its contribution even without increasing sales volume.

Getting Inside Box Two's Mind

When you present a PIP to a Box Two manager, what questions can you safely assume he will ask?

- *What is the net present value of this deal?* To get the answer, he will discount your proposal's future cash flow projections at the rate of his company's cost of capital. He will then calculate the cumulative value of these cash flows in terms of today's dollars in order to arrive at their present value. Finally, he will subtract the investment you are asking from the present value to learn the net value.

- *What is the return on investment from this proposal?* To get the answer, he will multiply his margins by his expected turnover. If his margins have been declining and you propose to improve them, you can leave his rate of turnover alone. If you cannot increase his margins, he will look to see if you are proposing to increase his turnover.

 ▪ *What is the payback period on the investment that is being proposed in the PIP?* Payback calculates the return *of* the investment, not the return *on* it. The manager will want it as soon as possible in order to limit his risk. He will usually calculate it by dividing his initial investment by the projected cash flows. Alternatively, he may simply add up each period's cash flows until the point where the investment has been covered.

Customer managers use a business shorthand to appraise your PIPs quickly in order to qualify them for serious consideration. They use two criteria in rapid-fire order to make a quick study of the key things they have to know up front:

1. How much money can they most likely earn if they invest in your proposals?
2. How soon will they be able to realize it?

These two quick screens will tell them if they are interested in going further with you, which means finding out how sure they can be about the "muchness" and "soonness" you are proposing.

Criteria of "How Much"

Customer managers use three criteria of muchness to determine how much they will get out of an investment in one of your Profit Improvement Proposals:

1. *Net present value,* which indicates the net value of all the future cash flows you will help them earn over the commercial life of your proposals, discounted back to their present value today so they have a common denominator of value. Bringing future values back to their present value, which discounts them, is made necessary by the time value of money. A dollar

in the manager's hands today is always worth more than the value of the same dollar in his hands tomorrow. Every manager has a minimum NPV standard for accepting proposals. You must PIP him above the standard to merit consideration.

2. *Accounting rate of return,* which indicates the average aftertax profit over a proposal's commercial life divided by its investment. AROR accounts for all the cash flows that accumulate over commercial life. Every manager has a minimum AROR floor that acts as a hurdle rate for considering your proposals.

3. *Aftertax cash flows,* which indicate a proposal's profit after subtracting for taxes and adding back depreciation and other noncash outlays. Cash flow is net income, commonly referred to as the bottom line. Cash flow is vital to every business. It can be even more important than profits because it pays for the continuity of ongoing operations. Depreciation is the reduction in asset value from use or obsolescence, based on periodically writing down a portion of an asset's original value so that it can contribute to the reduction of taxes, thereby influencing aftertax cash flow.

Criterion of "How Soon"

Customer managers use *payback* as their criterion of soonness to determine how soon they will be able to recover their investment in your proposals. The payback period is computed by dividing the total amount of an investment by the expected aftertax cash flows. Payback is an important determinant of the relative merits of competitive proposals. Once payback has occurred, the customer manager is "clean," removed from risk. From that point on, his interest will focus on the net present value, accounting rate of return, and aftertax cash flows of your proposals.

Practicing ROI-Talk

The accounting rate of return relates to the return on investment, ROI, which is used to evaluate total customer company performance. This total return on investment must be narrowed down to AROR in order to evaluate an *incremental investment,* such as a specific system. A system's AROR can, therefore, be considered as the added rate of profit that the system can add to the customer's ROI.

AROR/ROI Interrelationships

The interrelationship between ROI and AROR can be seen by the similarity between their formulas:

$$\text{ROI} = \frac{\text{net profit}}{\text{sales}} \times \frac{\text{sales}}{\text{investment}}$$

$$\text{AROR} = \frac{\text{net profit}}{\text{investment}}$$

For calculating the accounting rate of return, sales are eliminated from the ROI formula because total customer company analysis is not relevant for most incremental investments. The impact of most incremental investments, even huge capital-intensive systems, becomes swallowed up in a customer's total ROI. The consultant cannot identify an individual system's contribution when it is dispersed over such a broad base. Therefore, to make an incremental contribution measurable, its impact should be calculated according to AROR.

Net income is not the sole basis for determining AROR. Gross profit may be an appropriate measure of income if no incremental operating costs are involved or if operating costs cannot be separated on incremental sales. Contribution margin may also be an appropriate measure of income if no incremental fixed costs are incurred or if fixed costs cannot be separated.

System-Opportunity Identification

The return-on-investment approach is the best diagnostic tool to identify consultative sales opportunities. As the ROI formula shows, a consultative opportunity is always present when either a customer's operating profit rate or turnover can be improved.

Any opportunity that a consultant recommends must meet customer standards of what constitutes an adequate return on investment. A system whose promise of profit improvement falls below this standard will probably be rejected as not being worth the investment. It will usually be ruled out by one of three standards for determining whether a given rate of return on investment is adequate: its investment exceeds the basic cost of money, its payback is too risky, or the return falls below the amount that customers believe they have the right to expect from their technological sophistication.

The Return-on-Investment Yardstick

In order to tell whether the increased sales you propose from a profit-improvement project are good or poor, you will need an accurate yardstick. In many selling organizations, profit is commonly expressed as a percentage of sales price or as an absolute amount per unit. But any method of measuring profit as a percentage of sales is insufficient for consultative purposes since it takes into account only two elements of profit: sales revenues and cost. The difference between them is then calculated as a percentage of sales. Most companies call that difference profit. Profit, however, has a very important third component: *time.*

From the point of view of return, profit can be regarded as the ratio of income earned *during an operating cycle* to the amount of capital invested to produce it. Thus profits have two costs: time costs and costs of producing the product or service. When profit is compared with its funded investment, it is being expressed as a return on investment, or ROI.

Return on investment is an analytic tool that has three qualities in its favor for your purposes: (1) It is a fair measurement of profit contribution; (2) it is helpful in directing attention to the most immediate profit opportunities, allowing them to be ranked on a priority basis; and (3) it is likely to be readily understood and accepted by financial managers as well as sales and marketing managers of your customer companies.

Figure 5-6 represents the formulas for calculating return on investment. The formulas relate the major operating and financial factors required in profit making to the rate used to measure the profit that is made: the rate of profit per unit sales in dollars, the rate of turnover of operating funds, the funds required to finance business operations, and the total investment of capital employed, including working assets, plants, and facilities.

Figure 5-6.   Return-on-investment formulas.

A. Options for Improving ROI by Improving Turnover

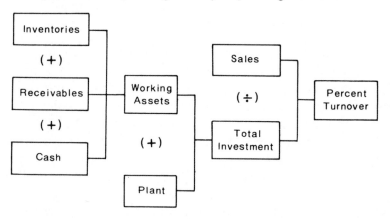

B. Options for Improving ROI by Improving Operating Profit

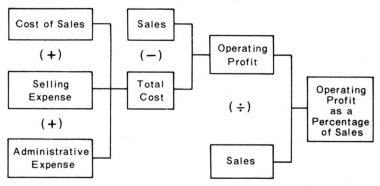

The customer's sole economic justification for investing in your profit-improvement projects is to earn a superior rate of return on the funds invested. This truism must be interpreted in two ways. One is in terms of income gained. The other is in terms of costs avoided in obtaining investment funds, costs of retaining such funds, and costs suffered by denying their use for alternative, potentially more profitable projects.

Return-on-Investment Diagnostic Techniques

Diagnosis lies at the heart of consulting. Diagnostic techniques that are based on return on investment lie at the heart of diagnosis. As Figure 5-6 shows, ROI is the product of the rate of operating profit expressed as a percentage of sales and the rate of turnover. Any time you want to improve a customer's ROI, you must first diagnose a problem in the customer's operating rate or an opportunity in the customer's turnover.

Part A of Figure 5-6 shows the ingredients of ROI expressed as turnover. If you examine each of those ingredients, you will find profit opportunities that can improve turnover. You can, for example, recommend a project to reduce your customer's receivables. This will reduce the amount of funds invested in working assets, thus reducing the customer's total investment base. As a result, you can improve your customer's profit without increasing sales volume.

Part B shows options for diagnosing profit improvement if your objective is to increase operating profit. You can recommend a project to lower the customer's cost of sales. This will reduce total costs and enable the customer to show an increase in operating profit.

Turning Over a Customer's Assets

When a customer invests his money to acquire your products or services, he obtains an asset. His goal is to turn it over as quickly as possible so that it will revert to cash. Then he can reinvest in another asset with you and start the process over again. If he makes good investments with you, he will end each investment cycle with more money than he started with. Asset turnover is the secret to making money. The more assets that are turned, and the faster they turn over, the more money will be made.

Accounts receivable and inventory are a customer's two major "current assets." Current assets, by being turned over, are more quickly convertible to cash than are fixed assets. Anything you can do to speed up a customer's asset turnover in these two areas will make money for both of you. If you and a customer allow these assets to build up—if a customer's sales decline and inventories grow or if your customer's customers delay paying their bills—both of you will be in trouble.

Ideally, customers would like to have zero investments in accounts receivable and inventory. Every day that you can help them condense their collection period is money in the bank. Every additional turn of inventory also improves profits. An item that turns over 1.7 times a year sits in inventory approximately seven months before being sold. If you can help move it in six months, using the "power of one," you can accelerate its contribution to earnings by one seventh.

Asset turnover is especially important in selling to a key customer's profit center managers. They are evaluated on the basis of return on investmet. Their ROI is calculated by dividing their earnings by the investment in their asset base. The higher their ROI, the greater the investment that top management will continue to make in their profit centers and the higher the reward each center's manager will receive.

The ROI of your customers is a good index of how good a partner you are. If you have the ability to affect inventory but you let their money remain tied up, you are a poor partner. If you have the ability to affect collections but you let their money remain tied up in accounts receivable, you are a poor partner. Increasing inventory turns and decreasing collection cycles will make you better.

Calculating Investment Risk

Whenever you make a proposal to a customer, you are challenging him to calculate a risk. If you ask him to invest with you to expand his capacity to produce his existing products, you are offering him a median risk. All other types of investment will have a higher or lower risk. Investments for replacement or repair are the safest. Past experience can accurately help foretell their probable cash flows. Cost reduction investments are somewhat riskier. No one can calculate the exact magnitude of their potential savings. The riskiest type of investment concerns new products or new market development where neither the costs nor the revenues can be predicted with certainty.

As soon as a customer invests with you, he incurs an opportunity cost equal to the return he could have earned from an alternative investment of the same funds. The opportunity cost is in addition to the direct cost he pays you and the indirect costs he incurs in implementation. The further away you take him from his median risk where he knows the return he can expect, the more risk-averse he will be and the more proof he will demand and the closer partnership with you he will expect.

Whenever risk increases, a customer will balance it against its return. In high-risk situations, he will be more interested in whether the return is sufficient to justify the risk than the rate of return itself, however high it may be.

The risk-return tradeoff is the basis of management. The only fully known sum of money in any transaction is its investment. Future benefits are always uncertain. As risk increases, the anticipated return must increase with it. If a manager is confronted with two equal investments that promise a similar return, he will probably choose the investment with the lower risk—that is, the one with the higher net present value per dollar invested.

Where risk is equal or minimal, it is not a factor. Under

these conditions, it will be better to make an investment rather than let money sit idle—and thereby incur opportunity cost— as long as a positive net present value can be returned. This means that it must equal or exceed the customer's cost of capital. As long as it does either one or the other, the investment will be acceptable. This is simply another way of calculating the worth of an investment based on its net present value. According to NPV, investing $50 million today for a stream of future cash flows with a value today of $59.755 million is an acceptable investment. In effect, the customer is paying $50 million for an asset worth $59.755 million, gaining $9.755 million of new value. Since the NPV is well over zero, this is a good investment. If it were only zero, the customer's wealth would be unchanged and his time wasted.

Risk, no matter how minimal, increases over time. That is one reason why a dollar today is always worth more than a dollar in the future. Two other reasons why money has a time value are inflation and the opportunity cost that is incurred when money is not productively invested. The delay in receiving money equals the cost of the return on the best alternate investment that could have been made for it.

Because money has a time value, every dollar returned by an investment is worth less as time goes on. In the way that customer managers think about investments, they say that if I have 91 cents on hand today, I can invest it at 10 percent interest and it will grow into one dollar within one year. Is this the best deal available to me at this time? Can I get a better rate of interest anywhere else? Can I get a quicker payback? Can I get a larger return?

The fear of opportunity loss, if it can be quantified, can be a powerful motivator to commit. Consultative sellers always calculate the value of a lost opportunity to invest with them, reminding their customers of how much it is costing them for each day, week, month, and quarter of deliberation and delay in closing on a PIP. This puts a penalty on "missing out on a good thing" and, conversely, awards brownie points for biting the bullet.

Specifying Instead of Being Specified

As a consultant, you must always keep in mind what you propose. Your Profit Improvement Proposals should tell you: Through them, you should be proposing improved profits as a result of solving a customer's business problems by the application of your technology to his operations.

You are not selling your technology. Nor are you selling solutions to a customer's business problems such as "improving materials flow" or "decreasing production backlogs." You are selling improved profits; they are your product and your proposals must set them forth in their major specifications of how sure your customer can be that he will receive the "muchness and soonness" in your proposal. A customer will not have the comfort level to partner with you if only you are sure. Your sureness is unimportant. You must make the customer feel sure. Unless you do, he will tell you that he is not comfortable. If he stays that way, you will not partner him to sell for you.

There are many short-term comfortable partners. There are fewer long-term comfortable partners. But there are no long-term uncomfortable partners.

You make a customer manager comfortable when you give him the evidence to prove where the return on his investment will come from and how it will flow. You may think, quite naturally, that the investment causes the return. Actually, it is the other way around. It is the promise of the return that causes the investment to be forthcoming, making the investment the result. If you do not make customers comfortable with the cause of their new profits first, they will be unable to envision a result.

When a customer signs off on a transfer of funds to you, he is committing to incur an asset. He owns something new. Its cost becomes a part of his balance sheet, increasing his indebtedness. The only valid trade-off for his debt is the added values he can receive from the improved operation, process, or function in his business that you will help him achieve.

To make this trade-off measurable, a consultative proposal

is modeled after proposals commonly prepared by Box Two for presentation to Box One. When you present it to your Box Two partner, you will be playing his role. He will be playing the role of Box One. The more closely you replicate your Box Two partner, the more closely he will relate to you as partnerable and the more readily you will be accepted into his internal hierarchy.

You, like Box Two, will become a specifier of profit-improvement solutions. Box One, who allocates assets to maximize their profitable return, will sit in judgment on both of you. Together, you will follow the official business proposal approach: First, diagnose a problem or opportunity in business terms; second, prescribe a solution in business terms; third, prove how the solution will work in business terms; and fourth, commit to controlling the solution to make sure it works in business terms, that is, improves the proposed amount of profits on time.

Seeking Simple Opportunities

A consultant can find many relatively simple ways to recommend profit improvement. If you sell to supermarkets, you can show each chain's central headquarters or even individual store managers how substituting your brands for others, or increasing the number and location of their shelf facings, may improve profit per case or per $100 of sales.

Profit improvement for a manufacturing customer may lie in improving the profit of dealers and distributors. By helping a customer's distributor organization increase its contribution—something the customer cannot directly control yet must nonetheless influence—you can help your customer raise the profit on sales made through this channel.

A distributor's largest single investment is likely to be in inventory. The key to distributor inventory control is finding the minimum investment required to maintain adequate sales and service. One way of measuring the utilization of inventory investment is to compare a distributor's inventory turnover with his industry's average. Inventory turnover can be computed by using this formula:

$$\frac{\text{Cost of sales for one year}}{\text{Average inventory}} = \text{inventory turnover}$$

If a customer's distributors are in a business whose inventory turns an average of 4.5 times a year, or once every eighty to ninety days, you can help a distributor whose turnover is lower than average see the problem this way:

$$\frac{\text{Projected cost of sales}}{\substack{\text{Projected average} \\ \text{inventory level}}} = \frac{\$370,000}{\$100,000} = 3.7 \text{ inventory turnover}$$

To help this distributor increase turnover to approach the 4.5 industry average, you will have to help the distributor reduce inventory investment. To do this, you must first find out what level of inventory investment can yield a 4.5 turnover. Divide the distributor's projected cost of sales by the desired 4.5 turnover, which results in an $82,000 inventory. It now becomes clear that you can help the distributor achieve profit improvement by reducing inventory investment by $18,000. Then you can turn your attention to optimizing the inventory mix.

The consultant's best approach to inventory reduction is usually through product-line smoothing. Distributors almost always carry too many items in their lines. An inventory burdened by too many items can cause a dissipation of the distributor's sales concentration, extra handling costs, waste through obsolescence or spoilage, and, of course, higher inventory carrying costs, higher insurance costs, and overextended investment.

To analyze a distributor's inventory, you can simply rank the products in the line according to their cost of sales and then compute their inventory turnover. Such an analysis could look like this:

- Products A, B, C, and D account for 57 percent of the cost of sales but only 34 percent of inventory. These products turn over inventory by an average of 6.2 times a year.
- Products E, F, G, H, J, and K account for 43 percent of the cost of sales but 66 percent of inventory. These products turn over inventory by an average of only 2.4 times a year.

The inventory turnover analysis in Figure 5-7 shows what it costs the distributor to carry inventory. By comparing the carrying costs of inventory to forecast sales volume, you can begin to learn more precisely what inventory the distributor should maintain. The first four products are apparently well controlled. They have an average turnover rate of 6.2 percent and one percent average carrying cost as a percentage of sales. You now know that you must concentrate on reducing inventory whose average turnover rate is only 2.4 percent and average carrying cost is 2.6 as a percentage of sales. This will help bring the distributor's inventory down to the $82,000 level that should contribute to the projected 4.5 inventory turnover.

Figure 5-7. Inventory turnover analysis.

Product	Percentage of Sales	Average $	Percentage of Average	Turn-over	Carrying Cost as Percentage of Sales
A	15%	$ 7,000	7%	8.2%	0.8%
B	17	9,000	9	7.0	0.9
C	14	11,000	11	4.7	1.3
D	11	7,000	7	5.8	1.1
Subtotal	57%	$ 34,000	34%	6.2	1.0
All other products	43	66,000	66	2.4	2.6
TOTAL	100%	$100,000	100%	3.7%	1.7%

Migrating Initial Sales

Key account penetration through Consultative Selling is a reciprocal process. Preliminary partnering makes possible initial entry at top-tier levels. Once entry has been accomplished, partnering should proceed apace so that migration opportunities open up beyond the initial sale. The purpose of preliminary partnering is to gain entry. The purpose of entry is to migrate, to penetrate a customer business in ever-expanding breadth and depth from your breakthrough point. The purpose of migration is to grow the customer's business and your business again and again.

In addition to the obvious benefit of providing ongoing high-margin sales opportunities, migration offers several other advantages. It helps amortize the investment in data collection. It helps develop new information sources about a customer business. It spreads awareness of your consultative positioning. And it helps deny opportunistic chances for competition to move in on a problem that you can, and should, solve. It helps prevent departnering.

Some migrations occur naturally—the solution of one problem leads progressively to the discovery of another, or a solution in one division stimulates customer interest about its transfer to a similar problem in another division. Other migrations will take place only as a result of effort. You will have to search out opportunities in the nooks and crannies of your customer businesses, relying on your partners to coach you about the most productive areas to explore and to point out the most cooperative guides to ask for advice.

The objective of penetrating a customer business in depth is to serve all major needs with your major products, services, or systems. This concept can be called maximizing "share of customer" as long as it is understood that it is not simply a volume criterion—it is a standard of the importance of your involvement. If you are significantly involved, you can become the preferred supplier of your customers' improved profits. Penetration in depth is inextricably tied to penetration in important areas of a business. Migration must be a selective policy whose aim is to consolidate your position as profit improver of the most vital functions you can affect.

The ideal migration timetable makes improving profit in one function the jumping-off place for improving profit in the next function. In this way, you can extract maximum learning value from each experience. You can also avoid stretching your resources too thin across more assignments than you can handle. It pays to remember that migration works both ways. One significant success encourages permission to try another. One significant failure discourages permission to try anything more at all.

Installing an initial system should therefore be regarded as planting the seed for follow-on sales opportunities, not the end of the sale. Once a sale has been made, the consultant has acquired a major asset: a more profitable customer. You can benefit the customer even further by additional profit improvement through one or more of three types of migration. You can offer to *supplement* the initial system with added components. Perhaps some components may have been sacrificed for financial reasons at the time the original system was approved. Or perhaps a greater need has become apparent only after installation. As a second type of follow-up, you can offer to *upgrade* the original components, up to and including the ultimate upgrading, which is total replacement of the system. Or third, you can offer to *integrate* an entirely new complementary system with the initial system.

These profit-improvement opportunities are not mutually exclusive. You can use all three approaches in sequence with the same customer. First, you can supplement the entry system. Then, at a later date, you can upgrade some of the original components. Finally, a complementary new system can be integrated with the original one. Then you can recycle the sales approach by offering to supplement the new system, then upgrade it, and eventually integrate a third system with the first two.

This recycling strategy is illustrated by the following scenario. It begins *after* an initial system is in place and producing prescribed profit-improvement benefits.

Cycle 1

1. Supplement initial system with add-on components.
2. Upgrade components of initial system with technically enhanced products or equipment.
3. Integrate a complementary new system with the initial system.

Cycle 2

1. Supplement new system with add-on components.
2. Upgrade components of new system with technically enhanced products or equipment.
3. Integrate a second complementary system with one or the other existing system.

Cycle 3

Repeat cycle 2.

Managing a Profit-Improvement Portfolio

The incremental value of a consultant's relationship with a key account customer is simple to calculate. At any given time, it is the sum total of earnings from all of a consultant's Profit Improvement Proposals. A few proposals will probably be spectacularly successful. But for the most part, steady, modest success is all that is required.

Each proposal should be successful in its own right. Beyond that, it should also lead naturally into the next successful project. As your profit-improvement contributions accumulate in a sausage-link chain, you will be building equity. This equity will consist of the value of the portfolio of Profit Improvement Proposals you have installed in each account. The reward for good work will be more work. By inviting you to remain in the game and try to improve profit one more time after each success, your customer is acknowledging a consultative partnership. As with all partnerships, "congratulations" is always followed by "you're vulnerable."

You, the consultant, are only as good as your last proposal. This should cause you to be financially conservative. Paradoxically, however, you will also have to be creatively daring in conceiving profit-improvement opportunities and planning to capture them. The net result of combining these two characteristics becomes the essence of your personal consultative style.

In setting about to construct a profit-improvement portfolio, you should start small. At the outset you must be content to make a single profit improvement in one business function or one product line in one account. Since the first proposal will probably be evaluated more critically than any of its successors, you must follow one injunction above all others: *The first time out, be successful.*

6

How to Sell
the Customer's Return

The penetration plan is your annual blueprint for getting into and staying in the business of a principal customer. The way you get in is by improving the customer's profit. The way you stay in is by continuing to improve the customer's profit, extending it to the solution of new problems, and never letting go. Last year's profit improver who has let go is last year's supplier of choice.

The databasing process for penetration planning requires answers to three critical questions that can determine up to 80 percent of your profitability on sales:

1. Who is my customer?
2. What can I do to improve my customer's profit?
3. What will my customer do for me in return?

The answer to the first question is crucial. Your customer is never a company as a whole, nor is it even a division. It is a specific business function manager within a division whose costs you can reduce or whose contribution to sales you can increase. If you are IBM, your customer is not PepsiCo. Nor is it PepsiCo's Frito-Lay division. It is the manager of Frito-Lay's inventory control function, for example, whose profit contribution you will be improving.

Similarly, if you are AT&T, your customer is not Merrill Lynch or, within it, the Diversified Financial Services division. Nor is it the division's real estate management functions. Your penetration plan may be directed to the division, but the business function manager in real estate telemarketing is your customer. It is that manager's profit contribution you will be improving. If you are Nabisco, your customer is not Grand Union supermarkets. It is the dry cereal department management group throughout the chain.

Planning to penetrate business functions within divisions or departments of customer companies is a far cry from vending commodity merchandise to purchasing managers on a price-performance basis. It is a totally different process: data-dependent rather than persuasion-dependent. Its database must therefore be structured to support the differences in sales strategy that a consultative approach demands.

Opportunity databasing hinges on one central concept: maximizing contribution. Two kinds of contributions are involved. One is your profit contribution to a customer. You must maximize it. The other is a customer's profit contribution to you. You must maximize that also. This defines the consultative concept of opportunity: the chance to be a maximizer of customer profits.

The role of a profit maximizer differs from the role of a needs analyst or a benefit provider or a problem solver. All these are intermediate steps. Through needs analysis, the provision of benefits, and the solving of problems, profits become improved. This is the ultimate step. If it does not take place, all the intermediate objectives can still be accomplished, but they will be in vain.

High-penetration objectives—superior profit objectives for your customer and for you as well—are financial objectives. Nothing supersedes them. They must come first in your penetration plan because they are the purpose of the plan. The only reason to plan is to be able to set and achieve high financial objectives.

The objectives of your plan should be databased in the following manner:

1. The most likely profit contribution that will be made *by you* to each customer:

   a. This year
   b. Next year
   c. Third year

2. The most likely profit contribution that will be made *to you* by each customer:

   a. This year
   b. Next year
   c. Third year

"Most likely" profits are a conservative estimate. They are a trifle more bullish than bearish, but only a trifle. They represent the contributions that can be expected if most strategies work according to plan and if there are no important hitches that have not been planned for. In practice, they should come out just about right.

If you help customers improve their profits from incremental sales, you will have to adjust the gross profits by the customers' effective tax rate before you commit to an objective. If you improve customer profits by cost savings that can flow directly to the bottom line, you can calculate the profits as net incremental gain. Only the net counts. Neither you nor your customers can take anything else to the bank.

The total annual contribution you expect to make to your customers will be the sum of all the Profit Improvement Proposals you plan to install in their business functions during a year. The contribution your customers will make to you will be the sum of your profits from the sale of each proposal that is collectible during the same year. Two ratios are helpful to monitor how effectively your resources are being allocated to obtain each customer's contribution. One compares profits to the expenditures required to achieve them; this is return on investment. The second is the more traditional ratio of revenues to expenses.

Taking a Selling Stance

Once you have defined a lead, there are three ways to get into position to propose as a consultant:

1. *Standing tall.* The best case is to have norms on the standard contributions that a customer's Critical Success Factors make to each of his Critical Success Businesses and Functions. This gives you the strongest ground to stand on. You can challenge customers to compare their current contributions against your norms. If your norms are better, you are in the best position to sell consultatively.

2. *One leg to stand on.* The next best case is to have norms from one industry that customers in another industry will accept as relevant and to bridge your applications expertise from the "norm industry" to the "no-norm industry." This can be done back and forth between the food processing and chemicals processing industries, for example, because their processing operations have many similarities. The sale of consumer packaged goods and financial services is also similar in many ways. Because you have only one leg to stand on, you are in a second-best position to make consultative sales.

3. *Legs firmly planted in midair.* If you have no norms that can be bridged, you will have to follow a four-stage process:

   a. Deduce a customer's Critical Success Businesses and Functions. Check your assumptions by tracking the strategic flow of customer funds to see that they are going to your assumed Critical Success Businesses and Functions. Double-check your assumptions against the life cycle position of each customer business or function to see which ones "must be" at critical stages or making critical contributions.
   b. Ask the customer managers which of the Critical Success Factors are their current hot buttons.
   c. Ask how much improvement they are committed to achieve and by when.

     d. Float "what if?" options to establish PIPable propos-
       als.

From the midair position, legs akimbo, many sellers are counseled to use a customer manager as a "coach." Help me, they plead. I am lost in the labyrinth of your business. Please shine your light on where I can find opportunities to sell you something. I promise you it will be to your advantage . . . an advantage that can be potentially even greater than going about your business.

Vendors seek coaches because they lack customer business knowledge. Consultants have customer business knowledge. They know where the leads are. As a result, consultants *act as coaches* to their Box Two partners.

Eschewing "Perceived Value"

Value exists only in dollars. In turn, dollars exist only in the form of specifically quantified amounts of money that accrue within a specifically quantified amount of time. There is no such amount of dollars as "more" or "a lot," nor is there a time for their accrual called "soon." To talk about profit improvement narratively instead of numerically is to speak an unknown language at the Box Two level of customer management.

At Box Two, quantification reigns. Dollars and time are expressed in numbers, not words. Some numbers are called "hard numbers" to indicate that there is a high level of confidence that they substantially represent real money and time. Other numbers are admittedly "soft" in their accuracy, useful to "ballpark" a proposal but not to buy into it or sell it. But hard or soft, the sign is always out at Box Two that says "Numbers Spoken Here."

Nonetheless, many sales representatives and managers prefer to remain innumerate. By avoiding the precision of numbers—a 2 is forever a 2, halfway between 3 and 4 and never any more or less—they may hope to fudge their commitments and thereby escape evaluation. I proposed that you would get more and you got more, they seem to want to say. What more do you want? And if you haven't gotten more yet, you should be getting it pretty soon. What's your hurry?

Hard numbers are admittedly hard to come by. Even good assumptions are not easy. Almost as much information and even more experience in a customer's business may be needed to float a soft number that is in the ballpark as to firm it up. A combination of ignorance and indolence often tempts sellers to fall back on something they call "perceived value"—alleged value that is not quantifiable or, more often, has simply not been quantified, but that the customer is expected to be able to agree undoubtedly exists. "Surely you agree that there will be an improvement?" the sellers suggest. If the customer agrees with their perception of value, they persist, "Surely you agree that it would be significant?"

In many instances, theirs is an honorable dialogue. Value does indeed exist and the mutual perceptions of seller and customer could be substantiated under audit. But no one can be sure of how much value is being proposed and how soon it can be accumulated. The gap that divides the perception of value from the certainty of value separates seller and customer from partnering. It also opens the door to a competitive proposal that quantifies its value. Even though the perceived value may actually be greater, no one will know for sure.

The implicit invitation that a proposal based on perceived value holds out to a competitor who is ready, willing, and able to quantify his value, even if it may be less, is one of the two major exposures that must be accepted by value perceivers. The other is the opportunity loss of the potential for maximum margins, since there is no way to relate margins to a perception of the value they should merit.

While there may be such things as soft, warm, and fuzzy perceptions of value, there are no fuzzy margins. Price always seeks a hard base. If value will not provide it, cost will. Instead of being able to command premium margins based on value, price will find its level at either the seller's cost or his competitors' prices. The value exchange that is inherent in Consultative Selling will have been preempted. Only a negotiated vended price will result, which will represent the penalty assessed on the supplier who sells perceptions as opposed to values. The cost of perception will be the difference between the vended price and the value price. In most cases, the cost of perceiving value will far exceed the cost of quantifying it.

Developing Your "What-Ifability"

The ability to propose a steady stream of investment opportunities or, more correctly, return opportunities to your customer partners is the engine that drives Consultative Selling. Proposals mean business. They make money for you and your customers, keep your learning curve strong by giving you access to new sources of information about customer businesses, and keep your partnerships active, alert, and alive. You should always have a minimum of three proposals in progressive stages of development. The one that you are working on should be on the table, the next one should be heating up in the oven, and the third should be in the freezer awaiting defrosting.

The proposals that are in the oven and the freezer represent your inventory. Until you sell them, they run up opportunity costs for you and your customers. You should turn them over quickly.

A consultative seller is continually diagnosing problems and opportunities and what-ifing solutions. Asking the customer "what if?" invites him to play strategic Ping-Pong with you. Each what-if should provoke either a "how?" or an enhanced what-if from your partner, building on your proposal or coming at it from a different cut. By presenting your proposals as questions, you circumvent most of the defensiveness that causes adversarial rejections and refusals to buy. Instead, you open your proposal to the customer, asking him in, so he can add his values to it and make it partly his own. Unless it becomes "his" in this way, he will not sell it with you. As long as your proposals remain "yours," you will be a vendor.

For example, a consultative seller might ask a supermarket customer: "What if you can acquire the equivalent of a $500,000 order each week—without incurring a single dollar for cost of sales? You can, if you can eliminate out-of-stock opportunity cost in a single best-selling brand in your dry cereals sections."

Or he might ask the same supermarket customer:

> What if you can offer your customers more advertised specials each week than your competitors can—in addition, what if you can also offer deeper price cuts on each of these specials? How much in new sales and profits can that earn for you each year considering that every single dollar of new earnings will be net, because all costs of each special will be fully funded by us?

> The funds required to support this donation will come from automating the checkouts at your stores, which will generate substantial savings of more than $90,000 per store annually. These savings will be derived from reducing the average time to check out each order by 30 percent.

> On a per-store basis, the operating costs break out like this: For a store with gross weekly sales of $140,000, savings are projected as approximately $7,650 per month by faster customer checkout and faster balancing of cash registers.

What-ifs like these fit right into your PIP proposals at the second stage of their presentation, as shown in Figure 6-1.

Eliciting the Magic "How?"

When your customer asks you how he can add the value you are proposing to his operation, he is opening your consultative sale. This answers the question "How do you open?" You do not. In Consultative Selling, the customer opens.

"How?" is the magic opener. It means "How can I be empowered?" "How?" comes in several forms. Some are non-verbal: facial expressions such as raised eyebrows, furrowed forehead, pursed lips, or quizzical looks and sometime nods. Fingers pulling at noses or earlobes, hands going to chins or

Figure 6-1.   PIP outline.

---

1. *Diagnose a customer problem or opportunity.* Demonstrate to the customer that you know something about his business that allows you to improve his profit. Based on experience in his business or industry, you know how you can capitalize on a market opportunity by bringing in new sales or how you can solve a marketing, manufacturing, or financial problem by cutting costs.

2. *Prescribe a value-adding solution to the customer's problem.* What-if the customer: Quantify the added value of applying your experience, expertise, products, and services to solve a customer problem or capitalize on an opportunity.

3. *Prove that the customer's added value exceeds price.* Prove that the value you promise to add to your customer's operations exceeds your price by expressing the price as an investment and the customer's value as a return on his investment.

---

backs of necks, and body leaning forward are additional non-verbal ways of asking "How?"

Verbally, a "how?" can be asked directly or indirectly as an expression of envy for your other customers whose profits you have improved, a revelation of wishes and wants that would constitute an ideal solution and how your proposed solution compares to it, or a request for added comfort expressed as a "Yes, but" reaction.

Qualified "how?"'s are often expressed in the forms of pseudoproblems that are designed to test and probe your solution, your experience, or your commitment. Customers also may want to know what their competitors are doing—"I wonder how they do this?"—or why their own people have not applied a similar solution long ago.

The entire Profit Improvement Proposal process is built around getting the "how?":

- In the *diagnosis,* get attention with the significance of the customer's problem or opportunity. "Aggravate him good."
- In the *prescription,* get agreement that the solution is

interesting. "Show the money." Create the tension from wanting to know "how."

- In the *proof*, resolve the tension by telling "how," and get acceptance that the "how" is doable and that therefore the prescription is achievable. "That's right."

Penetrating the High Levels

Objectives are a plan's purpose. Strategies are the methods of achieving objectives. In Consultative Selling, strategies are packaged in Profit Improvement Proposals. Each proposal represents a strategy to improve customer profit by solving a cost or sales problem. If the customer is a not-for-profit organization or a government agency, proposal strategies will focus on reducing costs and improving the dollar value of productivity. Either way, the mix of strategies must make a measurable impact on customer profit or operational performance, or both.

Profit Improvement Proposals are the sales vehicles for penetration strategies. They are designed to penetrate the customer's business at high-level points of entry. Each proposal contains a strategy for solving a specific customer problem. The sum total of proposals for the period of a year constitutes the annual top-tier strategy for a customer.

There are three steps to take before you can propose profit improvement:

1. Analyze a customer's business position.
2. Position penetration strategies.
3. Pinpoint penetration opportunities.

Analyzing a Customer's Business Position

A customer's business position determines your sales strategy. Each position presents a different penetration challenge.*

---

*For the full set of strategies for customizing Consultative Selling to a customer's business position, see Mack Hanan, *Successful Market Penetration* (New York: AMACOM, 1988).

1. *Penetrating a growing customer.* A growing customer is sales-driven. If you want to affect the sales function, you must increase its productivity so that it can generate more profits per sale or yield added profits from incremental sales. If you cannot affect sales but you can only reduce costs, the savings you achieve for a customer must be valued for their ability to support more sales. Your entire penetration strategy must focus on improving the customer's profit by increasing sales.

2. *Penetrating a mature customer.* A mature customer is driven from two directions at once. Sales must be increased, but not if this requires increased costs. If projected sales fail to result, the customer's stability can be threatened. Costs must be reduced, but not if this will reduce sales or market share. If sales fall, the customer's stability can be threatened. Your penetration strategy can focus on improving profit through sales increases or cost decreases, but it must avoid the unaffordable risk of increasing costs or decreasing sales in the process.

Positioning Penetration Strategies

The purpose of analyzing a customer's business position is to be able to custom-tailor your sales penetration. If a customer is growing or stable, you must present yourself as an improver of profit on sales. If the customer is declining, you must present yourself as a decreaser of costs.

Unless your sales position coincides with the customer's, you will never be able to create a partnership in profit improvement. The customer will not understand where you are coming from in your proposals. You, in turn, lacking a sense of your customer's objectives, will not know where the customer is going. As two unknowns, you will be talking past each other; you will be proposing to yourself.

To ensure that your sales positioning is in gear with how your customer is positioned, your penetration strategy should be preceded by a positioning statement. Here is a model statement:

In our penetration of the manufacturing functions of the ABC Company's XYZ Division, a stable business, we will position ourselves as the manufacturing vice-president's partner in profit improvement primarily by means of the reductions in cost we can deliver through our quality control system. We will also show how enhanced product quality can help improve profit through incremental sales.

Pinpointing Penetration Opportunities

A customer's inability to bring down a cost, and his need to increase profitable sales volume, are major business problems. Accordingly, they can be your sales penetration opportunities. In order to find out, you will have to identify them and then put dollar values on them and on the most cost-effective solutions.

Opportunities to penetrate a key account have a special genesis. A penetration opportunity does not automatically come into being simply because a customer has a problem and you happen to have a solution for it. Discovery is not opportunity. To determine whether a penetration opportunity exists, you must first analyze three specific dollar values.

1. *The dollar value of the customer's problem.* How significant is it? Is it making a significant negative contribution to customer profit? Does it justify a significant expenditure for solution?
2. *The dollar values of the profits from your solution* that will accrue both to you and to your customer. How significant are they? When will they begin to flow? How long before their total amount finally accrues?
3. *The dollar values of the costs of your solution* that will be incurred both by you and by your customer. How significant are they? Are they all up front or can they be paid for progressively out of the solution's improved profits?

Penetration opportunities are entry points. You should regard them as windows. An opportunity window opens for you when the following conditions are met:

1. The dollar value of the profits from your solution exceed the dollar value of the customer's problem.
2. The dollar value of the profits from your solution exceed the dollar value of the costs of your solution.
3. The dollar value of the profits from your solution exceed the dollar value of the profits from competitive solutions.

The first condition ensures that a customer problem is worth solving; that is, it is beneficial to solve. The second condition ensures that a problem is profitable to solve. The third condition ensures that your solution will be the preferred solution. All three conditions place the burden of proof squarely where it belongs—on your ability to create the most profitable solutions to customer problems in the business functions you can affect. This is the supreme standard of performance for Consultative Selling.

Prescribing Systems

A consultant's solutions improve customer profit in proportion to the consultant's skill in prescribing systems. Prescribing is the consultant's highest art. Good consultants are first-rate prescribers. They size up customer needs and specify the most cost-efficient systems to benefit them.

The ability to prescribe the right system the first time is a result of three factors. One is the consultant's experience. The second is expertise. The third factor is skill in solving customer business problems and helping capitalize on opportunities: in other words, helping a customer improve profit.

A system's combined advantage is expressed as a single benefit: profit improvement of the customer's business functions in which the system is installed. This benefit is a partial function of system price. It is also a function of the system's return on investment. The ability of a system to yield a return on investment that exceeds price endows it with premium-price capability.

Prescribing a system and pricing it for high customer

return are the two most demanding tasks of Consultative Selling. Together they determine the customer's value and the profit from the system. Because they have such a direct effect on both value and profit, the acts of prescription and pricing are the keystones of the consultant's selling proficiency.

The standard of performance for prescribing and pricing a system is met when the system's premium price is accepted as proof of its added value in meeting customer objectives.

When a consultant prescribes a profit-improvement package, he must follow the rule of "necessity and sufficiency." Components must be sufficient, but only those that are necessary to solve the customer's problem should be prescribed. This guideline helps protect consultants against underengineering or overengineering a system. If a system is overengineered, it may have to be overpriced; if it is underengineered, it may contribute to customer dissatisfaction and invite competitive inroads.

To avoid underengineering, you may have to acquire equipment or service components from other manufacturers to round out some systems. At times, it will be possible to market these components under your company's own brand name. This is the preferred way. But even if they cannot be branded, they should nonetheless be incorporated into the system if they are necessary to its objectives.

To be of maximum benefit to your customer and maximum profit to you, a system should have turnover built into it—that is, one or more of its components should be consumable. This allows you to generate an ongoing market for product-related services and consumable supplies, as a means of providing continuing sources of income for your business and continuing sources of knowledge about your customers' businesses.

A basic rule of system prescription can be stated in this way: *To maximize profit, standardize the hardware and customize the services and consumables.* When services and consumables are customized, a system's premium price is justified. When frequent turnover of those consumables is multiplied by premium price, maximum profits can result.

The following model prescriptions will help you formulate your own systems strategy:

- *An office communications system.* An office communications consultant defines the objective of office systems as improving the profit of customer word processing functions. Business communication is the vital customer process on which the consultant's systems concentrate. To solve problems of rising costs and inefficiencies in communication, the consultant prescribes a total communications system as opposed to the random use of a typewriter here, a dictating machine there, and a word processor and a copying machine somewhere else. The system is composed of input and output processing equipment, together with inspection, maintenance, repair, replacement, resupply, financing, and training services.

- *A fire protection system.* A fire protection consultant defines the objective of fire systems as improving the efficiency and reducing the cost of safeguarding customers' processing functions. The refining of chemicals is the vital customer process on which the consultant's systems concentrate. To solve the problem of rising cost for high-hazard protection, the consultant prescribes a total-risk management system as opposed to the random use of a fire extinguisher here, a sprinkler there, and shovels and a bucket of sand somewhere else. The system is composed of fire detection and extinguishing equipment, plus inspection, maintenance, repair, replacement, resupply, financing, and training services.

- *A materials cleaning system.* A materials cleaning consultant defines the objective of cleaning systems as improving the profit of customer electric motor rebuilding processes. Cleaning and repainting electric motors are the vital customer processes on which the consultant's systems concentrate. To solve the problem of rising costs for removing dirt, grease, rust, and paint, the consultant prescribes a total cleaning and finishing system as opposed to the random use of a sandblasting machine here, a blast room there, and steel grit abrasives somewhere else. The system is composed of blasting equipment, consumable abrasives, and related inspection, maintenance, repair, replacement, resupply, financing, and training services.

Deciding Which System to Propose

The return-on-investment approach is the most helpful tool for determining which of two or more systems to propose to a customer as well as how to price. A simple example will illustrate this point.

1. *System A* is forecast to improve customer sales by $200,000 and yield a profit on sales of 10 percent, or $20,000. The investment required from the customer is $100,000.
2. *System B* is forecast to improve customer sales by $300,000 and yield a profit on sales of 10 percent, or $30,000. The same $100,000 of customer investment will be required.

These two systems appear equally worthwhile in terms of their 10 percent profit yield on sales. But in terms of the return each system can achieve on the amount of customer capital it employs, System B is superior. With System B, $100,000 of capital can produce a $30,000 profit—a 30 percent return. System A also requires $100,000 of capital but can produce only $20,000 in profit, for a 20 percent return.

The difference between the two is the relationship of the improved sales volume to the capital employed. System A allows its capital to appreciate at the rate of 200 percent. With System B, however, the appreciation is 300 percent: It turns inventories into cash faster.

There is a shorthand formula you can use to determine return on investment:

$$\frac{\text{Profit}}{\text{Sales}} \times \frac{\text{sales}}{\text{capital employed}} = \% \text{ return on investment (ROI)}$$

In the case of System A:

$$\frac{20,000}{200,000} \times \frac{200,000}{100,000} = 20\% \text{ ROI}$$

In the case of System B:

$$\frac{30,000}{300,000} \times \frac{300,000}{100,000} = 30\% \text{ ROI}$$

In this simplified approach, the first fraction calculates the percentage of profit on sales; the second fraction calculates the turnover rate. When the two are multiplied, the result is return on investment. Any improvement in the circulation of funds invested in a system's total assets, working assets, or any component part of an individual asset will have a multiplying effect on profits.

Adding the Competitive Advantage

A system's marketability lies in its competitive advantage: the value added by improving customer profit. This customer advantage becomes the system advantage in the minds of customers, who evaluate systems both individually and competitively. A system does more than offer a customer advantage; the system comes to "own" the advantage as its single most crucial selling point. This is *preemption,* a system's ability to seize an advantage uniquely to itself.

The competitive advantage of a system acts as its market selecting mechanism. It selects customers in two ways. First, it seeks out and qualifies the segment of a market that has the greatest need for the system's advantage. Second, it comes to represent the system by acting as a shorthand way of describing its incremental contribution. The customer advantage determines the market and documents the system's capabilities.

A system's customer advantage must conform to three requirements:

1. It must confer a superior added value over competitive systems, as well as over the option of doing nothing, in at least one important respect.
2. It must be at least equal to competitive systems in all other respects.
3. It must not be inferior to competitive systems in any important respect.

A competitive advantage can be an attribute of the system. Or it can come from the way it is implemented, maintained, migrated, or marketed. The question of how much quality to build into a system therefore merits a minimal answer. Enough quality to deliver the customer advantage is enough quality. A maximum quality system as determined by the aggregate quality of its components may not be perceived as offering the maximum customer advantage. Minimal systems from the consultant's perspective are often preemptive systems from the customer's perspective.

The concept of competitive advantage is not just an argument against overengineering, overpackaging, or overcosting, although it speaks powerfully against all three. It is essentially an argument in favor of prescribing systems from a customer orientation. And it provides the direction for establishing a system's branding: the capture of customer preference because the *customer's profit is being improved best,* not because the *consultant's system is constructed best.*

Defending Against Desystemizing

A consultant's prescription for improved customer profit is always threatened by desystemizing. You should not fear the process. It plays the vital role of confirming the value of your prescriptive expertise and your ability to apply it to a customer's problems.

The essential consultative value is the ability to apply. This is what a prescription really is—an application of the consultant's expertise to a customer's business.

To this extent, you are an applications consultant. All the professional expertise in the world is valueless unless you can apply it to a customer's business. By protecting a system against customer attempts to desystemize it, you learn the extent of your prescriptive and applications skills.

Challenges to desystemize a system are actually a customer's attempt to test the worth of your applications expertise, which is the trump card that justifies premium price. Desystemizing is a price reduction strategy. Since premium price lies at the heart of Consultative Selling strategy, the system must be protected if premium price is to be maintained.

A system is only as good as its consultant's applications ability. Unless the consultant's expertise can be *branded*—that is, accepted as providing a value that exceeds its price and that cannot be obtained elsewhere—a system cannot be protected from customer attempts to desystemize it.

There are two basic desystemizing strategies:

1. Attempts to acquire only certain components of a system
2. Attempts to acquire only the consultant's prescriptive expertise and information base

When a customer threatens to desystemize your system, you have recourse to two strategies. One is the "yes" defense, which is effective against the only-certain-components attack. The other is the "no" defense, which is effective against the only-the-prescription-and-information-components attack.

The "Yes" Defense

A customer who does not want to pay premium price for a system but who still sees value in some of its components will try to cherry-pick. This is often like the Chinese restaurant approach of selecting one from Column A and one from Column B. When a system is attacked in piecemeal fashion, the best protective strategy is to say yes. There are three reasons this is so:

1. *You make a sale.* A partial sale is usually better than no sale at all. Penetration is established. At least some income is earned to pay off a portion of the sales cost.
2. *You have a foot in the door.* Even a partial sale gets you involved with a customer. This gives you an opportunity to apply upgrading sales strategies that can gradually result in your selling an entire system with additional components. This is the way many partial systems become full systems. In most businesses, customers tend to stick with their original system suppliers. Up to 90 percent of many systems sales come from add-on purchases by existing customers.
3. *You can gain information.* Every customer problem that is solved yields new information about the customer and the customer's markets. A new cost center may be found. A new way of reducing it may be discovered. A new sales opportunity may be identified. A new way of seizing it may be tried. Each time, something new will be learned to suggest the next proposal.

From these three reasons for saying yes to a customer, it is apparent that agreement to sell part of a system must be tempered by one consideration: The brandable components of a system must never be compromised. No matter what components are agreed on, the consultant's prescriptive expertise in profit improvement and the information base on which it depends must always be included in the sale.

In Figure 6-2 a consultant's recommended responses to customer requests are tabulated. Even though the components of the system are specific to materials cleaning, the responses are typical for all systems.

The "No" Defense

The most dangerous attack against a system is the attempt to select out its APDAB components: the consultant's *applications expertise and database*. This probe must be resisted at all costs. The consultant's expertise and data resources are your

Figure 6-2. Responses to desystemizing.

System Components	Recommended Responses by Seller to Customer Desystemizing
Swing table, blast-cleaning machine, and worktable	Yes
Operating supplies, including steel grit abrasives, and replacement parts	Yes
Environmental control: fabric filter dust collector to prevent in-plant and outside air pollution	Yes
Operating personnel training program on cost-effective operation and maintenance	Yes
Periodic inspection and maintenance-monitoring service	Yes
Profit-improvement planning service to reduce cost and improve profit from materials cleaning process	No
Customer information service on applying new developments in the technology of blast cleaning, equipment, components, and supplies	No

rock-bottom leverage against desystemization. If they can be obtained separately, there may be no incentive left for the customer to acquire the total system. But the key reason for protecting expertise and information is that their premium values support the umbrella of premium price over the entire consultative system. Without them, a system will degenerate into a commodity.

The best defense against this type of desystemizing is to identify the consultant's expertise and information with the system as a whole. "After all," you may reason with a customer, "my prescriptive expertise is based on managing systems composed of my company's equipment and services. I know these components. I have confidence in them. I can predict their contribution to improved profit. To ask me to apply my expertise to a system of foreign components deprives me of my quality control. It may defeat my ability and nullify my experience. It will certainly devalue my norm base, which, as you know, has been painstakingly built up from experience with my own equipment and services in solving a wide range of problems. It may not be valid for other suppliers' systems. For these reasons, I must say *no*."

No consultant likes to say no to a customer. Yet the desystemizing strategy of selecting only the consultant's expertise and information strikes so directly at the systems concept that there is no choice. It must be rejected. The only way to avoid answering with a "no" response is to see that it is not provoked in the first place. This is your principal educational task.

You can always be certain of two facts about a system. For one, no matter how novel the hardware components may be initially, they will eventually become commodities. For this reason, you cannot allow customers to regard hardware as the core of your systems. Second, the only component that can be branded against commodity status is the "software" represented by your own prescriptive and applications expertise. Every consultant must educate customers to accept this basic truth from the very beginning. This is not easily reconciled when hardware is exclusive, innovative, technologically sophisticated, and personally exciting to the consultant and even to customers. Nonetheless, it must be done. It is your only strategy for avoiding the recurrent need to say no and to redirect customer attention to saying yes to profit improvement.

Part III
Consultative Partnering Strategies

7

How to Set
Partnerable Objectives

Every business has natural partners. Who are yours? They are other businesses whose growth is dependent on you. Selecting your growth partners is the single most important act of Consultative Selling.

If you know who your natural partners are and what they need from you in order to grow, you can dedicate your Profit Improvement Proposals to them from the outset. Your business positioning can be a natural response to theirs. Your system capabilities can be exactly receptive to their needs. Your database can contain knowledge of their growth problems and opportunities. Your entire business can be the reciprocal of the businesses of your partners.

You have two types of natural growth partners. One is composed of businesses that are currently growing because of you. The other is composed of businesses that you could grow but are not currently growing.

Choosing Current Customers to Partner With

There are four questions to answer about your current customers in order to determine which of them you should partner with:

1. *Who are you growing right now?* Some of your growth partners will be customers you are already growing. You may not be aware of your contribution to their growth. You may think you are merely selling to them. But they are actually partners without portfolio. In order to determine whether any one of them should be selected as your partner, you will have to answer three more questions.

2. *How much are they growing you?* You may be unable to know the full extent to which you are bringing growth to a current customer. But you can much more easily calculate the profits by which you are growing as a result of the customer's business with you. There are four standards by which you should measure profits: their absolute value, their comparative value ranked against your customer list as a whole, their rate of growth, and the trend of their growth rate over the past three years.

3. *How much more can you grow them?* Growth takes place in the future. Consequently, you must add a fifth standard to your calculations: What is the most likely projected rate of improved profits you can plan for in the growth of their business over the next three years? If the projected rate of growth is becoming static or in decline, you may not have a true growth partner. Instead, you may have a mature customer to whom you can continue to vend products at competitive prices, whom you should sell to and profit from but not partner.

4. *How much more can they grow you?* Because growth partnerships must be reciprocal, you must elevate the most likely projected rate of your own profit growth over the next three years to see whether it is increasing, becoming static, or entering decline. If the projected incremental rates of growth are increasing for both your customer's and your own business, you have the ideal basis for growth partnering.

Choosing Prospective Partners

There are three questions to answer about prospective partners in order to determine which of them you should partner with:

1. *Who else can you grow?* Growable businesses that you are not currently growing are your source of consultative expansion. In order to qualify as a growable customer, a business must meet two criteria. Its business function problems must be susceptible to significant cost reduction by the application of your expertise. In addition, your expertise must be able to increase the customer's own profitable sales opportunities.

2. *How much will they grow you?* A business that is growable by you must be able to grow you in return if it is to be partnerable. Its contribution to your profit volume and its projected three-year rate of growth must meet or exceed your company's minimum growth requirements.

3. *How can you grow them?* For each growable customer that you determine is potentially partnerable, you must plan a growth strategy. The strategy will set forth the precise means by which you will add new profits to the customer's business. You will need to specify how much profit will accrue from reducing business function costs, how soon its flow will begin, and how long it will continue. You will also have to specify the amount and flow of profit from new sales opportunities that you can make available and the markets they can be expected to come from.

The businesses you are growing and businesses you are able to grow are the keys to your growth. The very fact of their growth or growability identifies them as consumers of cash. They are heavy users of money to finance their growth. If you can become an improver of their profits, you can become important to them as a money source.

Not only do they need cash, they need cash fast. They must channel it back into the two major cash-hungry functions of their business that control, or would otherwise constrain, their continued growth: manufacturing and sales. If you become an improver of their profits, you can become important to them as a source of fast cash flow.

Desperately Seeking PIPpability

A customer manager is constantly under Box One pressure to maximize his contribution to profitability. He is always in a state of dynamic tension. There is no steady state in which profit contribution can be maximized once and for all. Cost creep continually challenges control. Shifting demand, competitive campaigns, and margin slippages challenge earnings. Managers are reminded every day that the only constant is change.

The art of managing a business function or a business line is a perpetual tinkering process of adjusting the mix of the recources that go into it and the returns that come out of it. The manager's quest is to learn how few resources need to be invested to produce maximum return. The ideal answer is the fewer the better. But, in practice, managers are always in disequilibrium from the ideal. Investments turn out to be not as productive as they promise. Returns turn out to be not as great or as quick or as certain. The productivity of each dollar never seems to be maximized.

This provides the happy hunting ground for Consultative Selling. A manager who is desperately seeking maximum profitability is "eminently PIPpable" with Profit Improvement Proposals. As a result, a consultative seller's most partnerable position is to be desperately seeking PIPpability, the ability of the consultant to improve a manager's profits. The most PIPpable managers make the best partners. It is not that they are poorer managers and therefore have the most costs and smaller or more sporadic cash flows. Quite the contrary, the most eminently PIPpable managers are the best managers, alert to every prospect for a competitive advantage, filled with a sense of urgency to achieve it, and bold enough to sell the consultant's PIPs internally to their Box One funders.

Good managers have the same problems and opportunities that poor managers have. Good managers do something about them with a heightened aggressiveness, a foreshortened time drive, and a greater receptivity to partners who can help ensure their success.

The seller's search for PIPpability in a customer manager is the search for good managers with whom to partner. Poor managers may seem to need a consultative partnership. But only good managers are prepared to accept its offers and implement them with the skill and concentration they require. A good manager would still be a good manager without the seller's partnership. With it, however, he can be even better. This edge can be his competitive advantage, the value added by the seller.

The PIPpable partner is the manager who already wants to grow his contribution to profits or who is already growing it. He does not need persuasion to grow, only help. He is profit-responsible or profit-accountable and he is partnerable in his receptivity to joint approaches to achieving his objectives. If he is not profit-sensitive, he is not partnerable. But if he is not profit-sensitive, he is not a Box Two manager and therefore eminently *non*-PIPpable.

Growing From Your Partnerships

Partnering requires two choices. One choice is your selection of the customers you will grow. The second choice is made by your customers: Why should they partner with you?

There are three reasons:

1. *You are an important source of their growth profits.* The contribution of new profits that you can make to a customer must be significant. Only then will your partnership be important enough to both of you to merit top-of-the-mind attention, both his and yours.

To be an important source of growth for a customer means that you must account for worthwhile incremental profits. You must also be able to deliver them in a timely fashion, recognizing the time value that money has for him. In this, you must be dependable. He must be able to count on you to improve his profits when you say you will and by the amounts you promise. Your importance to him will be in direct proportion to your reliability.

2. *You are one of their best investments in profit growth.* When a partner does busines with you, he must perceive the price he

pays to be an investment rather than a cost. The distinction is vital because only an investment yields a return. He must understand that he is not investing in your products or services or systems, not even your solutions. He will be investing in new profits. The return he receives from his investment with you must be among the best yields he can make.

Just how high does a customer's return on investing with you have to be? You must compare yourself with his options. Normally a customer will invest in his own business in order to make profits. He has a "hurdle rate" that sets his minimum return. As his partner, you must offer him a better choice. You must make it more profitable for him to invest in your business. Either the investment he is required to make will be smaller yet yield a similar or faster return, or the return he receives from you will be larger even though the investment may also be corresondingly larger.

3. *You both have the same competitors.* When you sell products or services, positioning yourself as one of a customer's several alternate vendors, you are only concerned with defeating your own competitors—rival vendors. To be a business partner means that you must concentrate on defeating your *customer's competitors.* Unless you have the same objective, you cannot be partners.

A customer's competitors are the constraints on his growth. He has two of them. One is his current costs, against which he competes every day and which he must reduce if he is to improve his profits. You must help him. His second source of competition is in the area of sales opportunities. He competes for them every day too, trying to win customers against his competition. If he is going to improve his profits, he must increase his profitable market penetration. You must help him.

As your partners, your customers will grow you if you can make three transformations in your relationships with them.

You must first transform yourself from a supplier of products and services to a supplier of profits. You must change from a manufacturing or service business into a supplier whose product is profits.

You must transform yourself from representing an added cost to representing an added value. You must change your basis for doing business from selling performance values at a price to returning dollar values on an investment.

You must transform your outlook from competing against other companies in your own business to competing against the cost constraints and sales opportunity constraints of your partners. You must change your objectives to match those of your partners so that you can defeat the same competitors. Once you do that, your partners will grow you for the same reasons, and in the same ways, that they grow themselves.

Joint Venturing With Customer Managers

A consultative seller's partner is a customer manager who will sell their joint Profit Improvement Proposals internally. That is the acid test of partnership—not simply giving the seller access to himself or information about his business, not coaching and counseling the seller on how to penetrate his business, and not passively going along with the seller's penetration initiatives. A customer manager must be a seller to be a partner.

Consultative Selling partnership strategies are designed to give customer managers the mix of comfort and urgency they require in order for them to share in preparing and presenting a Profit Improvement Proposal to their Box One managers and in supporting it and implementing it for its full realization. This means that your proposals must become "our proposals," jointly prepared, presented, and achieved. Until this takes place, would-be consultants will be running up against one of the basic truths about all businesses: No one from the outside can get a hand on a customer's funds. Only the customer's own people are fundable, because only they are accountable for their payback and positive return. Without an internal seller as a client, a consultant has no one to sell to and no one to sell for him.

Box Two managers who make the best partners conform to a handful of characteristics:

1. They want to grow their business operations.
2. If you grow them, they can grow you.
3. You can grow them, as proved by your norms for expanding markets like theirs or cutting their significant costs.
4. They will partner with you to come closer to your norms by sharing data with you, contributing a team to work with you and your team, and acting as a testifier and reference site for you.
5. They can be an important influence on other customers in their industry, with prestige and a reputation that induce emulation.

Growability must be your key partnering objective. Only by growing can your partner ensure a fast turnover of your sales and their prolonged continuance. This requires a high turnover in the sales your customer makes to his own customers. If they become stable, turnover will stagnate. For this reason, stable customers—especially those with large shares of market that cannot be grown—are to be avoided. They make good customers but they are poor partners.

If you have a choice among growable customers—customers who meet your primary objective—what fine-tuning criteria should you apply to select among them? You should look for three attributes:

1. *Nascent opportunity.* You should seek the maximum opportunity to grow and be grown. Change is the mother of opportunity. A growable customer that is undergoing reorganization or restructuring to provide for further expansion offers enhanced partnership prospects. Change at the top tier is an added enhancement. Whenever major change is taking place, you have the chance to create a new role for yourself, meet new or newly perceived needs in new ways, and form relationships with new managers who can benefit significantly from your expertise.

2. *Positive attitude.* You should prefer to partner with cus-

tomers who prefer to partner. Their receptivity to your over-
tures will be greater. So will their awareness of and concern for
growth. At the minimum, you should expect them to be willing
to share data with you and to create a correlate profit-improvement team to work with yours.

3. *High repute.* You should understand that the most sophisticated customers make the best partners. They will have
the highest standards of performance. That will push you.
They will have the most intelligent managers in their industry.
That will pull you. Your contribution to them will most likely
be maximized; they will take what you give them and run with
it. Your odds for a successful track record will increase, as will
your ability to draw on them for references that will attract
other sophisticated customers to you.

Reducing Partnering to Common Denominators

All partnering is based on a few common denominators:

- Partners have a *common objective.* Each partner wants to
  improve profit.
- Partners have *common strategies* for achieving their objective. Their methods are based on mutual need-seeking
  and mutual need fulfillment. In both cases, needs are
  arrived at through negotiation.
- Partners are at *common risk.* Each partner has something
  of value to gain or lose.
- Partners have a *common defense* against all others who are
  not included in the partnership. Each party deals as an
  equal. Outsiders range from being less equal to being
  perceived as competitors.

Cooperative negotiation strategies enable partners to treat
each other as equals. This is the principal rule of partnerships.
There are ten additional rules that can help in partnering:

1. *Add value to each other.* Teach each other new ways to improve personal achievement and professional productivity so that both partners profit by the relationship.
2. *Be supportive of each other, not competitive.* Form a staunch team.
3. *Avoid surprises.* Plan work together and work according to plan.
4. *Be open and aboveboard.* Always level with each other.
5. *Enter into each other's frame of reference.* Learn each other's perceptions in order to see things from the other's point of view. Learn each other's assumptions to understand the other's expectations of the partnership.
6. *Be reliable.* Partners must be there for each other when they are needed.
7. *Anticipate opportunities and capitalize on them.* Forecast problems and steer the partnership around them. Keep the partnership out of trouble. If trouble is unavoidable, give the partnership a head start in solving it.
8. *Do homework.* Know what's happening. Know what may happen.
9. *Treat each other as people, not just as functionaries.* Be willing to provide the personal "little extras" that make a partnership a humane as well as a mighty force.
10. *Enjoy the relationship and make it enjoyable.* Both partners should prefer to work within the partnership rather than within any other relationship because it is one of the most rewarding associations either of them has ever had.

In Consultative Selling, partners share improved profit. This is the partnership's prime benefit. The second major benefit that partners can confer on each other is learning together just how their profits can be improved. A partnership should be a breeding ground for generating new knowledge of profit making and putting it to work with shared faith and apprehension. The act of learning together is one of the strongest bonding agents in a partnership. It is the growth element in the relationship because it ensures that *both* partners will grow.

The third attribute of a successful partnership is mutual support. Each partner takes on the parts of the relationship's labor that best fit individual capabilities. The complementary nature of the relationship enhances each of them. Conversely, each partner is diminished by the absence of the other.

Understanding a Partner's Motivations

The customer decision makers who must be partnered are multimotivated. They rarely act on the basis of one motive alone. Status, money, autonomy, and self-realization propel them. Of all their drives, three are likely to be major: power, achievement, and affiliation.

1. *The power motive.* Managers like to direct, influence, and control others. They like power. Power is measured by three standards: control over important resources, the ability to impose will on others, and the extent to which the flow of events can be influenced. Power can give its holder the right to act or to prevent others from acting. Power *over* people, or power *with* them, is called leadership.

The consultant must learn to cope with the power structure in customer organizations. Power can be recognized by its two faces. One is *personalized;* the other is *socialized.* Personalized power is based on a dominance-submission relationship, a win-lose type of interaction. It is self-aggrandizing at the expense of others. Socialized power, on the other hand, is used for the benefit of others. It helps make people feel confident and competent so that they can achieve common objectives. It is energizing, sustaining, and supportive.

2. *The achievement motive.* Managers are typically high

achievers. They are task-oriented: They initiate action rather than reacting. It is not money, power, or a need for the respect of their associates that primarily drives them. It is the urge to achieve for its own sake. Consultants who are also high achievers should find it mutually rewarding to negotiate with fast-track customer managers.

3. *The affiliation motive.* Both the power motive and the affiliation motive are geared to people. While power involves dominance, affiliation involves relating to other people in ways that maintain good interpersonal relations. The affiliation motive is people-oriented. Most effective managers rate high on affiliation, expressing their drive to relate to others with whom they identify. This is also true of the best consultants.

In the course of having their needs developed through negotiation, customers may have their first experience in being a partner. From it, they will derive their first impressions of your consultative skills. This impression forms the basis for respect. From the same experience, customers also derive their first impressions of your knowledge of their business and how to improve their profits. This impression forms the basis for confidence. To initiate customers into partnership, you must become aware of customer needs and how they differ from your own.

The Consultant's Need Set

There are three aspects of consultant needs. Each represents a certain type of income: *money income; psychic income,* representing such rewards as power, prestige, and promotion; and *self-actualization income,* including self-fulfillment, competence, and the realization of talent potential.

These needs are present in every consultant's motivation set. Yet they vary widely from one consultant to another. To negotiate effectively, your need set must be proportioned something like Figure 7-1. The money drive you have should be significant. But your use of it to give you power, especially

Figure 7-1.   Consultant motivation set.

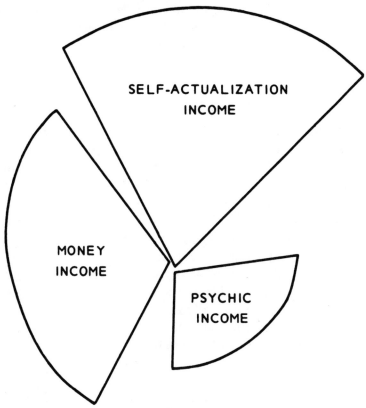

the power to dictate solutions or appropriate a customer's leadership, should be small. Although you may enjoy great prestige, you will always be required to work through your customer to accomplish your purposes. You can help a customer achieve power and promotion and thereby share vicariously in them. But you will often work unheralded, usually anonymously.

Consultants, on the other hand, must also have an unusually large amount of self-actualization in their need set. This aspect is the key to success. You must have, and be driven by, a need to realize your own fullest growth and development by growing and developing your customer partners. You must want to utilize all of yourself in your customer's behalf, engaging your full complement of skills and expressing your widest range of knowledge. You must need to translate these qualities into unique profit projects that only he and he alone should ever know have originated with you.

The Customer's Need Set

In Figure 7-2, three aspects of customer needs are illustrated in typical proportion. They contrast with the proportions shown in Figure 7-1 for the consultant's need set. The major difference lies in the relative significance of self-actualization income and psychic income. For the consultant, self-actualization must always take precedence over the psychic rewards of power, prestige, and promotion. For the customer, however, you should assume that power and promotion—which represent realizable objectives for a customer—supersede self-fulfillment. By remembering the primacy of power and promotion when you negotiate, you will be able to keep your customer's perspective in mind. You will also be able to visualize your role fairly accurately in the way the customer will see it: to help the

Figure 7-2.   Customer motivation set.

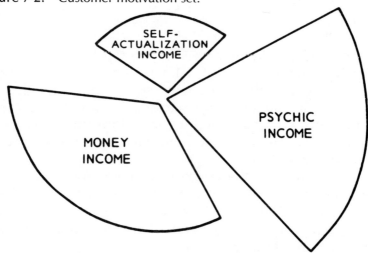

customer obtain increased power income and maximize money income as well.

You must achieve harmony in your relationships by integrating your needs with those of your customer. The initiative must be yours. It is your task to perceive yourself, first of all, in the power-accelerator role that your customer perceives for you. Second, you must devote your own self-actualization motives to your customer's best interests. And third, you must adopt a posture of empathy with your customer so that both need sets can operate as one.

Obsessing on Control

The Box Two mindset is obsessed with *control*. Every manager knows that costs must be controlled. So must sales, since too much demand that cannot be met can overwhelm manufacturing, inventory, and distribution just as seriously as too little demand can underwhelm them. If shipments get out of control, a manager gets into trouble. An uncontrolled rate of scrap or mean time between downtime or repair and replacement under warranty, or if market share deviates from plan, are all ominous signs that a manager is going to be off budget and off plan. This will bring him to the attention of Box One.

In most customer companies, deviations from plan call for Box One to "manage by exception"—to apply supervisory management practices and procedures to correct the exceptions and either get the manager back on plan or find a new manager who will be unexceptional. Box One's philosophy is often expressed like this: "When a manager goes off plan, I invite him to lunch. No one gets invited to lunch twice."

When a customer manager partners with you, his or her purpose is to reduce the risk of being invited to a "box lunch" by Box One. That is why you must be sure that you can help him achieve the new contributions to profits, either by cost reductions or revenue increases, that you have proposed to him and that he can achieve them within the time you propose. Otherwise you will expose him to catastrophic risk.

To be "in control" means that a manager is on plan—on budget, on time, attaining each milestone on schedule—so that payback of Box One's investment can be made on or before its due date and that the manager's return on investment reaches its projected rate. This is the way that your Box Two partner builds his track record as a good manager. As a good manager, he will again be favored to manage the next cycle of investment and you will again be favored to be his partner in replicating your mutual success. Together, you will become a reliable team.

All business is based on reliability. Customers prize reliability over every other attribute; they prize it in their people, their products and services, their operations and their reputations for their own customers' satisfaction. To be out of control is to be unreliable, which means that the profit contribution you and your partner have proposed cannot any longer be *counted on*. You should take these words literally. The expression "counted on" is a quantitative measure of your value and it says very clearly that you and your partner will "come in" with new profits as scheduled or you and your partner may be out.

Making Profit Improvement Proposals that can be counted on is your transcendent task. It is the basis for your partnered positioning. Take that away and you have what the computer industry calls vaporware and the food industry calls empty calories—promise without performance, the essence of unreliability.

In order to be an acceptable partner for a customer's Box Two manager, you must share his obsession with control. In consultative terms, control means two things: controlling a customer's costs to help him maintain low-cost production and controlling the flow of his revenues to help him maintain high margins or high market share.

To be admitted into a major customer partnership depends on a single compelling requirement: Can you bring more money to the customer's party than any other candidate for partnership?

If you "make partner," you can achieve control of the

contributions to costs, revenues, and earnings in the customer's business functions and lines of business that you affect. He will place responsibility for controlling these contributions in your hands, either as a dedicated supplier or a facilities manager of his operations. As his partner, he will count on you—counting dollar by dollar, in the most literal sense—to deliver your contributions "on the money" and on time.

By controlling your contributions according to the proposals you make to your customers, you control the continuity of your business with them. If your contributions slow or falter, your partnerships will be in trouble. Every time you deliver a proposed contribution, you earn the right to propose again. If you lose control of your ability to improve a customer's profits dependably, you will lose your customer.

So what is it that you can actually control? It is not the customer, nor is it the customer's business. You can control only the contributions you make to it.

As a result, PIP control becomes essential for partnering. Your PIPs must be reliable contributors to customer profits. The best way to ensure this is to set up a three-phase process of PIP control:

1. *PIP previews*. These will enable each manager-account representative team to preview the potential proposals in each account's penetration plan, rank them in priority order of their perceived sureness (dollar value and timeliness), and then certify their value before presentation.
2. *PIP reviews*. These will enable each team to review each proposal after its acceptance to warrant its deliverability and to schedule its monitoring and measurement milestones to make certain that its full proposed value is progressively delivered.
3. *PIP overviews*. These will enable each team to meet with its correlate customer team to agree on each PIP's contribution, to log it in their joint database, and to seek follow-on enhancements for it and natural migration opportunities in the near-term future. At each

overview, the partnership's norms for improved customer profits can be updated to keep them current.

Accounts that get out of control are caused by PIP management processes that become uncontrollable, either through
faults in the internal partnering of the supplier's managers
with their representatives or in their external partnerships with
customers. Through PIP management, the questions you need
to ask to know where you stand in account control always have
a forum:

- Are we making the profit contributions we are proposing?
- Are we measuring and monitoring them with our customers?
- Are we keeping up enough "PIP flow" to earn our
  partnership all over again every day?
- Are we maintaining our contributions above the level of
  the industry standard?
- Are we generating a steady state of future leads from
  each completed proposal?
- Are we making our competitors *beat us* in our norms or
  beat it?

Maintaining Professional Accountability

Partnership is a no-nonsense, no-surprises alliance. You must
embrace your customer partner's objectives and be incremental
to their achievement. You must supplement or complement
your partner's strategies so that the two of you pull together,
culturally and operationally. You must protect your partner
against the risks of failing to achieve your incremental contribution to his objectives or failing to achieve them on time. In
short, you must be accountable for your partner's success.

Once your partner agrees on your solution, he shoulders
the major share of risk. He is on the line with his top managers,
who are his lenders—in other words, your funders. He works

with them in a partnership similar to your own with him. It is based on no nonsense and no surprises. Once he has signed off on the loan he receives from his internal bankers, he is mortgaged to them. It is unthinkable to believe that he will not pay them back. It would be a shocking surprise if he did not earn the return on their investment on which he has signed off. Once he partners with you, there is no place for either of you to hide. He is responsible for making your proposal work. You are accountable to him for making sure it does.

Vendors are accountable for making their products work successfully. They can afford to ask only, What can I *sell*? As a consultative seller, you are accountable for making your partner successful. You must ask different questions: What can I *do for* my partner? What can I *do with* my partner that will ensure his success?

Partnering with you should be like taking out an insurance policy. Your partner must be protected by you, enhanced in his ability to make a superior contribution by the added assets you represent. He must be stronger as a lower-cost producer. Or he must be stronger as a market leader. He must know what you are insuring him against—unnecessary costs—and what you are insuring him for—higher-volume sales or increased profits on sales. This is how he will measure your contribution.

In vending, you are in the middle-man position between your customer and your competitors. From both sides you are subject to margin pressure in the form of greater discounts, bigger deals, and free services. When you sell as a consultant, however, your customer partner is in the middle between his supervisory manager, who is his lender and to whom he is responsible, and you, on whom he is dependent to fulfill his responsibility. If you fail him by turning out to be a liability instead of an asset, you put him at risk in his partnership with his own managers. For him, this is the ultimate risk. It is not just your project that is endangered; it is his career.

Your partner has no alternative except to count on you—in other words, to hold you accountable. As a professional consultative seller, you have no choice either. You must perform;

you must deliver; you must be prepared to pay the price of success if you want to collect its rewards. Are you there for your partner? He can never be too sure. Accordingly, you can never provide too much reassurance.

You assure your partner of your accountability by "being there," working with him and his people in high-visibility participation. You assure him by measuring and monitoring your joint progress toward his objectives and taking prompt remedial action if your evaluations indicate you are in danger of going off plan. You assure him by taking advantage of new opportunities as soon as they arise and being prepared for them with an inventory of Profit Improvement Proposals based on multiple what-ifs?

You cannot reassure your partner by telling him not to worry; he is paid to worry. Your assurance must come in the form of setting up an early-warning system to head off worrisome events, having remedies on hand for problems so you can nip them in the bud, and keeping your finger, along with his, on the pulse of your joint projects.

Measuring Your Added Value

Your need to be accountable is dictated by your Box Two partner's need to be consistent. The single most admired trait that Box One managers covet in the men and women who report to them is the consistency of their contributions to profits. Quarter after quarter, year after year, the managers who demonstrate consistency in their ability to "make their plans" are the managers who get the chance to do it again, to do it with greater budgets and even more responsibility, and finally to manage others who will do it for them.

Box One has little patience. Top managers believe that a manager who is going to be consistent is consistent from the start. Flashes in the pan get weeded out early as "brilliant but erratic"—in other words, undependable. From Box One's perspective, Box Two managers must serve an apprenticeship that proves they can maintain a consistent level of performance.

During this time, which can take up to 80 percent of a manager's career, he is developing his personal norms. Over the remaining 20 percent of career time, all the manager must do is to hold onto his norms and manage others to equal or exceed them.

You must manage your own norms as well. This means that you must know the value you add as a partner. If you remain ignorant of your value as a consistent profit improver, the only other contribution you make that your partners will be able to quantify will be your added cost.

Whatever business you are in, you must enter into a second and parallel business in order to measure your partnered value. You must become a tester of your value as well as an implementer and applier of it. To do this, you will need to develop a standardized test and measurement system to assess your value and to install it simultaneously with each major sale. Then you and your partner will have to measure its results at regular, periodic intervals.

You must know what to test for, how often and how to test for it, and how to interpret and apply your findings. There are three rules that should govern your assessment strategy:

1. Never install a product and service system without installing a measurement system to assess it.
2. Sell only the values you can measure.
3. Always measure the values you sell.

Selling and measuring are two parts of a single sale. Unless you measure your value, the basis of your partnerships will be ephemeral. They will be based on how much of a "good guy" you are, which is an implicit invitation to your competitors to devalue you.

If you are forced to undergo a devaluation or reevaluation by a partner, you will learn the hard way what partnership is all about. It is not about faith and trust. It is not about charity. Partnership is about proven value. Only when value cannot be measured and offered as proof does charity come into play.

Your value as a partner is nothing to get starry-eyed about.

It is measured in hard, cold cash: how much of it you contribute, how soon you contribute it, and how sure your partner is that you will contribute it consistently. The worst case is not failing to do these things. It is being able to do them yet not being able to prove what you can do. When that happens, you cannot sell yourself as a partner because you will not be able to put a value on your contribution. You will be unmarketable on the partner market.

8

How to Agree on Partnerable Strategies

A consultant's job can be defined in three ways: Bring back sales, bring back customer information that can lead to sales, and leave behind alliances with top-tier decision makers.

Sometimes a sale will build an alliance. More often, alliances help build sales.

There are four levels on which alliances must be structured in a key customer account. Three of them are in the upper management tier: top managers, financial managers, and function managers. The fourth is the purchasing level, where the traditional adversary relationship must be converted into a more partnerable affiliation.

The objectives of all key account alliances are similar, regardless of the level at which they are to be achieved. Their overriding goal is to ensure customer continuity. Unless key account relationships are continuous, there will be no way to maximize the profit opportunity that a major customer represents. Unless you can keep your key customers, everything else is academic.

Making Mutually Profitable Alliances

Three strategies will help you build lasting alliances: Collaborate, educate, and negotiate.

1. *Collaborate.* In key account situations, it takes two to make every sale. An unpartnered consultant cannot sell within a customer's company. There will be no one to sell *to.* There will be no one to sell *with.* There will be no one to *help sell.* For consultant and collaborator, there must be the same dedication, the same commitment, and the same conviction that a sale will add genuine values to both parties. When a sale is finally made, it should be impossible to tell who made it. This is the test of a true collaboration: The sale is the thing, not the seller.

2. *Educate.* You and your key customers must do more than buy and sell if your relationships are to be continuous. Along with making new dollars, you should both be making new information available to the people on each side who will be collaborating on proposing sales. Not only must you both *earn* as a result of your relationships, you must both *learn* as well. Professional growth and personal growth should attend profit growth.

3. *Negotiate.* The main subject area of the mutual education between collaborators is how to improve profits. This requires continuing back-and-forth dialogue. The flow of input must be unimpeded. The ideal environment will be rich in options— but sparse in negative thinking, put-downs, editorializing, or defensiveness against anything that is "not invented here." Free-swinging relationships where there is a high degree of give-and-take allow you and your customers to avoid losing out on important opportunities. They also allow you to cash in fully on solving the problems that come off the top of the customer's head.

Alliances With Top Managers

By selling as a consultant, you obtain access up and down the entire vertical chain of a customer's organization, perhaps including the chief operating officer, who is usually the president. If you sell to a division or subsidiary of a large customer company, your top ally may be its president. Selling to several divisions or to the corporate management itself will require you to partner at the top company level as well as at top divisional levels.

Customer presidents will join in alliances with key account representatives if, but only if, their self-interest is engaged. At their level, there are three principal interests:

1. *Financial improvement.* Chief operating officers are mainly preoccupied with bottom-line profits. They view their businesses as money machines. For most of their daily routine, they are on the lookout for as many ways as possible to convert investments—their allocation of resources—into superior return. If you can position yourself with them in this context, they can include your system among their investment options.

Presidents focus on returns. Their accountability to various constituencies demands it. Employees, shareholders, directors, and securities analysts all lean on them to produce increased profits. In selling to presidents in a consultative manner, you can help relieve some of this pressure. In your consultative role, you represent an added chance for them to earn new profits.

2. *People improvement.* Although presidents are fixated on returns, they never lose sight of where returns come from. Profits are made by people; they are a president's prime capital resource. If you can help improve the knowledge, competence, and productivity of strategically placed customer people, you can ally yourself as a partner in a major presidential mission.

What can customer people learn from you? You can improve their ability to reduce the costs of their operations so that they will become less of a drain on internal funds, or require a lower investment in their operations. You can also improve their ability to enhance sales revenues. If their abilities are upgraded in these vital areas, their profit contributions can be increased and their productivity stepped up by the amount they add to revenues for each dollar of investment in them.

3. *Operational improvement.* All customer operations are cost centers. By their nature, only a few can ever become profit

centers. If you can bring down a cost center's asset base by streamlining its operations, consolidating functions, eliminating steps in its processes, or reducing its need for labor, energy, or materials, you can create a common interest with customer presidents.

Presidents often ask themselves—and they are often asked by others—"How competitive are we?" By this, they mean many things: How good are our people, our products, our promotion? They also run an ongoing audit of their operations to determine how competitive they are. They call it productivity. It provides a useful index of just how effectively their operations are converting a dollar of investment into a dollar of sales.

When you help presidents improve their functions' productivity, you are assisting them in making their own businesses more competitive; that is, you are joining with them to help maintain their profitability, add to it, or regain it. These are always among the most paramount issues confronting decisions at the top tier.

Vendor sales representatives remain largely unaware of potential interfaces with customer presidents. Even if they have the awareness, they lack the ability to implement it so they can form alliances. They are often obsessed with a desire to "get upstairs." But it is the wrong obsession. The true objective is to be able to form a continuing alliance upstairs so that you can go back again and again—indeed, so that your presence will be regarded as an ongoing added value by customer people at the top.

Because vendors are unable to relate to customer presidents—what would they talk about, their own product?—many of them regard a presidential alliance as a preposterous assumption. In reality, it has a recognizable basis in fact. People at a customer's top tier are immersed every day in selling situations with their president. Everyone from top and middle management levels approaches the president with something to sell: a new business venture or new product idea, an expansion of staff or facilities, or a new market penetration. Top-tier managers approach presidents and their committees in a consultative mode: They request appropriations on the basis of their ability to contribute a superior return.

This is the only way to approach the top, because it is the only way the top approaches investing its funds. When you sell as a consultant, you must replicate the approach that is comfortable to top decision makers. Vendors, however, ask management to buy price performance. Not only is top management unskilled in making this type of commitment, it is also uncomfortable at being asked to play a purchasing role. Appropriately enough, it sends vendors back downstairs.

Alliances With Financial Managers

Customer financial managers, either controllers or financial vice-presidents, share their presidents' criteria for evaluating the desirability of major purchases. They, too, are motivated by return on investment. Forming alliances at their level will require, for the most part, a similar strategy.

Financial managers regard themselves as keepers of the corporate checkbook. In that capacity, they are just as concerned as their top managers about preserving capital. Even more than presidents, though, they focus on what goes out. They tend to be highly cost-conscious, auditing with exactitude the amounts of investment required to achieve a return as well as the size, timing, and certainty of the return itself. As the "point men" for the corporate struggle for funds, they more than anyone else are aware of the horns of the dilemma posed by an investment situation: What if I make the investment? Will a better one come along tomorrow after I am out of funds? What if I don't make the investment? Suppose a better one does not come along?

It is understandable that financial managers are cautious. If they are approached with a vendor's characteristic persuasiveness, their inherent defenses will be heightened. They find a safe haven in numbers—the financial facts of a proposition to buy. Numbers are their words. They speak of "reading" them, letting the numbers "tell" them things, and getting their "message." In order to partner with them, you must talk to them in their own language.

Financial managers are called money managers for good reason. Money is their unit of communication. For them, it talks. It converses with them in terms of its rate of return, its discounted cash flow, and its present value. Financial managers are always in the market for money. They want to invest it, to put it to work for their businesses so that it will earn more money, which in turn will give them more money to invest, and so on. They are the customer's investment managers. To form alliances with them, you will have to provide them with new investment opportunities in the form of profit proposals.

Controllers and directors of customer financial functions never lack for places to put money to work in their businesses. What they do lack, however, is the funds themselves. If you are going to have relevance for them as an ally, it will hardly ever be due to your products or services, unless they can be used in the operations of the financial function itself. Your relevance will depend on the new investment dollars you can produce and how quickly and dependably they can be obtained.

Alliances With Function Managers

Customer business function managers are immersed in the problems of supervising and administering their operations. They live in a world of people problems, productivity problems, manufacturing problems, quality control problems, inventory control problems, sales problems; whatever their function happens to be, it will have several of these problems as a normal consequence of its day-to-day activities. Business function managers always seek relief from their problems. They want their attendant costs removed. They want their opportunities expanded for greater sales revenues and productivity.

As a result, they want to be knowledgeable in three areas:

1. *How to improve their operations.* What options exist for improvement, how they work to deliver improvement,

and what mix of options will provide the optimal results.

2. *When to improve their operations.* What timing is optimal for the introduction of improvements, how they can best be sequenced, and when the payoff on an improvement can be expected.

3. *Where to improve their operations.* What parts of their processes are the best starting points, how they can be improved most cost-effectively, and where an improvement can next be migrated so that its impact can be multiplied.

With these principal concerns in mind, it is easy to understand why approaching functional managers by trying to sell them your product or service is unlikely to make a sale. Nowhere in their areas of concern is a concern for your products. They care only for how products can affect their operations and when and where to implement them. Their functions are the context for judging what fits and what doesn't, what works and what won't, what is a good buy and what isn't.

The vendor sales approach that says, "I want to sell you something" is meaningless when it is directed to a business function manager. It is, literally, out of context; that is, it has no perceived relation to the business function. To say "I would like to work with you" is equally meaningless. The only approach that makes sense is the consultative approach: "I can help improve your operation, both in performance and in profit." This addresses the business function manager's concept of a problem. It also addresses the function manager in your consultative role as profit improver.

Arguing Through Negotiation

Negotiation is the arguing style that partners use. It is designed to make sure that each partner wins something and that neither partner loses everything. If one of the partners comes away without a win, he has not been negotiated with; he has been commandeered. He has been mastered, not partnered.

What is it that each partner in a partnered negotiation must win? Each must win new, improved profits. The customer partner must have his profits improved by coming away with a lowered cost or higher revenues or earnings. The supplier partner must have his profits improved by coming away with a lowered cost of sale and a higher margin.

In vendor selling, "negotiation" centers on price. As soon as a price is proposed, discounting begins. Vendors often mistake this process for negotiation. They call it "negotiating price" when they really mean defending price. Defending price is not negotiation because the supplier cannot win. He can only limit his loss. If his margins are not directly attacked, he will be subjected to other forms of price pressure such as requests for free goods and services, advertising or promotion allowances, free carrying of inventory, and so on.

Because price does not exist in Consultative Selling, partners do not include it in their dialogues. Instead, they negotiate about the yield from the consultative substitute for price, investment. *How much* can it earn? *How soon* can it start to flow? *How sure* can we be—how can we be even surer—that we will receive the "muchness" we have planned as soon as we have planned for it?

These are the three subjects of partnered negotiation. Both partners want to maximize the sureness of their deals together. Without sureness, everything else is fanciful; Profit Improvement Proposals will be fiction, like a midsummer night's dream. Within the constraints that sureness imposes on the partners, how much return can they manage from their investments and how soon can they hold it in their hands?

In your role as a consultative seller, you must always be ready to propose more "muchness" or "soonness." The way you do this is by constant "what-ifing": What if we add this value to our proposal; what effect will we have on return? What if we subtract this value from our proposal? What if we combine these values in one proposal? What effect will that have on our return?

The best partnerships consistently earn the highest returns from their investments. They realize that each of them is making an investment of money, time, and resources and that each must maximize its payoff. As a result, it is not just the consultative partner who proposes and the customer partner who disposes. Both propose to add the maximum value to their mutual proposals. Both what-if each other so that their proposals are true joint ventures. Joint proposals, in which each partner is invested both personally and professionally, are the outcomes of partnered negotiation.

If you are asked how you know you are practicing partnered negotiation, a joint Profit Improvement Proposal is not only your best answer, it is your only answer.

Negotiating Styles for Specific Power Sources

The different needs of consultant and customer determine the negotiation process that bonds their partnership.

The ability to make decisions is solely within the customer's power. The consultant has no comparable power. Your only leverage against a customer's power is the ability to improve customer profits. With this ability, you can influence customer decisions. This means two things. You must know everything that is knowable about how a profit-improving system can be designed to meet customer needs. You must also know everything that is knowable about the customer's power structure.

Power is the ability to make, prevent, or influence a decision. Very few decision makers have that much power. Instead, power is typically limited and fragmented. You must find out who has what type of power. Only then can a Consultative Selling strategy be planned. It will be helpful for you to seek out three power sources:

1. *The power to say yes.* A yes-sayer is your prime partner. If you can identify a yes-sayer's needs and influence

that yes-sayer directly on a one-to-one basis, the maximum opportunity will exist for selling.

2. *The power to say no.* A no-sayer is your prime potential adversary. A no-sayer does not generally have the power to say yes, but may have the power to kill a proposal before it can come to the attention of a yes-sayer. To sell consultatively, you will have to neutralize no-sayers or convert them into allies.

3. *The power to influence the yes-sayers and the no-sayers.* An influencer has only implicit power. But that power can often swing the balance of decision making in your favor. Influencers can be especially important in helping override a no-sayer's objections. Your task is to mobilize an influencer's influence in a way that helps you sell.

How to Deal With Yes-Sayers

Yes-sayers have official power, the power of position. It is usually symbolized by a title that expresses power to compel compliance.

Appeals to a yes-sayer should be based on the projected improvements in profit that your system can contribute to the yes-sayer's operations. There are two supplementary appeals to which yes-sayers are usually responsive. The first is an appeal to maintain the organization's image of efficiency, modernity, and quality in the minds of its customers, competitors, employees, investors, and other constituents. The second is an appeal to the yes-sayer's personal need to manage a significant process improvement, preside over a respected and well-reputed operation, and take prudent risks.

Here is a checklist of appeals to yes-sayers:

- Profit improvement and increased cost-effectiveness
- Improved organizational image for operating efficiency, modern methods, leading-edge technology, and quality
- Compatibility of a system's benefits with personal values such as being on top of things, managing in a progressive fashion, and being a wise evaluator of innovation

How to Deal With No-Sayers

No-sayers often have official power; they may be second in command and report to a yes-sayer. Or they may have a political power base unheralded by a high title. Sometimes they are deliberately encouraged by a yes-sayer to perform a control function by acting as devil's advocates.

No-sayers perceive their roles as saying no. When they are unable to find any reason to say no, they use their favorite word anyway even in giving tacit agreement: "I can find *no* reason not to go ahead." You must communicate with no-sayers in their own terms. They must be deprived of any reason to say no and still be allowed to fully exercise their negative approach.

This means that you will have to demonstrate point by point why there is no reason that your system should not be employed. This may require infinitely detailed selling. The no-sayer may be interested in the system's contribution to improved profit. But an even greater interest may be directed to the bells, whistles, and flags of its composition, to the contribution to cost and effectiveness by each component, and to its competitive assets or liabilities. Risk-taking must be minimized in keeping with a no-sayer's value system that emphasizes caution, conformity, cost reduction, a tight control system, and the development of a high level of confidence before finding no reason not to go ahead.

To meet these needs, you may have to engage in exhaustively detailed multiple presentations. Here is a checklist of appeals to no-sayers:

- Cautious decision making based on fair and full evaluation of measurable facts and figures
- Conformity to standard industry practice
- Demonstrable cost reduction accomplished by new efficiencies or elimination of old inefficiencies
- A tight control system to measure operating cost efficiency and to apply quick remedial action
- Confidence acquired from independent evaluation of

claims, case histories based on customer testimonials, and personal visits to similar installations that are up and running

How to Deal With Influencers

Influencers may have either official or political pull that they apply to decision makers, often swaying them. Influencers are the most difficult power wielders to identify. Many of them are obscure. Since their power takes the form of personal influence, they may not hold high titles. In fact, many influencers are technical experts who function at middle organization levels but whose knowledge is called on by yes-sayers in their decision making.

In addition to the power they are given because of their expertise, influencers may hold political power that yes-sayers can use to feel out and manipulate reaction to their decisions. Holders of social power may also be influential in recommending action to yes-sayers.

Finding the hidden sources of influence in an organization is a difficult assignment. Once identified, they must be dealt with individually on the basis of their power. The influencer who holds expert power in technology, finance, or operations must be approached in technical terms with facts and figures from respected sources. Your company's technical support resources can help. So can case histories, customer testimonials, and demonstration visits to similar system installations.

Political and social power holders must be influenced in terms of their personal values and interpersonal relationships and how the system will affect them. You will also be wise to emphasize how these benefits can be communicated in the most positive manner throughout the organization so that the influencers' images will be enhanced in the eyes of superiors, peers, and the organization at large. No important organization toes can be stepped on. No empires can be invaded or eliminated, nor can entrenched power wielders be displaced. In short, the political and social structure must be preserved.

Here is a checklist of appeals to influencers with a technical power base:

- Facts and figures to bear out claims attested to by respected independent or third-party sources
- Case history documentation
- Customer testimonials
- Personal visits to similar installations

Influencers with a political and social power base can be approached according to this checklist:

- Beneficial effects on interpersonal relations of all people importantly affected, with specific reference to the absence of career threats and maintenance or enhancement of political and official position in the power structure
- Aid in communicating benefits throughout the organization and the community at large

Separating Partners From Nonpartners

Every decision maker can be considered as a fraction. The denominator is always the same: common needs and aspirations. Every numerator, though, is exceptional; numerators are composed of individual differences. In order to penetrate a customer organization, you have to analyze what is individual as well as what is common. This can be done by answering two questions: Who are the decision makers I can partner with? Who are the decision makers I will have difficulty partnering with?

Decision Makers Who Make Good Partners

There are six types of decision makers who have high partnering potential. Figure 8-1 summarizes their principal characteristics and most probable negotiating modes.

Figure 8-1. High-partnering decision makers.

Manager Type	Characteristics	Negotiation Modes
Bureaucrat	Rational, formal, impersonal, disciplined, jealous of rights and prerogatives of office, well-versed in organizational politics	Follows rules; stickler for compliance; more concerned with tasks than with people; logical strategist (but can be a nitpicker); predictable negotiator.
Zealot	Competent loner, impatient, outspoken, a nuisance to bureaucrats, insensitive to others, minimal political skills	Devoted to good of organization; aggressive and domineering negotiator, blunt and direct; totally task-oriented.
Executive	Dominant but not domineering, directive but permits freedom, consultative but not participative, sizes up people well but relates only on a surface level, cordial but at arm's length	Organization-oriented; high task concentration; assertive negotiator; adroit strategist, flexible and resourceful.
Integrator	Egalitarian, supportive, participative, excellent interpersonal skills, a born team builder, a catalyst who is adept at unifying conflicting values	Shares leadership; permits freedom of decisions and delegates authority; welcomes ideas; open and honest negotiator who seeks win-win relationships.
Gamesman	Fast-moving, flexible, upward-moving, impersonal, risk taker, one convinced that winning is everything, innovative, opportunistic but ethical, plays the game fairly but will give nothing away	Wants to win every negotiation; enjoys competition of ideas, jockeying for position and maneuvers of the mind; sharp, skilled, and tough negotiator; can be a win-win strategist.
Autocrat	Paternalistic, patronizing, closed to new ideas that are not invented here, not consultative or participative	Binds people emotionally; rules from position of authority; makes pronouncements of policy; a sharp trader who negotiates on a tit-for-tat basis.

1. *The bureaucrat.* Despite negative connotations of the term, it is generally not difficult to partner a bureaucrat. The bureaucrat is rational and systemized; policies, procedures, and rules govern all actions. Although friendships and jealousies abound among bureaucrats, and while politicking may be a favorite indoor sport, the selling climate is impersonal. Things get done systematically but not speedily. Divergent personalities and individual eccentricities are discouraged. The organization's way of doing things must be followed to the letter. Selling to a bureaucracy depends on understanding its traditional nature and cultivating its key decision makers. It is almost always a long-term process.

2. *The zealot.* Zealots are organizational loners. Although intensely concerned for their organization's welfare, zealots have an apostolic fervor for pet projects, which they always present as being precisely what the organization needs most. Zealots are usually competent. Other people's ideas, however, go largely ignored. Individual and organizational sensitivities are routinely stepped on. You may find zealots overly demanding and sometimes pests. Zealots negotiate by bludgeoning, although they welcome with open arms anyone who can help them attain their objectives. Zealots can be possessive. Since they tend to divide the world into "friends" and "enemies," you must be wary of becoming unduly identified with zealots and their causes.

3. *The executive.* Executives are professional managers, battle-wise, firm-minded, and strong-willed. They get the most out of people by accurately perceiving their strengths and limitations. Executives set a no-nonsense tempo in their organizations. They are sensitive to people but do not get involved with them emotionally. Negotiating with an executive is a straightforward matter of providing demonstrable benefits. An executive looks for incremental values. If they cannot be perceived, negotiation will most likely end promptly.

4. *The integrator.* Integrators are team-building managers. They are easy to negotiate with. Integrators perceive their role not so much as making decisions as managing the decision-

making process by consensus and collaboration. The integrator is a catalyst whose job is to create superior task accomplishment, individual growth and success, mutual respect, and cooperation. Since most of the integrator's decisions are group decisions, you must partner not only with integrators but also with their key group members.

5. *The gamesman.* Gamesmen run on fast tracks. Highly analytic, flexible, fast-moving, competitive, sharp, and aggressive, they love playing the game of business. Their preoccupation is with forming and re-forming winning teams. The consultant must become a team member. Like the executive, the gamesman relates without becoming emotionally involved. Wisely risk-taking, innovative, and strategically keen, gamesmen enjoy jockeying and maneuvering. Since gamesmen respect peers who are shrewd and adroit, they will challenge every negotiation skill that you possess. Yet gamesmen negotiate within the rules and will be cooperative as long as they believe they can win.

6. *The paternalistic autocrat.* Autocrats see their role as all-knowing, somewhat patronizing authority figures who demand personal loyalty from subordinates. Friction and conflict are smoothed over. Autocrats can be kind and considerate, but these traits are likely to vanish instantly if they are antagonized or not offered personal loyalty. On the other hand, if you can be "adopted" by an autocrat, a win-win relationship can develop.

Decision Makers Who Make Difficult Partners

There are six types of decision makers who have low partnering potential. Figure 8-2 summarizes their principal characteristics and most probable negotiating modes.

1. *The Machiavellian.* Machiavellians generally do not let ethics enter their negotiations. Although they can be ethical when it suits their purposes, they are cynical about people. Machiavellians depersonalize others. They concentrate on win-

Figure 8-2. Low-partnering decision makers.

Manager Type	Characteristics	Negotiation Modes
Machiavellian	Self-oriented, shrewd, devious, and calculating, insightful into weaknesses of others, opportunistic, suave and charismatic, can turn in instant from collaboration to aggression	An exploiter of people; cooperates only for selfish interests; totally impersonal negotiator, unmoved by human appeals; will win as inexpensively as possible, but will win at all costs.
Missionary	Smoother of conflict, blender of ideas, must be liked, identifies harmony with acceptance, highly subjective and personal	A seeker of compromise and leveler of ideas to lowest common denominator; negotiates emotionally with personal appeals to agree for his sake.
Exploiter	Arrogant, what's-in-it-for-me attitude, coercive, domineering, rigid, prejudiced, takes advantage of weakness, makes snap judgments unswayed by evidence	Exerts constrictive personal control over negotiation; makes others vulnerable by using pressure and fear to get own way; demands subservience; sees others as obstacles to be overcome.
Climber	Striving, driving, smooth and polished demeanor that masks aggression, opportunistic, without loyalty to others, goes with flow	Excellent politician; uses self-propelling change to call attention to himself; always thinking ahead; self-serving negotiator based on what-will-this-do-for-me?
Conserver	Defends status quo, resists change, favors evolutionary improvement, uses the system skillfully to safeguard personal position and prerogatives	Imposes own sense of order and nonimmediacy on negotiation; slows everything down; preaches traditional values; defensively blocks innovation and undermines agreements before implementation.
Glad-hander	Superficially friendly to new ideas but essentially a nondoer, effusive, socially skilled and politically skillful, superior survival instincts	Overreactive and overstimulated by everything, but impressed by little; promises support but then fades away; endorses only sure things that can do some personal good; never takes risks.

ning regardless of the loss incurred by their adversaries. Emotional considerations mean little. Machiavellians never get emotionally involved while negotiating. They use power, always seeking to augment it, and exploit others when it is necessary. Machiavellians lie plausibly, and they are experts at appearing innocent. They prefer ambiguous and unstructured situations, suspect the motives of others, and have little faith in human nature. Although they resist being influenced, they are superior at influencing. Machiavellians press to get all they can from every relationship. Trade-offs are a distasteful last resort.

2. *The missionary.* Missionaries are opposite to Machiavellians—wholly concerned with people, their feelings and reactions. Good human relations, harmony, and intimacy are their criteria for negotiation; confrontation and conflict are avoided. Missionaries often win popularity contests but less regularly win respect. Their strategies are almost always interpersonal. Negotiation means reaching agreement or delaying it in a pleasant manner. As a result, you may always be uncertain about when an agreement will be finalized. A negative reaction will be communicated as sweetly as a positive one.

3. *The exploitive autocrat.* Exploiters are arrogant, harsh, and vengeful. They demand subservience. Ruling by threats and fear, exploiters assume that consultants are incompetent and must be driven to do an acceptable job. This is McGregor's Theory X manager, distrustful of people in the extreme. Negotiating with exploiters is difficult. You must be ready to encounter exploiters on their own terms: strength for strength, force for force.

4. *The climber.* Climbers ceaselessly seek opportunities for self-advancement. Their loyalty, like that of Machiavellians, is to themselves. They use negotiating situations to propel themselves toward power and status. Climbers use aggressive strategies against the weak, and defensive strategies against those who attempt to constrain them. When blocked, climbers move laterally. Whereas a Machiavellian may be content to be the power behind a throne, climbers insist on being front and center. You must be wary lest climbers use you. Climbers can

also help you, but identification with a climber may invite hostility, particularly from other climbers.

5. *The conserver.* Conservers are hoarding types. They are basically stand-patters and status quo defenders. Anything new disturbs a conserver. Since they have usually gone as far as they are likely to go, conservers are generally jealous of whatever prerogatives they possess. In contrast to the Machiavellian, the climber, and the exploiter, who can become a consultant's helpers and recommenders, conservers are almost always hinderers. They safeguard their positions by throwing obstacles in your way. Sabotage of innovative change is their forte.

6. *The glad-hander.* Glad-handers are marketing personalities. Sociable, infinitely adaptable, extroverted, and superficially friendly, glad-handers are unprincipled. They are incapable of lasting loyalty. They are salable commodities, up for hire to the highest bidder. Yet they are charming and personable, possessing high social skills. You may be taken in at first by glad-handers because of their polished social veneer. But glad-handers do not wear well, especially under pressure. Partnering with glad-handers is a futile endeavor, but they can often be helpful in running interference to reach decision makers.

9

How to Ensure
Partnerable Rewards

You and your support staff are the essential partnering agents in Consultative Selling. Together, you compose a profit-improvement team for each of your customers. You, the consultant, are the leader of the team. You will partner with the customer business function managers whose costs you can reduce and with the managers of the customer's lines of business whose sales can be increased. The minimal resources you need as team leader, and their relationship to you, are shown in Figure 9-1.

Three types of support from within your company will be essential: financial, data, and technical. All supportive team members will play two roles. Internally, within the team, they will coach and counsel you in preparing and presenting Profit Improvement Proposals, as well as implementing them. Externally, they will create partnerships with their correlates in the customer's business—finance to finance, data to data, technical to technical.

Your first act as consultant should be to form your profit-improvement team on a customer-by-customer basis. Your second act is to consult with your customers on the organization of companion teams composed of their own staff support resources. As Figure 9-2 shows, a customer team is built around the decision makers who will be your partners. By melding the two teams, you create your partnership.

Figure 9-1. Consultative profit-improvement team.

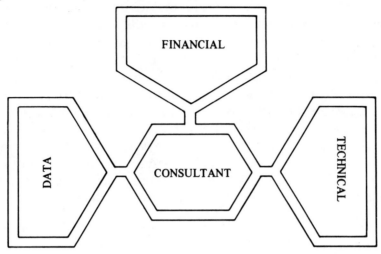

Figure 9-2. Customer profit-improvement team.

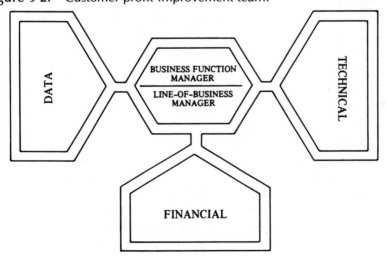

In Figure 9-2 you must be able to see yourself in the box marked "Consultant." This will enable you to be the partner in charge of your team. As such, you will be a playing coach, a manager who also plays a position, charged with setting each profit project's objectives and the most cost-effective strategy for achieving them. As the leader, the manager is surrounded by a minimal group of support players who contribute their specialties on the manager's command. If the supplier's business is small or just making its entrepreneurial entry, the leader and the minimal group of players may be virtually the entire corporate staff. As the supplier's business matures, the number of players will increase and many other specialists will become available for call when the plays they can make need to be incorporated into the game plan.

Partnering in Two Worlds

A supplier team's managing partner manages two kinds of alliances. One is with the partners who make up his own team; the second is with the customer's team. Fairly or not, the customer will tend to evaluate the caliber of the supplier's resources through its manager. He will also tend to evaluate the manager's company as a whole in the same way. Are these our kind of people? the customer will ask. Do they share our objectives? Can they implement? Will they be able to work smoothly with our people, gain their acceptance as full working partners, or will they prove disruptive and unproductive? When all is said and done, what will they have brought to the party—anything that we could not have done for ourselves or done better in partnership with others?

If there are to be affirmative answers to these asked and unasked questions, the supplier's managing partner will be largely responsible for them. The manager's self-conduct, and the way his project team is staffed, structured, and deployed, will be the main determinants.

These expectations require every consultative managing partner to be a remarkable person—remarkable in the literal sense of being worthy of remark. Four qualities are most often associated with remarkability:

1. *Empathy*. The ability to commit to the customer's profit objectives as if they were the manager's own.
2. *Drive*. The power to direct the supplier's resources against the customer's objectives in a true alliance of equals.
3. *Ability to share*. The need to reveal, and to have the customer team reveal, information vital to the partnership's success in a consistently open manner.
4. *Kingmaking ability*. The satisfaction of realizing personal ambitions and rewards by making the customer manager a king without rivalry, envy, or jealousy.

Sales representatives who make the best consultative sellers conform to a small number of common observable traits and characteristics. For men, being an only child or the oldest child seems to help. So does having a strong mother figure who induces a sense of responsibility at an early age. It is a bonus if she is a good teacher and a caring, consistent guide. For women, it appears helpful to have had to replace an older brother in carrying on the role model of a strong successful father. A woman ought to need approval from authority figures and be able to be persistent without nagging. It is also a predisposing factor if she has had to understand the world from the angular perception that is uniquely afforded to left-handed people.

Consultative sellers have responsibilities different from those of vendors. While their risks are not necessarily greater, their potential for bringing in significant rewards far surpasses a vendor's potential. It is only fair that consultants have a different basis for compensation. There are two main types of plans for incenting and rewarding them.

Plan One: Compensation Based on the Customer's Investment

There are two kinds of investment-based compensation plans. The "dumb" kind is entirely volume-driven, a lot of which the seller should probably have walked away from because he could not get the margins he needs to support his growth. The "smart" kind of plan is margin-driven. It is based on gross profits rather than actual dollar sales. The seller receives compensation, both commission and bonus, only on sales whose gross margin exceeds a hurdle number.

Plan Two: Compensation Based on the Customer's Return

Plan Two is partner-driven. Its purpose is to encourage the total commitment of the seller and his team to the customer. The plan rewards them for the same result that governs the customer's reward—the size of customer profits. This bases compensation not on what a customer spends but on what he earns from his expenditure, thereby bonding the seller to the customer's success. Behind this plan is the assumption that the purpose of partnership is not simply to sell; its true objective is helping a customer grow his business. Under the plan, both partners are rewarded as co-contributors to customer growth.

Plan Two removes all doubt from a customer's mind that his supplier is committed to their mutual success. It makes clear that supplier self-interest and the customer's interest are one and the same, giving the concept of partnership its ultimate reality.

Acknowledging the Rights of Partnership

You have the right to expect customer partners to acknowledge two responsibilities: to share access with you and your team and to share data. Your partners have rights as well. They are known as the "rights of partnership."

1. *Cure me.* Get things done, respond to my needs. Produce results fast because I have more needs.
2. *Talk my language.* Speak to me in profit-improvement

language. Show me that you identify with me and that you know my business.

3. *Don't surprise me.* Install a control system so I can be comfortable. Let me share in evaluating our work together.

4. *Level with me.* Tell it like it is. Criticize constructively. Tell me what's wrong, but let me know what's right, too.

5. *Get into my business.* Become a part of my team. Be around, ask questions. Don't be disruptive.

6. *Be reasonable.* Give a premium value in return for your premium price; superior profit makes price justifiable.

7. *Be competent.* Give me the best you have. Be a real professional.

8. *Teach me.* While you sell or perform, teach me how. Share your experience and expertise with me and my people.

9. *Take leadership.* Get out in front of my problems. Roll up your sleeves and get your hands dirty in my operations.

10. *Worry for me.* Think hard about my problems. Let me know what you think even without my asking. Give me immediate access to you when I am worried; be available. Put my needs first.

11. *Innovate.* Give me something that's better than you give anyone else. Make me preeminent; make me stand out. Apply yourself in a way that transcends normal boundaries. Offer me options.

12. *Be faithful.* Keep our business confidential. Make your relationship with me personal; don't pass me along to others.

13. *Be motivated.* Show desire to achieve our objectives. Be genuinely interested in my problems. Don't leave a single stone unturned in looking for solutions.

14. *Be flexible.* Compromise with me once in a while but don't give in on what you know is vital.

15. *Treat me like a person, not just a client.* Treat me like an equal; deal with me one-to-one. Don't talk down to

me. Throw in a few little extras every now and then. Advise me on closely related matters even if you're not being paid for them.

There is a good reason why there are so many rights of partnership for your customer. No matter how well you perform as a consultant, your customer always carries the burden of unequal risk. This is his counterpoint to unequal reward: He will gain more than you will, but he has much more to lose. You may have several customers to partner, but he has only one—his Box One manager, who cannot be disappointed. While you cannot balance the inherent inequality of your mutual risk, you can reduce it to its minimum by being faithful to the rights of partnership. In carrying them out, one commitment is paramount. You must be unwavering in your dedication to the customer's objectives. Both of you must work for them because both of you will succeed or fail with them.

Preventing Departnering

Departnering occurs when two conditions are met. An alliance that is incomplete or unfulfilled within itself is vulnerable. Then, when a more promising partner appears, it succumbs. Many troubled partnerships linger on because both partners temporarily subscribe to the belief that "You know what you've got, but you don't know what you're going to get." As soon as one partner believes that what he or she is going to get is better, the partnership will end. In Consultative Selling, this means that the customer will also be lost.

Because markets are tight communities, the loss of one key customer inevitably raises doubts, creates assumptions, and fosters anxieties that threaten the stability of other key customer relations. A domino effect can follow. The loss of one key account opens the door to competitors who, even if they have not been a cause of departnering, will be anxious to take advantage of its effects.

What leaves a partnership incomplete or causes it to be

unfulfilled? There are two major factors that predispose to eventual departnering: divergence of objective and inequality of risk.

1. *Divergent objective.* Partnerships rest on a common objective. Both partners must have the same result in mind before they partner, see the same result as being achieved while they are partnering, and be able to look back at the accomplishment of their result as a consequence of the partnership.

Consultative partnerships are known by the objective the partners have in common. The eternal question of what partners see in each other is easily answered: They want to achieve the same objective and they perceive the partnership as the optimal means of reaching it. This is their hidden agenda.

A consultative partnership is not a one-on-one situation. More accurately, it is a two-for-one relationship. Both partners share one objective—to improve the customer's profit. Unless this is accomplished, the consultant's objective of improving profit on sales will be impossible. For this reason, the customer's objective must come first for both of them. It is not philanthropy but enlightened self-interest that makes it so.

When objectives diverge, or simply appear to be going off in different directions or losing conviction, alliances atomize. A customer partner may acquire the belief that the consultant is more interested in self-promotion to the customer's top tier than in merchandising the partnership. The customer partner may feel used, demeaned, and taken unfair advantage of by helping the consultant develop business elsewhere, either inside or outside the organization. The consultant, on the other hand, may believe many of the same things about the customer partner. Whether such perceptions are true or not, they will have an erosive effect on the partnership.

Restating objectives and recommitting to them are essential elements in keeping partnerships on track. Objectives should be brought up for discussion at frequent intervals; this should be at the consultant's initiative. A good time to introduce them is when progress is being measured against them. At some of these checkpoints, the original objective may have to be downgraded. Perhaps it can be increased. In either event, keeping objectives current will perpetuate the values that both partners are working for.

2. *Unequal risk.* Partnerships are a means of reducing risk. Two parties can share the load, divide the responsibility, and parcel out the components of the risk that would otherwise be borne by one or left undone. Although risk can be reduced, it can never be eliminated. It must be shared as equally as possible if the partnership is to be preserved. Otherwise, one partner may accuse the other of "putting your hand out farther than your neck."

No matter how hard consultants try to bring into balance the risks inherent in improving customer profits, customers will always be left with the major exposure. They are exposed on their own behalf. They are exposed on their recommendation of the consultant. And they are exposed to their topmost tier of management. In any business situation, there can be no riskier combination of exposures.

Once customers commit themselves to work with a consultant to improve their profit, they must be successful. It is no wonder that they will be ultrasensitive to their own inherent risk and to the support they receive from you. They have a lot on the line.

Because customers bear the major share of partnership risk, you must take on the major share of reducing the risk and providing the reassurance that it has been reduced. There is no way you can have the same degree of risk as your customers do, but you can provide a greater degree of risk calculation and limitation. This must be your equalizer.

In Consultative Selling, you have several equalizing tools at your disposal. One is to be thorough in your fact-finding and in putting together your database on customer problems and opportunities. Another is to be diligent in obtaining feedback from your customers about their needs. A third is to manage your progress review sessions with care so that deviations from objectives are caught early and corrected, so that strategies can be revised to meet changed conditions, and so that opportunities can be capitalized when they are still fully available.

If you fail to keep a partnership's objective unified or its risks from being equalized, the result is fairly easy to forecast. Your customer will seek a new partner who meets two qualifications: a lowered risk and a more harmonious objective. In the process, the customer may find a partner who can deliver higher objectives. These may come in the form of greater profits, a more optimal mix, or a broader range of options to choose from. Improved objectives may also come from a quicker flow of profits, with new monies coming on stream sooner or existing costs being reduced faster.

When objectives fall out of harmony, and the inequality of risk becomes uncomfortably oppressive, the emergence of a new partner is inevitable. It invariably is a lengthy process for customers to decide to open up a search, evaluate candidates, and then hold their breath while they make a selection. But it always seems sudden to the consultants on whom the boom is lowered. Their lack of awareness is the proof of the pudding about how far the partners have drifted apart.

The history of terminated partnerships is filled with surprised consultants. "Why, it was only yesterday" they say, "that he was telling me what a great guy I was—how much we had been through together and how he would always be indebted to me." If it was not "only yesterday," it was "only last week" or "last month." The epitaph is generally the same: how great it *was*. Meanwhile, for the new partner, the benediction is how great it is *going to be*.

Appendixes

Appendix A

How Customer Managers Budget Capital Expenditures

Throughout business, there is an established method used by almost all customers to plan and evaluate their capital expenditures: what they should buy, when they should buy it, and what other options they should consider for investing their funds. The method is known as the capital budgeting process. This process contains four steps: (1) project planning, (2) evaluation and decision making, (3) control and audit of cash commitments, (4) postaudit evaluating and reporting of results.

The first step in capital budgeting proceeds on the assumption that a company has a formal long-range plan or, at the least, the proposed project fits into the mainstream of the corporation's interest. Implicit in a proposal is a forecast of markets, revenues, costs, expenses, profit. These aspects of capital budgeting are the most important, most time-consuming, most critical phase, and largely outside of the area of expertise of the financial executive. A major project generally affects marketing, engineering, manufacturing, and finance.

Adapted from "The Capital Budgeting Process," originally published as a monograph by Coopers & Lybrand, 1973, and reprinted by permission. Content and commentary have been contributed by Mack Hanan and J. P. Donis.

The uncertainties surrounding a long-range forecast are often great enough to throw doubt on the effectiveness of the entire decision-making process. Probability analysis of success/ failure becomes important in view of the uncertainties. A relatively simple approach to evaluating uncertainty is discussed later. However, sophisticated probability analysis and computer simulation can be beneficial in giving credibility to major long-range projections in the face of great uncertainty. Unless this phase of capital budgeting is made reliable and meaningful, the decision-making phase simply becomes an exercise in arithmetic.

The second stage, project evaluation and decision-making methods, has received major attention in accounting and financial publications. There is general agreement that the time-adjusted cash-flow methods (net present value and discounted cash flow [DCF] rate of return) are most meaningful guides to the investment decision; however, there is still place for cash payback analysis in appraising the financial risks inherent in a projection. These methods will be examined and brought into perspective for use in the proposed model. Within certain limits, and they can be identified, these measures will give the best tools for appraising proposals. They do not produce the magic "go, no-go" answer. They give management guidance. No matter what quantitative guidelines are developed, qualitative factors will be important in the final decision; the personal judgments and preferences of the project sponsor and management cannot be discounted.

The third step, control and audit of cash, is the simplest step in the budgeting process once the source of funds has been determined and committed. After approval, the project should be treated as any other budgeted item, with payment schedules determined and variances reported and explained. Major overspending can impair the validity of the investment decision, and even invalidate the entire process.

A caution is appropriate at this point. When a proposal calls for a specific investment, it is implicit that no more than that amount will be spent. Overspending of any significant amount cannot be permitted. Similarly, a project sponsor should not come back the next year for additional funds because he underestimated his original request. When either of these events occurs, it becomes necessary to refigure the entire project on the total cash outlay. Unfortunately, at this point the company is already irrevocably committed to the project, and the new calculations are after the fact.

The fourth step, post-audit evaluating and reporting of results of investment, is a task that everyone agrees needs doing, but is rarely done. As will be reviewed below, capital investments are projected on an incremental basis, on a cash basis, and on an internal rate of return basis over the life of the investment. Regular financial records and reports are on an annual basis, on an accrual basis, or on a rate of return by individual years. A major problem is that many projects become an integral part of a larger, existing investment and the new project cannot be separated from the existing one. The post audit of the incremental segment may become obscure or meaningless. As a result, many incremental investments cannot be appraised against objectives, for example, a large rate of return. The large projected incremental rate of return may become diluted when merged with a larger investment. There may be general disappointment because the new investment results have not lived up to forecasts and, yet, the projected earnings and cash flow of the incremental investment may be right on target. New criteria for post audit may have to be determined to affect post audit for many projects at the time the original projections are made so that management knows how it will measure results against plan. One criterion may be cash flow. Another criterion may be the development of pro forma statements comparing financial income before and after the additional investment, that is, a financial model. The main point is that good budgeting calls for comparisons of projections and results, and though the project evaluation criteria may not be susceptible to audit in many cases, it should not preclude the establishment of other criteria for postaudit purposes at the time the original projection is made. The use of pro forma statements indicating total results as well as impact on earnings per share before and after the investment may be the appropriate basis for appraisal of the additional investment.

Principles of Capital Investment Analysis

This section describes the specific concepts used to evaluate major capital expenditure projects and programs within the scope of the capital budgeting process. The underlying concepts and methods used are examined to bring into focus the economic consequences of a capital expenditure.

When a capital expenditure is proposed, the project must be evaluated and the economic consequences of the commitment of funds determined before referring it to a budget committee for review or to management for approval. How are the economic consequences described best? This is done in two steps:

First, set up the project into a standard economic model that can be used for all projects no matter how dissimilar to each other they may be.

$$\text{Benefits} - \text{costs} = \text{cash flow}$$

To describe the formula in accounting terminology:

Benefits: Projected cash revenue from sales and other sources
Costs: Nonrecurring cash outlays for assets, plus recurring operating expenses
Cash flow: Net income after taxes plus noncash charges for such items as depreciation

Thus, if the model were stated in a conventional accounting form it would appear as:

Add: Cash revenues projected (benefits)
Less: Cash investment outlay and cash expenses (costs)
Total: Cash flow

The "benefits less costs" model is usually developed within the framework of the company's accounts and supported with prescribed supplementary schedules that show the basis of the projection.

It should be apparent that in setting up an economic model, the conventional accrual accounting concept, net income after taxes, has been abandoned. The established criterion is cash flow—net income after tax plus noncash charges.

Second, adjust the cash flow into relevant financial terms. The cash flow projected for each year over the life of the proposal has to be translated into financial terms that are valid; that is, translate the annual dollar cash flows to a common dollar value in a base year. This concept must not be confused with attempts to adjust for changes in the purchasing power of the dollar.

The calculations assume no significant erosion in the purchasing power of the dollar. Should this occur, the time-adjusted common dollar concept may require adjustments for the diminished real value (purchasing power) of future dollar payments. The common dollar value concept used in capital budgeting adjusts for time value only. This is achieved through the development of the concept of discounting and present value that will be examined in the next section. An examination of how a simple two-step model is developed will illustrate the rationale of this approach.

In the first step we set up the economic model: Benefits minus costs equals cash flow. To complete this model, we need to identify in detail all economic benefits and costs associated with the project. Benefits typically take the form of sales revenues and other income. Costs normally include nonrecurring outlays for fixed assets, investments in working capital, and recurring outlays for payrolls, materials, and expenses.

For each element of benefits and costs that the project involves, we forecast the amount of change for each year. How far ahead do we forecast? For as long as the expenditure decision will continue to have effects: that is, for as long as they generate costs and significant benefits. Forecasts are made for each year of the project's life; we call the year of decision "year 0," the next year "year 1," and so on. When the decision's effects extend so far into the future that estimates are very conjectural, the model stops forecasting at a "planning horizon" (ten to fifteen years), far enough in the future to establish clearly whether the basis for the decision is a correct one.

We apply a single economic concept in forecasting costs: opportunity cost. The opportunity cost of a resource (asset) is what the company loses from not using it in an alternative way or exchanging it for another asset. For example, if cash has earning power of 15 percent after taxes, we speak of the cash as having an opportunity cost of 15 percent. Whenever an asset is acquired for a cash payment, the opportunity cost is, of course, the cash given up to acquire it. It is harder to establish the opportunity cost of committing assets already owned or controlled. If owned land committed to a project would otherwise be sold, the opportunity cost is the aftertax proceeds from the sale. The opportunity cost of using productive equipment, transportation vehicles, or plant facilities is the incremental profit lost because these resources are unavailable for other purposes. If the alternative to using owned facilities is idleness, the opportunity cost is zero. Although opportunity costs are difficult to identify and measure, they must be considered if we are to describe the economic consequences of a decision as accurately as possible. An understanding of this concept of opportunity cost is probably the most critical to this economic analysis and is generally quite foreign to the manager.

At the end of the first step, we have an economic model for the project's life showing forecast cash flows for each year. In the second step we convert the results into financial terms that are meaningful for decision making. We must take into account the one measurable financial effect of an investment decision left out in step 1: time. Dollars shown in different years of the model cannot be compared since time makes them of dissimilar value. We clearly recognize that if we have an opportunity to invest funds and earn 15 percent a year and we have a choice of receiving $1,000 today or a year from now, we will take the $1,000 today, so that it can be invested and earn $150. On this basis $1,000 available a year from now is worth less than $1,000 today. It is this adjustment for time that is required to make cash flows in different years comparable; that is, discounting.

This time value of funds available for investment is known as the opportunity cost of capital. This should not be confused with the cost of raising capital—debt or equity—or with the company's average earnings rate. Like the opportunity cost of any resource, the opportunity cost of capital is what it will cost the company to use capital for an investment project in terms of what this capital could earn elsewhere.

The opportunity cost of capital is alternatively referred to as the minimum acceptable rate of interest, the marginal rate of interest, the minimum rate of return, the marginal rate of return, and the cost of capital. Whatever the term used, and they are used loosely and interchangeably, it reflects the rate the corporation decides it can be reasonably sure of getting by using the money in another way. It is developed through the joint efforts of management, who identifies relevant opportunities, and the controller, who translates management's judgment into a marginal rate.

Another simple economic concept must be introduced: incremental cost, sometimes called differential cost or marginal cost. By definition, it is the change in cost (or revenue) that results from a decision to expand or contract an operation. It is the difference in total cost. In performing the capital budgeting analysis, we deal with incremental costs (revenues) only. Sunk or existing costs are not relevant to the evaluation and decision.

Throughout this study all references to costs and revenues are on an incremental basis.

Rationale of Discounting and Present Value

Discounting is a technique used to find the value today or "present value" of money paid or received in the future. This value is found from the following formula:

Future dollar amount × discount factor = present value

The discount factor depends on the opportunity cost of capital expressed as an interest rate and a time period. Figure A-1 illustrates how discount factors are usually displayed. The discount factors are grouped according to the annual interest rate, expressed as the present value of $1.00, and then listed according to the year the amount comes due. The table should be read this way: When a dollar earns 10 percent per year uniformly over time, a dollar received at the end of the second year is equivalent to (worth) about 86 cents today.

Arithmetic and Concept of Present Value

To adjust the model's results for the time element, we "discount" both the positive and negative cash flow forecasts for each period at the company's marginal rate of return to determine their present value. This discounting process makes the forecasts equivalent in time. We can now add the present values of these cash flow forecasts to derive the net present value (NPV). The NPV is a meaningful measure of the economic consequences of an investment decision since it measures all benefits and all costs, including the opportunity cost of capital.

When the net present value of a proposed investment is determined, we are ready to decide whether it should be accepted. This is done by comparing it to the economic consequences of doing nothing or of accepting an alternative. The

Figure A-1.   Present value of $1 at 10 percent.

Year	Present Value (Today's Value)
0–1	$0.9516
1–2	0.8611
2–3	0.7791
3–4	0.7050
4–5	0.6379

general rule followed in comparing alternative projects is to choose the course of action that results in the highest net present value.

Figure A-2 illustrates the cash flow forecasts and time-value calculations for a typical proposal to invest in a new project when the alternative is to do nothing, that is, maintain liquidity rather than invest. A discount rate of 10 percent is assumed as the company's marginal rate.

The proposed project will cost $500 in year 0, and cash operating expenses thereafter will be $200 per year for four years. Assume the cash benefits will be positive but decline over the four years and total $1,450. The cash flow is negative in the year of investment but positive in the succeeding years, and there is a net positive cash flow over the life of the project of $150 before discounting. When the cash flow forecasts are made equivalent in time by multiplying each annual cash flow by the present value of the dollar for each period, the time-adjusted cash flow is determined, and the net present value is found to be $60. The proposed investment is better than doing nothing because all costs are covered, the 10 percent opportunity cost of the corporation's funds is realized, and in addition, the project will yield an additional $60 return.

Figure A-2 indicates an NPV of $60. Depending on the cash flow and/or the discount rate, the NPV could be negative or zero. If the NPV were zero, the company would have

Figure A-2. Arithmetic of determining net present value (NPV).

Year	Benefits	Costs	Cash Flow	PV of $1 @ 10%	Discounted Cash Flow
0	$ 0	$ (500)	$(500)	1.000	$(500)
0–1	425	(200)	225	.952	214
1–2	425	(200)	225	.861	194
2–3	350	(200)	150	.779	117
3–4	250	(200)	50	.705	35
TOTAL	$1,450	$(1,300)	$ 150		$ 60 NPV

projected earnings exactly equal to its marginal rate of 10 percent. If there were no alternative projects, and the only alternative were to do nothing, the project with the NPV of zero would be accepted because the company would earn its marginal rate of return. (As explained later, the NPV of zero would yield the discounted cash flow rate of return, that is, 10 percent.) If the NPV were negative because of an inadequate cash flow, assuming the same 10 percent marginal rate required by management, it would mean the project would earn less than 10 percent, and it would be rejected.

There are a number of evaluation methods that are employed in capital budgeting; however, after critical examination of all methods, only the arithmetic developed in this simple model will be used to examine three methods used in evaluating capital budget proposals: (1) cash payback, (2) net present value, (3) discounted cash flow (DCF) rate of return—sometimes referred to as the "internal rate of return."

Cash payback is commonly used by businessmen evaluating investment opportunities, but it does not measure rate of return. It measures only the length of time it takes to recover the cash outlay for the investment. It indicates cash at risk. In our model there are costs of $500 committed in year 0. To determine payback we merely add the unadjusted cash flow for each year and determine how many years it takes to get the outlay back. In the first two years $450 is recovered, and by the end of the third year $600 is recovered. By interpolation we find cash recovery to be approximately 2.3 years. It is obvious that the rational businessman does not commit a large sum of money just to recover it. He expects a rate of return commensurate with the risks and his alternative use of his funds in alternative investments (opportunity cost). In our example the calculation of payback reveals a relatively short exposure of funds and cash flow continuing beyond the payback period. It is interesting information in overall project evaluation, but not conclusive. Our model will automatically throw off payback as a by-product as we calculate the crucial time-adjusted net present value of the investment and DCF rate of return.

A version of cash payback that has come on the scene

recently to aid in the evaluation of ultra-high-risk investments is described as the cash bailout method. This approach takes into account not only the annual cash flow as shown in Figure A-2, but also the estimated liquidation value of the assets at the end of each year. If the liquidation value of a highly specialized project is zero, then cash payback and cash bailout are the same. But if it is assumed in our example that the liquidation value of the investment at the end of year 1 will be $275, the cash bailout would be one year (cash flow $225 plus liquidation value $275 = $500 original cash commitment).

We consider net present value as described a valid basis for determining the economic consequence of an investment decision. Many business economists use it as their sole criterion for the go, no-go decision for investment. We recognize this method as paramount throughout our analysis but prefer using it in conjunction with other measures rather than as the sole criterion.

Arithmetic and Concept of Discounted Cash Flow Rate of Return

We are now ready to examine the concept of DCF-ROR. It is completely different from the return on investment (ROI) commonly used by businessmen. The conventional ROI is computed for an accounting period, generally on the accrual book figure; investment is taken at original cost although it is sometimes taken at half original cost; no adjustment is made for time value when looked at in the long run.

We are talking about a very different rate of return on investment: The discounted cash flow rate of return is the interest rate that discounts a project's net cash flow to zero present value. Let us expand Figure A-2, which shows a $60 NPV when a discount factor of 10 percent is used, to Figure A-3, which adds a discount factor of 18 percent and yields a $0 NPV.

The DCF rate of return is 18 percent. By definition the

Figure A-3. Arithmetic of determining DCF rate of return.

Year	Cash Flow	PV of $1 @ 10%	Discounted Cash Flow	PV of $1 @ 18%	Discounted Cash Flow
0	$(500)	1.000	$(500)	1.000	$(500)
0–1	225	.952	214	.915	206
1–2	225	.861	194	.764	172
2–3	150	.779	117	.639	96
3–4	50	.705	35	.533	26
TOTAL	$ 150		$ 60 NPV		$ 0 NPV

DCF-ROR is the rate of return on the project determined by finding the interest rate at which the sum of the stream of aftertax cash flows, discounted to present worth, equals the cost of the project. Or, stated another way, the rate of return is the maximum constant rate of interest the project could pay on the investment and break even. How was the 18 percent determined? By trial and error.

There are many analysts who use the net present value method exclusively; some use the DCF rate of return; others use the two methods to complement each other. Using NPV, positive or negative dollar values are determined with the cost of capital as the benchmark. Excess dollar PV is evaluated and a judgment is made. The DCF rate of return approach ignores the cost of capital in the calculation and determines what the rate of return is on the total cash flow. The result of this approach on our example is to convert the $60 NPV into a percentage. It works out to 8 percent on top of the 10 percent that had been calculated for the NPV. Many businessmen prefer working with the single figure of 18 percent for evaluating a project against a known cost of capital, instead of describing a project as having an NPV of $60 over the cost of capital. It is our feeling that the two methods complement each other, and under certain circumstances one may give a better picture than the other.

Let us reexamine this special DCF rate of return to see

what distinguishes it from the conventional rate of return. It is time-adjusted to base year 0, so that all dollars are on a common denominator basis; it is calculated absolutely on a cash flow basis; the investment is a definite time-adjusted value; the rate of return is determined at a single average rate over the total life of the investment. Certain implications of this statement require explanation.

The DCF rate of return is calculated over the full life of the project, and the accountant's yearly ROI cannot be used to test the success/failure of the new investment. If the planned life of a project is ten years, and if it can be segregated from other facets of the operation, the DCF rate of return has meaning only when the full economic life of the project is completed. However, in this case it is possible to monitor results on a year-to-year basis by examining the actual dollar cash flow and comparing it with the projected cash flow. (Observe the assumption that the project is separate and distinct from the rest of the operation.)

The one thing that disturbs businessmen most with the DCF rate of return concept is the underlying mathematical assumption that all cash flows are reinvested immediately and constantly at the same rate as that which yields a net present value of 0. In our example in Figure A-3, 18 percent was used as the discount factor as a constant. Another case could just as easily have indicated a 35 percent rate of return, with the implicit assumption that the cash flow was reinvested at 35 percent. But if the earning experience indicates a cost of capital of 10 percent, how can we reconcile the assumption that we can continue to earn 35 percent on the incremental flow?

Even though a company's average earnings reflect a cost of capital of 10 percent, the demands on incremental new investment may well have to be 18 to 35 percent to compensate for investments that fail to realize projected earnings. Opportunities to invest at 18 percent or 35 percent are not inconsistent with the average earnings of 10 percent. However, if it is felt that a projected rate of return of 18 percent, in our example, is a once-in-a-lifetime windfall and no new opportunities can be found to exceed the average 10 percent rate, then we are in trouble with our DCF rate of return concept. The reinvestment rate will not stand up. In this situation we have to combine both net present value and rate of return to explain the situation in this way: The 10 percent rate of return of this project covers the opportunity cost of money and throws off an additional $60 cash flow. If other projects of the same magnitude can be found so that the total cash flow generated can be reinvested at the same rate, there would actually be a rate of return on the project of 18 percent (the DCF rate of return). The lack of other good investment opportunities is a constraint on the full earning capacity of the project.

We have examined three methods of evaluating investment opportunities. Cash payback evaluates money at risk. Present value measures the ability to cover the opportunity cost of an investment on a time-adjusted basis of money and indicates by a net present value whether the project under consideration will yield a "profit" or a "loss." The discounted cash flow rate of return is an extension of the net present value concept and translates it into a single rate of return that when compared with the opportunity cost of capital gives a valid basis for evaluation.

Since NPV and DCF-ROR concepts take into account the opportunity cost of capital through the discounting technique, it may be stated as a principle that all projects under consideration where this opportunity cost is covered should be accepted. This proposition is both theoretically and practically sound, but three factors need to be considered: How do you determine the minimum acceptable rate of return (the opportunity cost of capital) to select the proper discounting factor? How can you assume no constraints on the supply of capital so that all worthwhile projects can be accepted? How do you take risk into account when examining indicated results? These questions will be examined in the next three sections.

Minimum Acceptable Rate of Return—Cost of Capital

How do you determine the minimum acceptable rate of return (cost of capital) used in discounting? Again a caution: The cost of capital concept used here is not the same as the cost of borrowing. This is probably the most critical factor in the evaluation process. It is a unique and personal rate to each company. There is no guide to look to in other companies. Two companies looking at a potential investment, say an acquisition, may place two completely different values on it. To Company A, with a minimum required rate of return of 10 percent, the investment could be attractive, while to Company B, with a required rate of return of 25 percent, the investment would be totally unacceptable. The difference is centered in the cost of capital to each company, its opportunity rate of return—the rate that can be expected on alternative investments having similar risk characteristics. An example of the arithmetic involved in reaching this conclusion can be seen when we modify Figure A-2 to include both a 10 percent and 25 percent discount factor and assume that both companies A and B are the potential sole bidders for an investment with an asked price of $500 and a net cash flow of $150 (see Figure A-4).

The investment is very attractive to Company A but completely unacceptable to Company B—it would realize less than its objective of 25 percent. If Company A were in a position to know the cost of capital of Company B, it would know that Company B would not bid at all for this investment. Company A would know that it would be the sole bidder.

Figure A-4.   Comparison of NPV using 10 percent and 25 percent discount factors.

| | | (A) | | (B) | |
Year	Cash Flow	PV of $1 @ 10%	Discounted Cash Flow	PV of $1 @ 25%	Discounted Cash Flow
0	$(500)	1.000	$(500)	1.000	$(500)
1	225	.952	214	.885	199
2	225	.861	194	.689	155
3	150	.779	117	.537	81
4	50	.705	35	.418	21
TOTAL	$ 150		$ 60 NPV		$ (44) NPV

If a company has successfully earned 25 percent on the capital employed in it, an investment opportunity to be attractive would have to yield at least that rate. The 25 percent represents the cost of capital to that company and an investment opportunity offering only 15 percent would be rejected. A second company with a 10 percent cost of capital would find the same 15 percent potential attractive and accept it. Thus the same 15 percent opportunity investment is attractive to one and unattractive to the other. Both companies analyzing the identical situation reach different logical conclusions.

Cost of capital in our anlaysis is *always* considered to be the combined cost of equity capital and permanent debt. We evaluate economic success/failure of a project without regard to how it is financed. Yet we know that money available for investment is basically derived from two sources: debt with its built-in tax saving so that its cost is half the market price for money (assuming a 50 percent tax rate), and equity, which has as its cost the opportunity cost of capital of the owners.

It is necessary at times to break down the combined cost of capital into its components of cost of debt capital and cost of equity capital to put it in terms understandable to the businessman who commonly measures results in terms of return on equity. To illustrate this cost of capital concept, we will assume that a corporation is owned by a single individual whose investment objectives are clearly defined. The total capitalization of the company is $100, made up of $30 permanent debt capital and $70 owner's equity capital. If preferred stock was outstanding at a fixed cost, it would be treated the same as debt. The aftertax interest rate of the debt money is 2.75 percent. The aftertax dollar return on the combined debt and equity capital of $100 under various operations would appear as shown in Figure A-5.

To restate these dollars as rates of return on the investment of $100, $30 debt, and $70 equity, the percentage return on capital would be as shown in Figure A-6.

If the company has been earning an average of $10 on the total investment of $100, and the cost of debt is $.825, the earning on owner's equity is $9.175. Stated as a rate of return,

Figure A-5.   Aftertax dollar income on investment of $100.

Income on Total Investment (Before Interest)	$30 Debt × 2.75% Cost of Debt Capital	$70 Equity Income on Owner's Equity
$ 8.00	$0.825	$ 7.175
9.00	0.825	8.175
10.00	0.825	9.175
11.00	0.825	10.175
12.00	0.825	11.175

Figure A-6.   Aftertax rate of return on investment of $100.

Rate of Return	Cost of Debt Capital	Rate of Return on Owner's Equity
8%	2.75% ($0.825 ÷ $30)	10.25% ($7.175 ÷ $70)
9	2.75	11.68
10	2.75	13.11
11	2.75	14.54
12	2.75	15.96

the $10 earned on $100 is 10 percent return on the total investment (combined cost of capital), and because of the leverage built into the capital structure with long-term debt, the $9.175 earning on equity yields a return on equity of 13.11 percent (cost of equity capital). When there is a 30 percent debt structure and the average cost of debt is 2.75 percent after taxes, we can readily convert return on total investment into return on equity by reading our table. It is quite simple to create similar tables for each company and its debt/equity ratio (e.g., with a 50/50 ratio and debt cost of 2.75 percent, a 10 percent return on total investment yields a 17.45 percent return on equity capital). If there is the opportunity to invest the company funds in alternative situations or reinvest the funds in the business and continue to earn at least 10 percent on the combined debt/equity funds, we would describe this as the opportunity cost of capital. This is the critical rate used in discounting: The discount rate used to determine net present value and the benchmark for comparing discounted cash flow rate of return are based solely on the combined cost of capital. The rate of return to the stockholders can be derived and compared with their opportunity cost, that is, their ability to invest their funds elsewhere and earn at least the same rate.

Having decided that return on combined capital is the appropriate criterion for evaluating investment, it is necessary to follow through with this concept when projecting revenues, expenses, and net benefits. If we are to determine net benefits (cash flow) on combined capital, all charges against that capital must be excluded from the expense projections. If interest were charged in the projection, there would be double charging. This is not a novel method; it is used regularly by investment analysts who often determine income before interest on funded debt and before taxes.

As noted, interest expense on long-term debt is not included in the current expense projection because it is covered in the combined cost of capital computation. The interest on short-term debt may be a direct charge to operations if its cost is not in the invested capital base. If the major financing is handled through equity and long-term debt and the short-term borrowing is negligible, this method is acceptable. However, many companies live off their current borrowings and the short-term debt is actually part of the permanent capital. The true leverage would then be reflected in the return on owner's equity when compared with the return on total investment. Once more, a caution: When this method is used, the interest expense on current debt must be excluded from projected costs.

The capital funds of a company constitute a pool of monies for all projects. A particular borrowing rate for additional capital, at a time when a new project is introduced, becomes part of the pool of funds and it becomes part of the average cost of debt relative to total capital. With the addition of new funds, it is the average long-run cost that is significant and not the current borrowing rate. The relevant comparison of the projected rate of return is with the average rate for the pool of funds and not the cost of the incremental funds.

In the case of the individual ownership of a corporation, the historical earnings rate can be determined along these lines and a cost of capital for opportunity cost evaluation can become a valid benchmark. If average earnings rise from $10 to $12, there is a new cost of capital, a new cutoff rate for accepting or rejecting projects. This does not imply constantly changing cutoff rates. Some years will be more profitable than other years, some years the cost of debt may be higher or lower than other years, but the earnings of the company are the average adjusted for trend. There is not much logic in setting a cutoff rate at 25 percent when the average is 10 percent, just because there was once an isolated year that had unusually high earnings. Many good projects would be rejected because of an unrealistically high cutoff point. The reference point should be actual accomplishment and reasonable expectations, not wishful thinking.

When the assumption of the individual ownership of a corporation is abandoned in favor of a public corporation with a myriad of stockholders, the cost of capital concept gets into difficulty. It is difficult enough postulating the opportunity cost of capital for even a small family, but when we try to postulate the investment objectives of all the different stockholders in a large corporation, things become really complex. One stockholder wants cash dividends; another wants growth and reinvestment of earnings; still another wants fast capital appreciation. The opportunity cost of capital to each owner goes undetermined. We are not going to grapple with the problem of cost of capital for publicly owned corporations here, because it is a problem that is extremely complex and can be highly theoretical. It is sufficient to note that some large public corporations have been able to develop a cost of capital for their capital budgeting evaluations with some success. Other public corporations have conceded that they cannot develop a cost of capital for all their stockholders and have resorted to a cutoff rate commensurate with their earnings experience. This latter approach violates the opportunity cost concept for the individual owners, but practical considerations have made it necessary to recognize the opportunity cost of the corporation as a person with only minor reference to the real persons who own it.

Constraints on Supply of Capital

How can you assume no constraints on supply of capital for investment? Theoretically, if the earnings of a corporation are great enough and growing fast enough, there is no limit on the amount of debt and equity available. In good basic economic theory, companies should continue their capital expansion until the marginal cost of capital equals its marginal revenue; or stated simply, it is worth borrowing as long as the earnings exceed the cost by even a small amount. The principal limit on debt to the successful corporation becomes the ability of the mangement to live with it—at what point do the managers start losing sleep because they are so heavily leveraged? However, there are other practical constraints. General business conditions and the state of optimism/pessimism may lead to a limit on the amount of capital a management is willing to commit. There are constraints on the amount of risk a management may be willing to assume; there may be limits on the ability of an organization to handle certain ventures. There are probably other contraints, real and imaginary. In the budgeting process all categories of investments must be classified and weighed. The degree of risk willing to be assumed, and a commensurate return, is something that exists only in the mind of individual managements.

There is no nice formula that can set this. Depending on the management's philosophy, and assuming constraints on availability of capital, the selection may result in the rejection of good safe investments promising a 10 percent return, and acceptance of promotional investments with a great risk promising a 60 percent return, and vice versa. Another constraint mentioned is organization, which may be the decisive factor in choosing between an investment that will make few demands on management and one that will make great demands on management. The latter may offer a superior projected return, yet it may be rejected, reluctantly, because management does not have confidence in its ability to cope with it even though the indicated economic rewards are greater. The practical problems of project selections are varied and complex. While the techniques discussed are hardly the *sine qua non,* they do lend objectivity and direction.

Describing Risk and Uncertainty

How do you account for risk in evaluating the net present value or DCF rate of return? A more accurate term is uncertainty, but risk and uncertainty tend to be used interchangeably by businessmen. The technical difference between the two terms is found in the ability to determine probability of future outcome. Risk, with respect to outcome, implies that future events can be determined within a range of known probabilities, while uncertainty implies that probabilities of outcome cannot be established. Not all proposals have exactly the same element of risk. One investment risk category, the outlay of funds to introduce labor-saving equipment, can be evaluated quite accurately; the projected benefits may be almost a certainty.

Management could even decide to accept all such proposals where indicated NPV exceeds the combined cost of capital. Another category of risk may be the introduction of new product lines. The difference in uncertainty between the two categories is obvious. There probably would be no blanket acceptance of proposals for new products at the cost of capital cutoff rate.

The discount factor remains constant no matter what the risk. The recognition of the different risk categories results in a subjective evaluation of the uncertainties of the venture and a markup on the cost of capital for the go, no-go decision. For example, with a cost of capital of 10 percent, a proposal is made to invest in replacement equipment. There is a modest NPV, little uncertainty. All such proposals would be segregated and acted upon and probably accepted. The second situation, introducing a completely new line or lines whose success is highly uncertain and producing a modest positive NPV, would hardly be acceptable. All such risky proposals would be segregated and judged individually within this special group. To compensate for the uncertainty, a minimum acceptable cutoff rate may be two or three times the cost of capital rate. Average success/failure may actually fall to the 10 percent average cost of capital to the company.

The determination of the projected rate of return on an investment from the NPV can be arrived at by raising the discount rate until the NPV is zero. This is the DCF rate of return, which is the projected average return on the investment. If such a rate came to 18 percent against a cost of capital of 10 percent, it is still left to the judgment of management whether the additional 8 percent rate of return is adequate to cover the uncertainty of successs/failure. This is how risk is usually evaluated—purely subjectively.

There are more exact and sophisticated methods that we will describe. Risk implies probabilities of success/failure. The fact that the project evaluation method we describe here is quite precise and yields a definite answer must not blind us to the reality that decisions are always made in the face of uncertainty. The rate of return description of a project's economic consequences is a single, uncertain prediction of projected revenues and expenses. We cannot ever completely remove this uncertainty. The best we can do is to describe the probable range and intensity of uncertainty involved and the economic consequences of forecasting errors. Next, we briefly discuss three methods that have been found helpful in performing this work.

Sensitivity Analysis

Sensitivity analysis seeks to determine how much a project's net present value or DCF rate of return will be affected (its "sensitivity") when a single factor, or specific group of factors, changes by a given amount. Let's say that for a given project we have been able to predict the volume of product sales with relative certainty, but the price forecast remains very doubtful. To make a sensitivity analysis, we would repeat the evaluation using different prices; this would show how much the NPV changes with each price change.

When used with discretion, the results of sensitivity analyses are helpful in estimating the economic consequences of specific forecasting errors. As a minimum requirement, each project evaluation should describe the effect of a wrong forecast in the factor or factors judged most uncertain. However, with analysis of this type we are measuring the effect of change of a single factor or group of factors while all other factors in the projection are held constant. When other components of the projection change, and they are ignored, the new answers may have serious limitations. For example, to change projected prices but to hold volume and costs constant may be unrealistic. We become "practical" at this point and settle for simple sensitivity analysis and get rough answers, because manually reworking the model to reflect all possible changes in the figures to determine new cash flows becomes an almost impossible task. In this area computer programs really become significant. Hundreds of single factors can be tested against all other factors and the arithmetic can be worked accurately in minutes instead of in weeks.

Probability Adjustment

Probability is the preferred method of organizing estimates of both the range and intensity of uncertainty for the decision maker. In using this method the decision maker computes a reasonable range of possible outcomes for the economic model from very unfavorable to very favorable. From them, it is possible to estimate the probability that each will occur. If the unfavorable outcome seems more likely than the favorable one, the project is probably unwise, and vice versa.

An example of probability analysis after the initial projection has been made can be prepared as a test of its validity. No one can forecast with complete confidence and certainty the annual cash flows resulting from projected volume, prices, or even costs. The probability of achievement can be examined by preparing a table of possible deviations from the forecast. Assuming the initial annual cash flows had been projected at $10,000, a reappraisal by management might indicate the following possible results:

> 5 chances in 100 annual cash flow will be $14,000
> 25 chances in 100 annual cash flow will be $12,000
> 45 chances in 100 annual cash flow will be $10,000
> 20 chances in 100 annual cash flow will be $ 8,000
> 5 chances in 100 annual cash flow will be $ 0

It is apparent that the projected $10,000 annual cash flow has been reassessed as being the most probable, and there is also an indication of a 30 percent chance that it will be exceeded. However, there is a 20 percent chance that it will be less, and a 5 percent chance that it will fail completely.

There is no precise formula for testing the validity of the judgments that lead to predictions of chances of success/failure. They are based upon subjective judgments of experienced and responsible executives. If this type of analysis does nothing more than force an orderly reappraisal of a project, it will serve its purpose. In this example, the conclusion may be that the $10,000 annual cash flow forecast looks reasonable and the initial projection would be allowed to stand. If, on the other hand, the probabilities of achieving less than the $10,000 had been greater, it would probably lead to a write-down of the cash flows.

The introduction of probability analysis also opens the way to very sophisticated statistical analysis of projected results. Computer programs have been developed that measure probabilities of success/failure of the principal factors making up the projection (volume, prices, costs), and it is possible to determine projected results by taking into account any combination of favorable and unfavorable events. The DCF rate of return is then stated as rates over a range of probabilities. This approach may be extremely beneficial in evaluating major projects, but one must bear in mind that the mathematics is still based on human judgments of chances of success/failure.

Decision Tree Analysis

Some large projects present a wide variety of alternatives with varying degrees of uncertainty. In such cases it may be helpful to clarify the choices, risks, cash flows, and information needs involved by developing a decision tree analysis. This analysis does not require any new measurements. The physical act of preparing a decision tree can, however, force the recognition of alternatives and possible ramifications of a decision that otherwise might not be seen. A simple decision tree is shown in Figure A-7.

The choice confronting the project sponsor in this analysis is to build a small plant or a large plant. He must evaluate the probabilities of high demand or low demand and the consequences of each with the alternative plants. If a small plant is

Figure A-7. Decision tree.

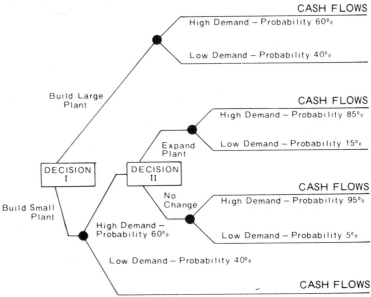

built and volume develops, a second decision becomes critical: Expand or don't expand. The evaluation of these alternatives and the calculation of their economic consequences is facilitated when constructed along these lines.

Project Evaluation

Evaluating components of an investment program for a company is complex at any time. There are many categories of investment: (1) revenue-producing projects, (2) supporting facilities projects, (3) supporting services projects, (4) cost-savings projects, and (5) last but hardly least, in this era of air and water pollution control, investment required by public authority that will yield no return. Each must be evaluated to determine its incremental consequence.

When a project is isolated from the rest of the operation, evaluation is relatively clear. But sometimes a planned major investment embraces several auxiliary projects which, evaluated by themselves, are not very meaningful. When this occurs, it is necessary to construct a master model that includes all of the projects. Some of the auxiliary projects may not come into being for several years after the main investment is made, and may or may not produce a new positive cash flow. The master model in simple form may take on the appearance shown in Figure A-8 if individual projects of the types (a), (b), (c) above are assumed (the figures do not add up—only format is demonstrated).

If the three projects are interrelated, they should be pro-

Figure A-8. Master project.

Project	NPV	0	1	2	3	4	5	. . .	15
(a)	100	(30)	(2)	14	14	13	13		40
(b)	40	—	—	(15)	5	5	5		20
(c)	(26)	—	(2)	(2)	(4)	(4)	(4)		(10)
TOTAL	114	(30)	(4)	(3)	15	14	14		(50)

jected as a single entity. In our example, (a) is assumed to be a major facility that to be successful needs (b) added in three years as supporting facilities; (b) would have no basis for existence if (a) were not created. Project (c) may possibly be identified as a new computer/information system that will produce only costs, but would not exist if (a) and (b) were not created. All costs and all benefits for all corollary investments need to be projected as far into the future as possible to get a true evaluation. Investment evaluations that are made of a project with all the certainty of a DCF percentage can be grossly misleading if the supporting investment of satellites is not taken into account. Actually, these are not separate investments. There is only one—Project abc. The evaluation has to be of the new single entity. The post audit can be of only the conglomerate single entity (abc).

Projects of the cost-savings category are generally easiest to identify and evaluate. There are relatively clear-cut choices: Invest $40,000 today for new labor-saving machines that will reduce labor costs $12,000 per year; the machines will last eight years, and quality of performance will be unchanged. Determine the NPV and/or DCF rate of return and accept/reject. Such investment opportunities constantly arise, but it is almost impossible to project them as part of a master project. As a result, such investments are evaluated as isolated investment opportunities that may occur in three years, or eight years, or never. When they occur, if of major proportions, they affect the potential return on the total investment.

A cost-incurring project, such as spend $100,000 to prevent air pollution or be closed up, is one of the few black-and-white decisions a manager faces. Ideally it would be expensed. It may have to be capitalized and written off and in addition have annual related operating expenses. This nondiscretionary investment falls into the same general category as support project. The cash flow is always negative and must be included as an integral part of the master investment. A large enough commitment may sharply reduce the original projection and a revision may be necessary.

Selecting Among Projects

On the basis of the techniques for evaluating planned capital investment, it is now possible to move to the methods of selecting among projects. As noted above, in theory, selecting among projects is easy. Invest in anything that when discounted at the appropriate marginal rate will yield a positive NPV. Practically, for many reasons, there are constraints on capital in the minds of most managers. Let us look at the project selection problems that are involved for projects under consideration in a particular risk category when there is a limit on capital.

We have selected the NPV method as the best approach to analyze proposed projects of varying lives. Comparing projects under the DCF-ROR method can be misleading because of the different life factor and the reinvestment factor inherent in each ROR. Excess NPV avoids this difficulty. When the various projects are converted into a profitability index, selection is further facilitated. The profitability index is the ratio of the NPV to investment. For example:

$$\frac{\text{Present value of expected benefits}}{\text{Investment}} = \frac{\$132,000}{\$100,000} = 1.32$$

In selecting projects when a limit is imposed upon the amount available for investment, we look for the combination that will maximize combined net present value without exceeding the imposed limit. We know that we have reached this goal when we can no longer increase the combined net present value by substituting one project for another and still satisfy the constraint.

A way to achieve a satisfactory combination of projects is through trial and error. As a guide we can use the profitability index (see Figure A-9). However, such ratios are not foolproof. This is illustrated where there are three possible projects requiring a total of $1,500 in initial outlays, but where $1,000 is the imposed limit.

The choice is between investment in A + C (cash outlay

Figure A-9.   Profitability index.

Project	Net Present Value	÷	Investment: Cash Outlay	=	Profit-ability Index
A	$1.000		$600		1.67
B	700		500		1.40
C	500		400		1.25

$1,000) or investment in B + C (cash outlay $900). Since A + C have a combined greater NPV than B + C ($1,500 vs. $1,200), A + C should be selected even though C's ratio (1.25) is less than B's ratio (1.40). Such differences are common. The profitability index must always be used judiciously. When there are numerous projects to choose among, the combining process becomes more difficult.

Summary

After examining working concepts of what is involved in the capital budgeting process, the reader can appreciate the many problems that must be resolved when attempting to be "objective" and "scientific" in his capital commitments. The first step is planning the new investment. This is critical. Investments with long life expectancy are wrapped in a shroud of uncertainty, yet plans and projections based on intuition and a minimum of facts are often made with an aplomb that gives the impression of certainty. Hard conclusions and decisions are often reached on the basis of very soft facts. The recognition of uncertainty and its proper evaluation is probably the most important step in the analysis of an investment. Yet this is the area where we often become "practical" because the task is so difficult both in gathering the necessary data and in evaluating them. If all the sophisticated measures of evaluating uncertainty are attempted manually, the paperwork literally becomes overwhelming and it becomes advisable to turn to computer programs for help with the mathematics.

The use of the computer is accepted practice in the capital budgeting procedure. The description of the manual methods of computation already described, and those that follow in the model, assume an aura of certainty. Every attempt is made to approximate the greatest probability of certainty, yet the calculations that evolve from a single measure must be evaluated in the light of uncertainty. The computer programs based upon sensitivity analysis, decision tree analysis, and probability analysis that have been mentioned can now extend our computational abilities.

A program based on a technique known as "Monte Carlo Simulation" makes possible the "simulation" of future events by sampling values from our estimates under favorable and unfavorable circumstances and making all necessary cash flow calculations by random chance. This is an important step forward in the sophisticated handling of uncertainty on the basis of the principles we have very briefly examined. Suffice it to state at this juncture that where computational speed and accuracy are beneficial, computer programs based upon sound theory and principles exist or are being developed. Our primer has recited the principles on which programs have been developed and can be employed advantageously in many situations.

After the development of a plan on an incremental basis, we spent a good deal of time developing and examining recommended criteria for evaluating projected investments. A simple two-step model was developed. The first step, with three elements, is applicable in all situations:

Benefits less costs = cash flow

This is the basis for preparing all projections. The next step is to adjust the cash flow to eliminate time differences. All cash flows are adjusted to year 0, which becomes the common denominator for evaluations. The adjustment is made by discounting future values to present values. The mechanics of discounting are not difficult to master but the determination of a discount factor is. The discount factor is the interest rate that equates with the company's combined cost of capital. This is a relatively new concept and should not be confused with the traditional cost of borrowing. Cost of capital is the rate earned on the combined capital of equity holders plus the permanent debt used as part of the capital of the company. This simple explanation stands up for the company with a sole owner who can evaluate the rate of return with his own opportunity cost of capital. When a public corporation becomes involved, the calculation of equity cost of capital could become extremely complex if an attempt were made to take into account the opportunity costs of the various stockholders. For our examination we have simplified the problem by recognizing a combined cost of capital where opportunity costs can be determined. This rate becomes the discount value and is used for discounting.

When proposed investment benefits are discounted at a rate consistent with cost of capital, we have a net present value that tells us that the project will yield more or less than the cost of capital. This rate becomes our cutoff rate when we consider whether to accept or reject. Many analysts use this NPV as the sole criterion for evaluation of the project. We recognize the importance of NPV but carry it a step further to discounted cash flow rate of return (DCF-ROR), because the latter changes the excess NPV dollars to a single percentage rate of return that is often easier to comprehend. These two measuring devices that are time-adjusted through the discounting methodology are teamed up with several other criteria to bring the maximum information to bear on the analysis. The most prominent of these is cash payback, which is introduced to reflect money at risk only, and not a rate of return. All these calculations were built on judgments by responsible executives. The final calculations are presented to a budget committee for its appraisal of the facts. The validity of the mathematics used in the projection and final evaluation are dependent on the skill, objectivity, and integrity of the people making the multitude of subjective judgments that are needed at many stages in the development of the projection.

When an NPV or DCF-ROR is determined for a project, and if the company's alternative to investment is to do nothing, the choice is clear. When the choice of capital commitment is among several projects and there is a limit on the amount of capital available for investment, we have chosen to compare projects using NPV rather than DCF-ROR. We are not committed to saying NPV is better than DCF-ROR in all situations, or vice versa. Each has features that work better in some situations.

We recognize the need to control authorized cash expenditures once a commitment is made. Projections of NPV or rate of return are made. If cash expenditures exceed estimates, the projected benefits are meaningless. Practically, this has been a pitfall for many good capital budgeting procedures. If large overexpenditures are made, a new projection should be prepared; however, this only yields a new rate of return after the fact. By that time we are merely generating statistics.

Postaudit of investment is difficult. It is often neglected. If a plan of postaudit is not determined and agreed upon at the time a commitment is to be made, the probabilities are there won't be one or a postaudit will be attempted and it may not be satisfactory. As all investments are projected on an incremental basis, and the results are usually part of a larger investment, there is an inability to sort out the results of the incremental portion and identify its NPV or DCF-ROR. It is not fair to management, and it is poor budgeting procedure, to establish a value upon which important decisions are made and then announce you cannot compare the results with the budget. NPV and DCF-ROR indicate expected results over the complete life of the investment, but there is a desire and need to appraise results on an annual basis. For those investments that can be identified apart from other investments, the postaudit can be in the form of tests of cash flow and adjusted financial statements. When the investment becomes an integral part of existing investments, the incremental portion cannot be identified and plans must be made to postaudit on the basis of the new combined investment. This will involve the preparation of a "master" investment projection at the time the incremental investment is planned. A financial model should be prepared, combined cash flows can be computed if desired, and a postaudit can be performed for the master investment. It is important that this step be taken or failure of the postaudit is almost a certainty.

Appendix B

How Customer Managers Make Lease-vs.-Buy Decisions

Ownership may be effected through outright purchase without indebtedness, through financed purchase, or, for all practical purposes, through a long-term lease. In an outright purchase, the buyer has full rights of ownership. Where the buyer obtains financing (before or after the purchase), his ownership is diminished by the limitations on his control of the asset. For example, in an installment purchase, the buyer's right to sell may be restricted by the lender's lien. In a long-term lease, the lessee lacks not only the right to sell but also all of the asset's residual rights except for any purchase options available.

Short-term leasing is an alternative to the above forms of ownership. Here, the lessee is freed of almost all the risks of ownership, including obsolescence and maintenance, but the amount of the rental naturally reflects these advantages. In choosing between some form of ownership (as described above) on the one hand and short-term leasing on the other, management is faced with such *operational* considerations as

Adapted from "Leasing vs. Buying," originally published in *The Lybrand Journal*, Fall 1972, and reprinted by permission of Coopers & Lybrand. Content and commentary have been contributed by Mack Hanan and J. P. Donis.

maintenance, risk of obsolescence, and the degree of control desired. If ownership is selected, a further decision—this one involving essentially *financial* considerations—is necessary with regard to the form of ownership. It is with this second, basically more complex, decision that this article is concerned. The focus will be specifically on the choice between outright purchase and long-term lease as a form of ownership.

Outright Purchase vs. Long-Term Lease

The decision to buy or lease can be made only after a systematic evaluation of the relevant factors. The evaluation must be carried out in two stages: First, the advantages and disadvantages of purchase or lease must be considered, and, second, the cash flows under both alternatives must be compared.

Figure B-1 shows the principal advantages and disadvantages of leasing from both the lessor's and lessee's standpoint. This listing is only a guide. For both parties, the relative significance of the advantages and disadvantages depends on many factors. Major determinants are a company's size, financial position, and tax status. For example, to a heavily leveraged public company, the disadvantage of having to record additional debt may be considerable, even critical; the disadvantage may be insignificant to a privately held concern.

Analysis of Cash Flows

A cash flow analysis enables the potential lessee to contrast his cash position under both buying and leasing. This is essentially a capital budgeting procedure, and the method of developing and comparing cash flows should conform to the company's capital budgeting policies and practices. There are several comparison criteria in current use, among which the three commonest are rate of return, discounted cash flow, and net cash position.

(Text continues on page 280)

Figure B-1. Leasing advantages and disadvantages.

Lessee Advantages

• *One hundred percent financing of the cost of the property (the lease is based on the full cost) on terms that may be individually tailored to the lessee.*

• *Possible avoidance of existing loan indenture restrictions on new debt financing.* Free of these restrictions, the lessee may be able to increase his base, as lease obligations are generally not reflected on the balance sheet, although the lease obligation will probably require foot-note disclosure in the financial statements. (It should be noted, however, that a number of the more recent loan indentures restrict lease commit-ments.)

• *General allowability of rental deductions for the term of the lease, without problems or disputes about the property's depreciable life.*

• *Possibly higher net book income during the earlier years of the basic lease term than under outright ownership.* Rental payments in the lease's earlier years are generally lower than the combined interest expense and depreciation (even on the straight-line method) that a corporate property owner would otherwise have charged in the income statement.

• *Potential reduction in state and city franchise and income taxes.* The property factor, which is generally one of the three factors in the allocation formula, is reduced.

• *Full deductibility of rent payment.* This is true notwithstanding the fact that the rent is partially based on the cost of the land.

Lessee Disadvantages

• *Loss of residual rights to the property upon the lease's termination.* When the lessee has full residual rights, the transaction cannot be a true lease; instead, it is a form of financing. In a true lease, the lessee may have the right to purchase or renew, but the exercise of these options requires payments to the lessor after the full cost of the property has been amortized.

• *Rentals greater than comparable debt service.* Since the lessor generally borrows funds with which to buy the asset to be leased, the rent is based on the lessor's debt service plus a profit factor. This amount may exceed the debt service that the lessee would have had to pay had he purchased the property.

• *Loss of operating and financing flexibility.* If an asset were owned outright and a new, improved model became available, the owner could sell or exchange the old model for the new one. This may not be possible under a lease. Moreover, if interest rates decreased, the lessee would have to continue paying at the old rate, whereas the owner of the asset could refinance his debt at a lower rate.

• *Loss of tax benefits from accelerated depreciation and high interest deductions in early years.* These benefits would produce a temporary cash saving if the property were purchased instead of leased.

Lessor Advantages

• *Higher rate of return than on investment in straight debt.* To compensate for risk and lack of marketability, the lessor can charge the lessee a higher effective rate—particularly after considering the lessor's tax benefits—than the lessor could obtain by lending the cost of the property at the market rate.

• *The lessor has the leased asset as security.* Should the lessee have financial trouble, the lessor can reclaim a specific asset instead of having to take his place with the general creditors.

• *Retention of the property's residual value upon the lease's termination.* The asset's cost is amortized over the basic lease term. If, upon the lease's expiration, the lessee abandons the property, the lessor can sell it. If the lessee renews or purchases, the proceeds to the lessor represent substantially all profit.

Lessor Disadvantages

• *Dependence upon lessee's ability to maintain payments on a timely basis.*

• *Vulnerability to unpredictable changes in the tax law that (1) reduce tax benefits and related cash flow or (2) significantly extend depreciable life.* The latter measure would lessen the projected return upon which the lessor based his investment.

• *Probable negative aftertax cash flow in later years.* As the lease progresses, an increasing percentage of the rent goes toward nondeductible amortization of the principal. Both the interest and depreciation deductions (under the accelerated method) decline as the lease progresses.

• *Potentially large tax on disposition of asset imposed by the Internal Revenue Code's depreciation recapture provisions.*

1. *Outright purchase.* The cash outflows in an outright purchase are the initial purchase price or, assuming the asset is purchased with borrowed funds, as is almost always the case, the subsequent principal and interest on the loan. There will also be operating expenses, such as maintenance and insurance, but these items are excluded from the comparison because they will be the same under both purchase and leasing, assuming a net lease. The charge for depreciation is a noncash item. Cash inflows are the amount of the loan, the tax benefit from the yearly interest and depreciation, and the salvage value, if any.

2. *Leasing.* The lessee's cash flows are easier to define than the buyer's. The lessee pays a yearly rental, which is fully deductible. The lessee will thus have level annual outflows offset by the related tax benefit over the lease period. Salvage or residual value does not enter the picture because the lessee generally has no right of ownership in the asset. Figure B-2 is a comparison of cash flows developed under both buying and leasing.

3. *Comparing the cash flows.* Once the annual cash flows from outright purchase and leasing have been developed, the next step is to contrast the flows by an accepted method (such as discounted cash flow) to determine which alternative gives the greater cash benefit or yield. In so doing, some consideration must be given to the effects of changes in the assumptions adopted. Examples could include a lengthening by the IRS of the depreciation period or a change in interest rates. In this manner, a series of contingencies could be introduced into the analysis, as follows: Assume a ten-year life and a borrowing at 10 percent. If outright purchase is better by x dollars, then:

- A two-year increase in depreciable life reduces the benefit of outright purchase to $(x-y)$ dollars.
- An upward change in interest rate reduces the benefit of outright purchase to $(x-z)$ dollars.

Probabilities could be assigned to the contingencies, for example: that the depreciable life could be extended by two

Figure B-2. Buying vs. leasing: a comparison of cash flows.

	Buy								Lease			
Period	Debt Service[a]	Principal Repayment	Interest Payment	Depreci-ation[b]	Interest Plus Depreci-ation	Tax Benefit at 50 Percent	Aftertax Cash Cost	Cumula-tive Aftertax Cash cost	Rental[c]	Tax Benefit at 50 Percent	Aftertax Cash Cost	Cumula-tive Aftertax Cash Cost
1	$ 11,507	$ 3,614	$ 7,893	$ 12,500	$ 20,393	$10,197	$ 1,310	$ 1,310	$ 10,990	$ 5,495	$ 5,495	$ 5,495
2	11,507	3,912	7,595	11,667	19,262	9,631	1,876	3,186	10,990	5,495	5,495	10,990
3	11,507	4,234	7,273	10,833	18,106	9,053	2,454	5,640	10,990	5,495	5,495	16,485
4	11,507	4,583	6,924	10,000	16,924	8,462	3,045	8,685	10,990	5,495	5,495	21,980
5	11,507	4,961	6,546	9,167	15,713	7,856	3,651	12,336	10,990	5,495	5,495	27,475
6	11,507	5,370	6,137	8,333	14,470	7,235	4,272	16,608	10,990	5,495	5,495	32,970
7	11,507	5,813	5,694	7,500	13,194	6,597	4,910	21,518	10,990	5,495	5,495	38,465
8	11,507	6,292	5,215	6,667	11,882	5,941	5,566	27,084	10,990	5,495	5,495	43,960
9	11,507	6,810	4,697	5,833	10,530	5,265	5,242	33,326	10,990	5,495	5,495	49,455
10	11,507	7,372	4,135	5,000	9,135	4,567	6,940	40,266	10,990	5,495	5,495	54,950
11	11,507	7,979	3,528	4,167	7,695	3,848	7,659	47,925	10,990	5,495	5,495	60,445
12	11,507	8,637	2,870	3,333	6,203	3,101	8,406	56,331	10,990	5,495	5,495	65,940
13	11,507	9,349	2,158	2,500	4,658	2,329	9,178	65,509	10,990	5,495	5,495	71,435
14	11,507	10,120	1,387	1,667	3,054	1,527	9,980	75,489	10,990	5,495	5,495	76,930
15	11,507	10,954	553	833	1,386	693	10,814	86,303	10,990	5,495	5,495	82,425
	$172,605	$100,000	$72,605	$100,000	$172,605	$86,302[d]	$86,303		$164,850	$82,425	$82,425[e]	

NOTES

(a) $100,000 of debt borrowed at 8%. The debt service, payable quarterly in arrears, will be sufficient to amortize the loan fully over 15 years. (b) Asset cost of $100,000 will be depreciated over 15 years using the sum-of-the-years' method. It was assumed that the asset had no salvage value. (c) Rental on a 15-year lease will be payable quarterly in arrears. The rental was based on an interest factor of 7¼%. It was assumed that the lessee's credit would require 8% interest. Since the lessor retains the depreciation benefits of the asset, he can charge a rent based on 7¼% even though he has financed the acquisition at 8%. (d) Present worth of $86,302 cost of buying, at 8%, is $41,198. (e) Present worth of $82,425 cost of leasing, at 8%, is $47,034.

COMMENT ON NOTES 9(d) and (e): When comparing the cumulative aftertax cash costs, buying is the more expensive alternative by about $4,000. However, present-valuing the annual outflows results in buying's being the most economical alternative by approximately $6,000.

years, 30 percent; or that interest rates could rise by one half a percentage point, 10 percent. Once the contingencies have been quantified, an overall probability of achieving the expected saving can then be calculated.

It must be stressed that the rate of return—the product of the cash-flow analysis—is not the exclusive or even, in some cases, the main determinant in deciding whether to buy or lease. Such factors as impact on financial statements, desire for operational flexibility, and loan restrictions, as well as other accounting, tax, economic, and financial considerations may be collectively at least as important. These aspects are essentially nonquantitative, but they can be evaluated with a satisfactory degree of accuracy by weighing the advantages and disadvantages.

Tax Considerations

There are two ways in which a lease can be treated for tax purposes, as a true lease or as a form of financing. If the lease is viewed as a true lease, the lessee is entitled to a deduction, in the appropriate period, for his annual rental expenses. (Normally, the appropriate period is the period in which the liability for rent is incurred, in accordance with the terms of the lease, granted that the timing of the liability is not unreasonable.) If the lease is viewed as a form of financing, the lessee is deemed the property's equitable owner and is thus permitted to deduct the depreciation and interest expense.

The test the IRS applies to determine whether a lease is a true lease or a form of financing is basically an evaluation of the purchase options. If the lessee can purchase the property for less than the fair market value or for an amount approximately equal to what the debt balance would have been had the asset been bought outright, the transaction is viewed as a financing agreement. If the lessee has a purchase option in an amount substantially exceeding the probable fair market value or the debt balance, the transaction would probably be recognized as a lease.

The Business Relationship

A final aspect of the lease-buy decision relates to the lessor-lessee relationship. If the lessor encounters financial difficulties, under certain circumstances the prospective lessee can be adversely affected. That is, depending upon the terms of the lease and the lessor's financing arrangements, a lender might look to the property to satisfy a default by the lessor. Although careful wording of the agreement can afford a measure of protection, it is essential that the lessee look into the prospective lessor's financial condition, business reputation, and client relationships. If the findings are favorable, negotiations may be carried out with a minimum of delay and expense. If the findings are unfavorable, the prospective lessee might still wish to proceed, relying on the protective clauses in the agreement, or he might abandon the lease (at least with that party) entirely.

Index